D1522724

# The Liberal Polity

*Also by Craig L. Carr*

THE POLITICAL WRITINGS OF SAMUEL PUFENDORF (*editor*) (*trans. Michael J. Seidler*)
ON FAIRNESS

# The Liberal Polity

## An Inquiry into the Logic of Civil Association

Craig L. Carr

GRAD
JC
574
.C38
2006

First published 2006 by
PALGRAVE MACMILLAN
Houndmills, Basingstoke, Hampshire RG21 6XS and
175 Fifth Avenue, New York, N.Y. 10010
Companies and representatives throughout the world

PALGRAVE MACMILLAN is the global academic imprint of the Palgrave Macmillan division of St. Martin's Press, LLC and of Palgrave Macmillan Ltd. Macmillan® is a registered trademark in the United States, United Kingdom and other countries. Palgrave is a registered trademark in the European Union and other countries.

ISBN-13: 978–0–230–01964–5 hardback
ISBN-10: 0–230–01964–1 hardback

This book is printed on paper suitable for recycling and made from fully managed and sustained forest sources.

A catalogue record for this book is available from the British Library.

Library of Congress Cataloging-in-Publication Data
Carr, Craig L., 1948–
    The liberal polity : an inquiry into the logic of civil association /
    Craig L. Carr.
        p.   cm.
    Includes bibliographical references and index.
    ISBN 0–230–01964–1
    1. Liberalism—Philosophy.   2. Civil society—Philosophy.   I. Title.
    JC574.C38 2006
    320.51—dc22                                        2006045008

10   9   8   7   6   5   4   3   2   1
15   14   13   12   11   10   09   08   07   06

Printed and bound in Great Britain by
Antony Rowe Ltd, Chippenham and Eastbourne

For
*Gary*

*Children, love one another, and if that is not*
*Possible at least try to put up with one another.*

Goethe

# Contents

# Acknowledgments

This work was a long time in the process of becoming, and a great many debts, both intellectual and personal, were incurred along the way. It is a pleasure to acknowledge them here and to offer my most sincere thanks as modest payment. My thoughts on toleration, and liberalism more generally, have been greatly influenced over the years by many profitable and enjoyable discussions with Mike Seidler and Mike Philips. Bill Lund graciously read an earlier version of the manuscript and offered many helpful comments and some much-needed advice. Bob Duff, Jim Stemler, and Martin Monto helped me think through some of the more sociological dimensions of intergroup conflict. I was also blessed with a number of excellent graduate students during the time the manuscript was in progress, many of whom helped immeasurably with the tedious job of research. My thanks to C.J. Gordon, Gary Gingrich, and Christian Woldmann for all the help. Thanks must also go to Stephen Moore not only for his dedicated help as a graduate assistant, but also for his helpful insights into the nature of toleration. Lastly and especially, I want to thank my friend and colleague Gary Scott, who has taught me so much over the years about international law and the meaning of friendship. Since it is all but certain that this work would never have happened without Gary's kindness and support, it is only appropriate that it be dedicated to him.

# Introduction

The purpose of this inquiry is to put some answers to the following two questions. First, under what conditions, if any, is it possible for human beings holding disparate, conflicting, and perhaps even hostile beliefs and viewpoints to live together peaceably within a common polity? Second, and assuming a plausible answer to the first question, is it reasonable to hope for something more in this regard than peaceful coexistence? That is, should we be content merely to put up with those whose ways may be strange and objectionable to us or should we seek instead to cultivate a sense of respect and appreciation for all this otherness? The answers to be developed and discussed below are by no means the only ones that have been, or that might be, put to these, related, questions. Nor are they necessarily very novel or original—originality at this point in the history of theorizing about politics seems largely a matter of subtlety and nuance, in any event. Whether they are the best answers that have been, or might be, put to these questions is for others to decide. I will, however, argue on their behalf that given the socio-political circumstances under which many human beings presently live, there is good reason to think that they are the most appropriate and generally acceptable answers available to us.

The answers I shall develop are unlikely to be terribly popular with most of those thinkers who take seriously the project of theorizing about civil life—for I intend to approach these questions as practical political challenges and not as moral problems to be resolved by appeal to moral insight. This crosses against the current of most political theorizing, which supposes that political problems are fundamentally and importantly moral in nature. My argument turns the relation between politics and morality on its head, so to speak, by claiming that political thought can and should inspire a partic- ular morality of civic association—a political morality, in effect—without itself being rooted in a more comprehensive and foundationalist moral viewpoint.[1] Popularity, however, is hardly an adequate test of theoretical merit and does little, by itself, to testify to the sufficiency of argument that supports any given theory. The sufficiency of argument is what matters, and so, at the risk of sounding like the Devil in a den of Daniels, I will set aside concerns about popularity and let the argument take us where it will.

The questions posed are, needless to say, eternal and enduring ones that have troubled political philosophers throughout the ages. If they did not matter from a practical point of view, on the other hand, they would hardly deserve much time or attention. The recorded history of humankind is awash in the blood humans have spilled by their own hands. The modern state received its initial defense at the hands of political philosophers who saw in the European state system a method for realizing a modicum of peace, tranquility, and security both within the state's borders and between neighboring states. In the wake of the over three hundred and fifty years since the Peace of Westphalia, the optimism with which modern political thought embraced the state hardly seems justified. States have continued to fight one another, and even though the horrible weapons of modern warfare now make the cost of total war too terrible to imagine, the threat of war and the specter of international conflagration remain unsettling possibilities. More recently, state-sponsored or -supported international terrorism has introduced another source of instability and unrest amongst the community of states. But international warfare and terrorism are only the most drastic ways that human beings inflict terrible cruelty upon themselves. We also see within states continued human predation, and the Enlightenment hope that the modern state would bring justice and security for all living within its borders now begins to seem like a naïve dream. Even in the most benign and wealthy of states, there is travail, vicious conflict, continued oppression, horrible poverty, and ongoing bloodshed. Perhaps this is simply the human condition; perhaps we are hardly justified in hoping for anything better. But justified or not, anyone who would like to see things otherwise has reason to think about how the human condition might be improved. Insofar as it makes sense to think of such improvement in political terms, those who put faith in the possibility of a better civil condition also have reason to consider and explore the conditions under which a general peace might be sustained within the polity and a compelling vision of social justice cultivated there. This, in any event, would appear to be the underlying logic that sets one to theorizing about politics and continuing to cultivate Enlightenment optimism in the modern state as the institutional *sine qua non* of human flourishing.

## The politics of the modern state

The modern state system has in recent times felt a tug from two separate directions. On the one hand, economic concerns have spilled over state borders and encouraged the evolution of a global economy. As regional economies grow and states become more economically dependent upon their neighbors, authority shifts from state government to regional unions of states, and the treaty relations that give rise to these unions become social contracts in their own right in which states give away a degree of their sovereignty in the name of regional economic well-being. Additionally, the timely—if not belated—recognition that certain collective action problems spill over state borders to affect regions—and even the entire planet—encourages additional treaty relations that give birth to regional and even global regulations and further limit state sovereignty. In fact, international lawyers even now talk about how regional and global multilateral treaties make international law that is binding even on states that are not signatories to them.[2] In law as well as in life, necessity is invariably the mother of invention, and the management of regional and global problems requires the development of regional and global authorities capable of meeting this challenge. Yet the trend toward regionalism and interdependence—or better, interconnectedness—diminishes the place of the state in our lives, erodes state sovereignty, and foreshadows a coming global federalism.

At the same time that the state is being challenged by creeping regionalism and globalism, we are also witnessing a rebirth of more particularized cultural, ethnic, and even religious identifications. These pressure the state from within and push toward the formation of smaller, more homogeneous self-governing nation-states. Many states have in the past had remarkable success in suppressing, marginalizing, or appeasing the minority groups in their midst. But this success has begun to wear thin for a variety of reasons, and for different reasons in a variety of places, and we now find cultural and ethnic groups insisting that the state recognize them, protect their ways, and permit them greater jurisdiction for self-governance.[3] The pressures of multiculturalism—an awkward notion that only captures one dimension of the struggle over group autonomy present in many modern states—sit strangely beside the opposite and external pressures of cosmopolitanism, and together they anticipate problems for the future of the state system as we have come to know it.

These separate and distinctive pressures introduce differing and perhaps competing targets of theoretical inquiry. They invite those who feel drawn to theorize about politics to make some hard choices about where to focus their attention. Political thinkers might and often do want to press their concerns into the international area. There is much for them to think about in this venue and much in the way of important insight for them to contribute to the larger field of interstate studies. The rise of regionalism and globalism, the expansion of international law, the emergence of human rights-based challenges to state sovereignty, the logic of the trend toward cosmopolitanism (if there is such a trend), and the cultivation of some intelligible understanding of the notion of 'spaceship earth' are all subjects that invite theoretical reflection and critical discussion.[4] They introduce issues of the first importance for the future of the state and the evolution of political life more generally. They give rise to new and pressing political problems that are sure to encourage new ways of theorizing about public life and the proper nature of civil association across the planet. But they are not the problems I want to address here.

My focus, instead, is directed toward the internal pressures that threaten the state from within, pressures displayed by calls for group recognition and the growing momentum that pushes in the direction of increased group autonomy. The fact of pluralism—internal group differences based upon religious, cultural, ethnic, ideological, or simply lifestyle factors— has moved into the political forefront of many modern states. As groups become inclined to insist upon greater autonomy and more jurisdictional control over their 'own' affairs, the legitimacy of state rule is put into greater doubt. The call for group self-rule can take several different forms. In its most extreme form, it reaches its peak in secessionist movements, as groups struggle to break from their host state and become polities unto themselves. In its less extreme forms, groups work to free themselves from the often comprehensive jurisdiction of the state and assume greater authority over group affairs. Sometimes, this form of independence involves efforts by groups to gain exemptions from state law or policy in order to go their own way and live by their own customs and traditions. At other times, it involves group claims to rights that protect them against intrusion from the 'outside' society around them and insulate their way of life against outside aggression or interference.[5]

The exact shape that self-rule movements or demands for greater autonomy take depends, of course, upon both the groups in question and the state involved. It is a feature of the particularities and histories of groups and of the states they reside within or between. Acknowledging the fact of particularity introduces barriers to the theoretical project of coming to grips with deep-seated and contentious diversity—barriers that will be explored shortly. Particularity, however, also poses specific and occasionally unique practical challenges to state sovereignty and state legitimacy. While the nature of these challenges are group and state specific in the way intimated by the fact of particularity, they can be characterized in terms of discernible general trends. Sometimes groups look to the state for support in the process of promoting their own ways and pursuing their own customs or traditions, and sometimes they see the state as a part of the problem rather than as a possible remedy. In either case, traditional views of sovereign authority are called into question in a manner that invites some revisionist thinking about state sovereignty and the nature and legitimacy of political authority more generally.

To undertake such a revisionist project is, in part, to inquire into the adjustments that modern states should make in order to accommodate those groups insisting upon increased jurisdictional autonomy or protective group rights. But it must also involve—and perhaps more importantly— the articulation of the important, and perhaps necessary, role the state plays in supporting groups themselves and nurturing a social environment where they can practice the independence and autonomy they may happen to desire. Effective revision, that is, works in two seemingly contradictory directions. First, it must reconfigure the jurisdictional relationship between groups and the state in a manner that allows groups the degree of independence they desire or require in order to sustain themselves. Second, it must demonstrate the necessity of political authority and the corresponding importance of civic identity with the polity regardless of a citizen's group affiliation(s). The internal pressure generated by groups seeking greater independence does not necessarily render the modern state otiose or unnecessary, and there are reasons to think it remains a vital component of public life. So, at the same time that the jurisdictional boundaries between groups and political authority may need to be reconsidered, there is a corresponding need to reassert the continued necessity of civil association in the form of the modern state.

Consequently, the revisionist project needs to demonstrate to those groups seeking greater independence or autonomy that the state is necessary for, and not a hindrance to, the full exercise of this autonomy. It is an accommodationist project insofar as it attempts to facilitate group diversity and difference at the same time that it endeavors to build a political unity constitutive of a common political identity. Yet, in the presence of the tremendous religious, cultural, and ideological differences on display in many modern states, it is important to ask initially whether such accommodationism is even possible, let alone desirable—hence the purpose behind asking the first of my two questions. In the presence of group pressures for secession or increased autonomy, and when confronted with the ugly realities of intergroup hostility and conflict present in many contemporary states, it is of the first importance to ask whether it is possible for disparate, conflicting, and possibly hostile worldviews to coexist within a common polity, or whether it is possible to imagine viable grounds for political unity in the face of such diversity.

Since I want to put an affirmative answer to this question, we are led naturally to my second question. If it is possible to imagine conditions that would support political unity in the face of group diversity, it is also important to ask about the nature and extent of the unity that is politically possible and desirable. If peaceful coexistence is not a theoretical possibility, it hardly seems acceptable to defend the continued presence of the state against groups whose members insist upon increased self-rule or even separation and independence. But if it is possible in theory to craft a vision of peaceful coexistence, no matter how hostile the groups involved may happen to be, we should also ask whether the state should undertake an effort to cultivate a sense of mutuality, respect, or comradeship beyond the simple maintenance of social tranquility. I shall put a rather negative answer to this question and for reasons easily anticipated. Any state that attempts to accommodate groups whose members have (or think they have) reason to dislike others is faced with the ticklish problem of managing the intergroup conflict resulting from intergroup hatred and animosity. To demand respect, comradeship, or the appreciation for 'otherness' may require at least some groups to change their ways, and the second question that entertains us here asks if this is necessary or possible within the context of political unity. Concluding, as I shall, that it is neither possible nor necessary for a viable political unity to require or promote love or respect for others beyond a minimal respect for them as fellow citizens supports the need to place clear limits on the ends of civil association in the name of group integrity. This too may prove integral to the accommodationist enterprise.

## Liberalism and the modern state

The political problems posed by the fact of pluralism are hardly new. In their most current western manifestation, these problems arose, not surprisingly, with the emergence of the modern state and the fracturing of religious belief in Europe. Perhaps ironically, the development of state sovereignty in Europe—presumably a necessary feature of political life if a state is to be capable of meeting its intended purpose of sustaining a viable government within a given jurisdiction—took place alongside the emergence of religious difference and disagreement. The presence of religious diversity inevitably rendered the ideal of absolute sovereignty suspicious. Absolute political authority is inconsistent with truth if one is convinced that truth is on your side and the sovereign is not. When this happens, people must make choices. They can either find an absolute sovereign who is of the correct faith or they can look for alternative strategies of compromise. In the Europe of the seventeenth century, a compromise of sorts seemed the more reasonable strategy to many political thinkers, and so the political tradition of modern liberalism was born.

Today, the notion of liberalism houses a number of contentious political viewpoints which seem to have little in common save for various commitments to liberty, some vision of human equality, and an emphasis upon the rhetoric of rights.[6] Seen from a more historical vantage point, however, liberalism can be considered a response to the need to domesticate political authority in order to preserve it. By defending individual liberty, the formative thinkers of the liberal tradition laid the foundation for a decentralized political environment in which individuals were free to worship as they saw fit and expand commercial activity as they wished. The result is a theory of civil association that defends, among other things, the necessity, value, and significance of the state at the same time that it champions an ideal of religious toleration that is both respected and policed by political authority. Insofar as political accommodation of this sort looks like just the thing to guide efforts to draw a viable line between what belongs to Caesar and what belongs to the individual or group, it would seem that there should be something in the liberal tradition that could service the search for answers to the questions I have asked.

This accommodationist spirit is kept alive by those contemporary liberals who suppose that liberalism must support the legitimacy of the state by demonstrating the acceptability of its political principles to all prospective citizens. Stephen Macedo expresses the point well when he tells us, 'The liberal project is to find regulative political principles for people who disagree.[7] But political accommodationism is not all there is to classical liberalism; nor is it necessarily the motivating force that animates most contemporary liberals. Traditionally, liberalism has always had a foundation in an underlying and supporting moral point of view. The liberal defense of religious diversity, it should be remembered, was situated within a volatile political condition in which competing sects presumed to have a privileged handle on religious truth. Where conflict rages over such basic questions, peace can plausibly be found only by fabricating grounds upon which a (shaky) truce can be built or by discovering a bedrock of rational insight that the warring factions can recognize and accept regardless of whatever it is that sets them apart and in opposition. Classical liberals—Locke in particular comes to mind here—generally seized upon the latter strategy. This meant revealing the moral common ground shared by competing religious views, defending its objective validity, and then describing how the state was charged with policing the moral obligations just uncovered and how its authority was itself circumscribed by these very obligations.

In its classical form, then, liberalism married a practical political aim—the domestication of political authority and defense of the modern state—with a specific moral agenda. Or perhaps it is more accurate to say that the moral agenda provided the normative baseline that seemed to make political accommodation possible. In recent times, however, this moral foundation has hardened considerably, and liberalism now is, or has become, a moral tradition—a theory of the good one wants to say—in its own right.[8] Liberal morality is accompanied by an ontology that pulls individuals into the foreground and minimizes the individual's group attachments and social identifications. The resultant moral valorization of the individual that was inspired by Kant and Mill, each in their own way, and that characterizes liberal thought in its contemporary maturity has transformed liberal visions of the state into an instrument dedicated to the defense of those liberties supportive of the demands of liberal morality. As a result, liberalism's traditional accommodationist aim has been effectively divorced from its moral agenda, and modern liberalism, or the various liberalisms that lay claim to the title, can now be regarded largely, though perhaps not exclusively, as an ideology that champions the moral worth of the independent and autonomous individual.[9]

No doubt many self-proclaimed liberals will dislike characterizing liberalism as a kind of ideology. The notion of ideology, at least since Marx, has been associated with a false but firmly held belief system, and few liberals savor the idea of thinking about liberal morality as false. It is possible, however, to characterize liberalism as an ideology, or better a worldview, for the purpose of illustrating its presence in the minds of its adherents as a belief system, and put aside questions about whether the moral convictions associated with it are objectively true or valid. As ideology or worldview, liberalism has both ontological and moral dimensions. It inspires in its faithful a particular way of seeing the world and a particular way of valuing what one now sees. Contemporary liberals characteristically see autonomous individuals, and they characteristically valorize these individuals by insisting that they possess a dignity or 'incomparable worth' that makes them deserving of respect.[10] Correspondingly, liberals increasingly regard group attachments and identifications as contingent and revisable aspects of one's life. Associational identification matters, if it matters at all, because it is (or should be) the result of free and independent individual choice. As we make our lives for ourselves, we elect to join certain associations or to adopt certain group identifications. Such choices, however, are generally considered reversible; and consequently, they do not irredeemably fix our identity. They are subject to change and revision, and may even be discarded like old shoes when we no longer want to have much to do with them.

Some external critics of liberalism who hang together or are pushed together under the banner of communitarianism object to liberal individualism because they think it is harmful to individual well-being (by producing atomistic, estranged, or morally insipid creatures where human beings used to be) or because they believe it is simply and myopically wrong (since in truth we are not the independent, atomistic, and autonomous creatures that liberals mistakenly believe us to be).[11] There is no reason to be concerned here with the validity of these communitarian attacks, although there may be reason to have sympathy for communitarian claims about the human need for community and associational identity with specific others. But there is reason to suppose that communitarian concerns have a certain political currency in the increasing group claims for autonomy and protected rights and even in the more strident secessionist demands. There are those who take group identifications most seriously, not as a matter of philosophical insight but as a matter of practical politics. The voices calling for recognition, self-rule, special rights, and sometimes separation even arise frequently and significantly in states with long and cherished liberal pedigrees, like the United States. Communitarianism in theory is not the only opponent of contemporary liberalism; groups practicing their own brand of communitarianism are increasingly political opponents of the liberal worldview as well.

Increasing separatist demands, growing insistence upon self-rule, and continuing claims to special protections against the dominant culture suggest that perhaps the modern liberal state has been transformed into something like the antithesis of the classic liberal vision. How could it be that a political doctrine devoted to the toleration of diversity and respect for liberty should now confront claims suggesting, in effect, that it is neither tolerant enough nor free enough? The answer is not difficult to discern. As liberalism has hardened into a worldview, the liberal state has become committed to the defense of liberal ways and to governing according to the requirements of liberal morality—vague and uncertain though these requirements may be at times. Consequently, the liberal state becomes the opponent of those non-liberal or evidently illiberal groups that have survived in its midst, overshadowing them with liberal agendas, encouraging, if not demanding, conformity to liberal ways, and eroding their religious, cultural, or ideological integrity in a spirit of what might be called liberal righteousness. Alternative non-liberal worldviews are thus marginalized, demonized, or both by a state powered by its own distinctive but not universally shared moral perspective. If liberals were on the other side of this coin, would they not begin to see all this as a form of imperialism? And in the face of pressures toward liberal conformism, is it any wonder that groups seeking to defend their identity and preserve their integrity would agitate for greater independence from the liberal state?

Group demands for self-rule and special rights may be, and likely will be, endorsed by liberals, to be sure, if the groups in question practice ways that are not offensive to the fundamental standards of liberal morality. In fact, liberals might, and often do, boast that liberalism supports an exceptional diversity of ethnic, cultural, and religious practices.[12] Things become problematical from a liberal viewpoint, however, when the claims advanced, rights asserted, and group autonomy demanded involve group efforts to do things that contradict the requirements of liberal morality. Examples of group practices offensive to liberal morality are legion: some cults brainwash and imprison children; some religions oppress or endanger their children; some groups refuse to allow their children access to proper political and/or social values; some groups preach and practice racial, religious, and/or ethnic hatred and intolerance; some groups oppress women or practice the ugly ritual of female genital mutilation; some groups fix the religious, cultural, and ideological beliefs of their members and will not tolerate dissent; some ideological groups not only espouse but work to implement political doctrines that are elitist, racist, or inegalitarian, and so forth.

What are liberals to do with groups like these? As worldview, liberalism can tolerate any and all groups that are willing to respect and practice liberal ways. But a good many liberals think that liberalism must be a 'something' and not just an 'anything' as Richard Flathman puts it.[13] Liberalism stands for something and because it does, liberal states cannot tolerate everything. In particular, they cannot tolerate what their own worldview inclines them to regard as intolerance in others.[14] Groups that brainwash children should not be tolerated because children should be educated in a manner that enables them to operate maximally as autonomous beings; groups that endanger the health or safety of their children should not be tolerated because the well-being of the child, as liberals understand this notion, should be promoted; groups should not harm or mutilate their members because this hinders the ability of these individuals to live good and fulfilling lives, as liberals understand this notion, and so forth. If liberalism is to be a something, liberals must stick to their moral guns and faithfully dedicate themselves to the promulgation of liberal ways. The imposition of group ways on others, it may be insisted, is hardly imperialistic, righteous, or oppressive if these ways are right and proper—a claim that has an unhappily familiar ring to it and one that those liberals who prefer to consider liberalism a political doctrine are unwilling to accept.

If liberalism is to endure as a viable tradition of political discourse, it must surely be a something and not an anything. Yet if we take this to mean that liberals must be willing to impose their moral scheme on non-liberals, we reach something of a paradox. As a moral doctrine, liberalism demands a type of conformity; it cannot and will not tolerate illiberal ways. As a political doctrine, on the other hand, liberalism is dedicated to tolerance in order to cultivate social peace and tranquility throughout the polity. But given the realities of pluralism, liberalism cannot realize both these ends at the same time; thus, to render liberalism coherent, one of these ends must be allowed to trump or determine the other. In classical liberal thought, liberalism's moral foundation controlled the reach of its commitment to toleration. Locke, for example, presumed that good Christians would acknowledge his case for natural rights, and that this would establish a common ground from which to develop a solid liberal defense of the state. But Locke had little use for Catholics or atheists, and he did not extend the requirement of toleration to them.[15]

Such claims were politically awkward even in Locke's day by virtue of the fact that Catholics at least had a real and significant social presence. But they are considerably more awkward in the modern liberal states of the early twenty-first century because these states typically have a far greater diversity of non-liberal and even illiberal influences. I suspect that liberalism has never been entirely free from the paradox resulting from the contradiction between its political purpose and its moral agenda, but as states born within and inspired by liberal viewpoints mature, they increasingly find themselves confronted with non-liberal groups that both reject liberal morality and still insist that liberals honor their political commitment to tolerate and honor diversity and difference. The multicultural pressures discussed above simply illustrate one dimension of the practical political difficulties that arise as the paradox within the liberal tradition manifests itself more concretely in the political life of the modern liberal state.

The paradox to which I am calling attention is nicely, albeit unwittingly, characterized by Charles Larmore:

> Liberalism has been the hope that, despite this tendency toward disagreement about matters of ultimate significance, we can find some way of

living together that avoids the rule of force. It has been the conviction that we can agree on a core morality while continuing to disagree about what makes life worth living.[16]

Larmore supposes that political accommodationism is possible only if people can first agree on a core morality capable of supporting formative political principles. If such a morality cannot be found, Larmore worries that the future will be one (or continue to be one) 'where ignorant armies clash by night.'[17] And he worries that if liberal morality cannot suffice as the basis for the needed core morality, liberalism will become, as I have suggested that it has, but one more 'partisan ideal.' The paradoxical aspect of such a liberalism emerges once we appreciate that in the face of extraordinary moral and ontological diversity, it is simply not possible to forge political accommodation upon an antecedent moral foundation. If we begin to theorize by arguing from an antecedent moral perspective, we are sure to encounter other moral (and accompanying ontological) viewpoints that see things differently and that sense a source of oppression where liberals hope to achieve accommodation. Thus, in a world as diverse as the one we now must confront, Larmore's moral focus works against his accommodationist desires.

To dissolve the paradox, liberals must make a difficult choice. They must decide if liberalism is going to be a moral or a political doctrine. This is at bottom a choice about what matters, or what should matter, to people who look to liberalism for guidance in addressing the problems of public life. If the choice is to hold dear to liberalism as a moral doctrine, that is, if it is the basic moral commitment to the autonomous individual as a being of incomparable worth that matters most, the traditional liberal effort to address and resolve problems created by group diversity and worldview pluralism is badly circumscribed. But this puts the point too lightly; if the choice is for liberalism as a moral doctrine, then from the viewpoint of anyone who worries about the fact of intergroup conflict and animosity, liberalism becomes a part of the problem rather than the source of a possible solution. This, some will say, might be unfortunate, but it is the price of seeing to it that liberalism remains a 'fighting faith,' that it is a something and not an anything. For many, and perhaps most self-proclaimed liberals of any variety of stripes, the cost will seem well worth it. Contemporary liberals are increasingly comfortable with insisting that liberalism put to the service of political life cannot be fully or devotedly accommodationist. The liberal state, from this point of view, must insist upon a degree of conformity, but there is solace to be found, the refrain goes, in the fact that this is a morally proper and defensible conformity—small solace, to be sure, to those non-liberal groups that happen to disagree with this.[18]

Nonetheless, critics of moral liberalism have pressed their arguments with effect by demonstrating that a morally inspired liberalism has little of value to offer as a viable theory of civil association simply because moral liberalism cannot realize the accommodationist goal that has also been a traditional feature of liberal thought.[19] It seems worthwhile, then, to consider how things might go if we elect to make the other choice and develop a theory of liberalism as a political doctrine, and as it happens, this is what I intend to do here. Liberalism's traditional political agenda need not, and perhaps should not, be derived solely from its own moral basis, and once the contentious nature of this moral basis is exposed, the political agenda takes on added pertinence. It would, I suspect, be a good thing if human beings holding disparate normative and epistemic views could learn to live together in relative peace and amity and without feeling threatened, oppressed, or marginalized by their political neighbors. It would, that is, be good if people belonging to diverse and hostile groups could hit upon some political strategy for getting along with one another in spite of the very important moral and ontological issues that may happen to divide them. It would be good to bring about a brokered peace and promote political unity in pluralist polities that suffer from intergroup conflict and hatreds. But these are not intended as moral claims; they rest instead upon the, perhaps naïve, intuition that social peace and tranquility are desirable as the precondition for anyone's ability to live her or his life as she or he sees fit. Social peace is here to be considered a practical and not necessarily a moral good. This claim too will need some defense, but for the present I shall leave it as an initial presumption that warrants exploring the accommodationist path contemporary liberals have not taken. Political accommodation, then, is the possibility introduced and supported by liberalism as a political doctrine, and while classical liberalism probably never really lived up to this vision (even if it was sometimes advertised in this way), the hope of avoiding a future 'where ignorant armies clash by night' makes it desirable to see if this possibility can be effectively articulated and defended within a coherent theoretical framework. It may be that liberalism's accommodationist ideal cannot be fully realized, but we still might be able to do more toward the realization of this end than is possible under moral liberalism.

## Practical liberalism

Insofar as intergroup conflict poses a real and pressing political problem in at least some modern states, an exploration of the possibilities opened up by taking liberalism as a political doctrine seriously may prove to be of some practical political value. While this will hardly make this method of resolving the liberal paradox any more favorable to those liberals who wish to insist that liberalism must be regarded essentially as a moral doctrine, it does, nonetheless, suggest the practical value of raising and exploring the two questions that direct and inspire the discussion and argument that follows.

On the other hand, while the decision to consider the possibilities associated with taking liberalism as a political doctrine seriously does necessitate the abandonment of foundational moral argument, it is not correspondingly necessary to abandon the need for centering principles of civil association; it does not, or does not necessarily, eschew principle for process. Accommodation is only possible if we manage some kind of agreement on something, and the something in question must enable us to go on. It must inspire a way of being with others—a form of accommodation—capable of forming unity even in the presence of diversity. So it is, in the terms made fashionable by John Rawls, a constructivist project.[20] Words, of course, cannot compel; they can only cajole. A theory is only as satisfying as the reasons it gives to support, require, or encourage concession to its first principles. And here is the central challenge associated with regarding liberalism as a political doctrine: It invites us to imagine the most diverse and disparate group setting imaginable, and it then requires us to construct arguments sufficient to entice or logically require all these disparate elements to accept the same (unifying) first principle(s) regardless of whatever it is that they happen to believe or hold dear.

Since there are so many liberals defending so many different versions of liberalism, it has become popular to locate specific versions of liberalism within the larger context of liberal argument by assigning the version a particular thinker wants to promote a name that associates it with an identifiable category of liberal thought. Accordingly, it would seem reasonable to call the construction of liberalism I shall offer here 'political liberalism.' But this label has been put to good use already by those liberals whose moral convictions incline them to emphasize things like state neutrality and the primacy of the right over the good.[21] I am also attracted to the title of pragmatic liberalism, but this too has been taken by liberals with theoretical agendas quite different from mine.[22] Some who have imagined a similar construction of liberalism have, somewhat derisively, called it 'realist liberalism,' a not altogether inaccurate title.[23] But I want to avoid this label largely because the notion of realism has received so many diverse interpretations that it now seems to obscure more than edify. The view of liberalism to be developed here also bears some resemblance to the notion of agonistic liberalism introduced by John Gray; but as we shall see, the differences between the theory articulated below and the concerns of Gray are important enough to advise against borrowing this title as well.[24]

Of those few thinkers who have been inclined to consider liberalism as a political doctrine in a reasonably favorable light, some have called it 'vulgar liberalism' because of its distance from the more noble version of liberalism as moral doctrine, while others have called it a 'liberalism of fear' because, like Hobbes, they think it is fear that unites rather than shared moral insight or objective moral truth.[25] These accounts of liberalism as a political doctrine make a certain amount of sense, but such unflattering labels tend to put things in an unnecessarily negative light and risk under-representing the theoretical value of the accounts they introduce. I will settle, then, for the reasonably modest, and probably rather nebulous name '*practical* liberalism' largely for lack of a better alternative. This name may well have been applied elsewhere as well. But some kind of shorthand terminology seems desirable, and since the term 'practical liberalism' is as descriptive of the nature of the liberalism I propose to defend here as any of the alternatives, and may even stir the passions of those thinkers who are wedded less to a moralized version of liberalism than to the other possibilities, I will make do with it.

Liberalism made practical takes political accommodation as the central challenge facing the modern pluralist state. It presumes, accordingly, a social condition of group conflict and hostility, and endeavors to imagine in theory a stable political unity, in terms of a *modus vivendi*, that makes accommodation possible with the least cost to the independence of those groups constitutive of the polity. To do so, it relies upon argument that is as neutral as possible between moral and ontological points of view, as it must if it is to avoid all moralized viewpoints and knowledge claims that might be considered objectionable, suspicious, or false by any conceivable group that might happen to be present in the social environment. This is a prerequisite for any theoretical argument that hopes to show how political unity is possible in spite of the fact of deep normative and ontological diversity. Such a liberalism will need to rely, as one might suppose, upon a particular construction of the familiar notion of prudence if it is to succeed. This will invariably elicit the charge (if charge it is) of Hobbesianism, and a liberalism that appeals to prudence in the name of political unity might accordingly be dismissed as but the latest variation on a political theme introduced and inspired by Hobbes. But recourse to prudential argument is hardly sufficient to make political argument Hobbesian. There is more to Hobbes than prudential reasoning—just as there is more to practical liberalism than prudential argument, and there is no reason why liberal argument cannot avail itself of the counsel of prudence.

In any event, practical liberalism as envisioned here hardly qualifies as Hobbesian. It involves the articulation of distinct and principled limits upon political authority, and it introduces distinct and principled demands that must be respected and met by the citizenry. Unlike Hobbes, and like traditional liberals, it supposes that social peace and public tranquility cannot be established by recourse to political power alone, and it agrees with traditional liberals that the goal of social peace is attainable only with the establishment of a political morality that promotes social justice and supports the legitimacy of the state. It also shares with traditional liberalism a skepticism about political power and an appreciation for the importance of political morality as a basis for political unity, and this is perhaps sufficient to justify placing such a vision of civil association within the family of theories that comprise the liberal tradition. In short, it seeks to develop or construct the demands of a political morality that follows from a constitutive principle that is supported and defended explicitly by prudential argument.

However, unlike both Hobbes and traditional liberals, practical liberalism deliberately avoids supposing that the craft of theorizing about politics should start with the independent individual and puzzle over how to blend these distinct beings together into a civil association that still allows them a degree of independence. There is no hint of individualism to practical liberalism. Instead, it presumes a social background of group conflict and hostility based upon deep-seated normative and ontological differences. It will be supposed here that the social conflict inspired and driven by deep normative and ontological disagreement over things that matter, and matter greatly, to persons is best understood in terms of intergroup conflict. Correspondingly, persons shall be regarded, insofar as any sort of account of persons is appropriate for the argument to follow, as largely group-centered beings for whom meaning and purpose in life is derived from and intimately linked to membership in some formative group, or collection of groups.

This, of course, invites additional comment about the nature of groups as well as some further discussion of persons as group-centered beings, and I shall have something to say, though perhaps not enough, about both these matters as things proceed. But two points should be emphasized at the outset. First, by viewing persons as group-centered beings (rather than as, say, atomistic individuals in competition with similar others for mutually desired but unhappily limited social resources), I do not intend to make any epistemological claims about human nature or the natural condition of humankind. I want only to call attention to the fact that normative belief and ontological viewpoint are often fixed by a person's group affiliations and developed or modified through involvement and/or deliberation with others who share at least key elements of one's basic understanding of things. That is, normative belief and ontological viewpoint are generally shared with distinctive others and this sharing becomes a source of individual identity premised upon the unity it creates and the difference it generates between group members and group outsiders. Of course, persons can and generally do belong to more than one identifying group along with any number of interpersonal associations that have little or no normative or ontological significance for their members. The fact that persons can belong to more than one group is illustrative of the fact that normative belief invariably has room for disparity. It may be conjoined, for example, if one's identification with group A constitutes only a part of a person's normative horizon, a horizon completed by one's identification with other groups, perhaps, or even by one's own studied reflection. But group belief may also be layered, like a cake, if some larger groups subsume smaller units (or unities) within them. The Christian faith, for example, has fragmented into several distinctive sects, but they continue to have in common enough to enable them to see themselves as a group of Christians. As we shall see, the fact that persons can belong to more than one group is of considerable political importance. It introduces the possibility of achieving a type of group unity amidst the fact of group diversity, and if this were not possible, it would make little sense to try and fashion, in theory, a form of *civil* association, that is, the formation of a distinctive political group, amidst the deep normative and ontological diversity introduced by the fact of ethnic, religious, cultural, and ideological difference.

The second point to be emphasized at the outset is that it is probably best not to ask too much of any effort to provide an exact accounting of what counts as a group. While it is important to say something about the nature of groups, insistence upon a precise and compelling definition of a group seems neither very possible nor terribly necessary. The request for a definition itself suggests the presence of an essentialism that may simply be misguided. What matters for present purposes is that groups should be understood in terms of the basic normative and ontological viewpoints reflected in and held by their members. These are the factors responsible for the type of social conflict that invites us to ask the questions that serve as the focus of this inquiry. Thus, the notion of a group, as it is used here, is perhaps best understood in practical, political terms. Groups are the repositories of the normative and ontological differences that generate the conflict that is socially destabilizing and therefore politically problematic. We can recognize groups practically if and when they place themselves in opposition to some set of others/outsiders and identify them as people who are damned, disgusting, and/or misguided by virtue of who they are or what they believe. The social conflict of concern here, in other words, takes place between some generally recognizable set of 'we's' who happen to be opposed for moral, religious, or ideological reasons to some generally recognizable set of 'they's,' and while the 'they's' may also regard themselves as 'we's,' this is not necessary for intergroup conflict to exist between these two 'groups.'

The consequent emphasis given to intergroup conflict under practical liberalism may seem to be grounds for initial suspicion about the value of the inquiry to follow. Critics may suppose that the central concern for inter-group conflict makes practical liberalism more appropriate for a place like the Balkans, but not for liberal democracies that boast a much higher degree of social homogeneity and far less intergroup conflict and hostility. This is a significant challenge; any political theory is only as pertinent as the social problem it seeks to address. Moreover, all theorizing about politics must proceed by imaging some baseline condition that situates the discussion and vindicates the prescriptions offered. Cultivation of the sociological back-ground that houses the theoretical project is thus an important initial step for the process of theory articulation. Where once it mattered to liberal theorists to get something we might call human nature right in order to craft a civil arrangement appropriate for its subjects, it now matters to practical liberalism to get clear on the social dynamics of intergroup (and intragroup) life. This is the project of the first two chapters to follow. The sociological backdrop to be introduced there is inspired by the very real fact of group diversity that exists in modern liberal democracies, particularly the United States—the specific context of my theoretical project.

There is, to be sure, a long and rather ugly history of intergroup conflict and hostility in the United States, and in this it is probably little different from other western democratic states like Great Britain, Canada, and Australia. But the United States is not the Balkans; we find in the US a dominant liberal tradition that has done much to shape the nature of intergroup politics on display within its borders. This liberal ethos seems to dominate the social landscape and even adheres in some fashion to religious groups that are not traditionally overly liberal. The presence of dominant liberal mores does not mean that such states are normatively homogeneous, however, or that they lack enough intergroup conflict to worry about. Instead, the presence of dominant social influences intro-duces the ugly possibility of group domination and encourages us to see pleas for group independence, increased group autonomy, or special group rights as a reaction to a form of oppression. So, the predicament that inspires practical liberalism should not be identified solely, or even chiefly, as social chaos sparked by intergroup warfare. The motivating impetus to take practical liberalism seriously is also, and perhaps more immediately, given by the destabilizing possibility of group domination and the struggles of minority groups to escape the clutches of more dominant groups. Once again, then, practical liberalism assumes a traditional liberal agenda: The search for a political *terra firma* lodged securely between equally unpalat-able extremes of social chaos and imperious domination by the socially powerful.

The aim, of course, is a theory of political legitimacy—for the stakes at issue, as modern states face pressure from ethnic, cultural, racial, religious, ideological, and lifestyle groups within their borders, are understandable in terms of the state's legitimacy—its right to rule those under its claimed jurisdiction. Non-liberal theories construct this legitimacy by cultivating homogeneity, eliminating diversity, and encouraging individual identific-ation with the civil *patria*. Liberal theories, on the other hand, ideally try to build unity amidst diversity, sometimes because liberals have a certain fondness for diversity and sometimes, as in the case of practical liberalism, because they recognize that group diversity is simply a fact of social life. Once again, practical liberalism follows this standard liberal design, and like traditional liberalism, it acknowledges the need to articulate a viable theory of toleration. Chapters 3 and 4 take up the case for political unity and demonstrate the requirements of a principled form of civil association in terms of the demands of toleration as required under practical liberalism. The price of toleration is high, particularly for those liberals who insist that liberalism should remain a moral doctrine that takes individual autonomy seriously, but there is no reason to think that the price of social peace should not be high.

Yet liberals and non-liberals alike may want or expect more from civil association than merely social peace. A polity united only by standards of toleration will seem to many too impoverished, too minimalist to be worthy of respect or recognition. Republicans and a good many liberals will insist that we should expect more from the polity than this, and perhaps argue that a polity held together only by a shared willingness to tolerate all manner of diversity is too thin to last long. These are, to be sure, important concerns, and they occupy my attention in Chapters 5 and 6. The critics who introduce these worries are mindful that political life involves something more than the construction of public institutions; there is also something we might call a political ethos that emerges from a political tradition. Politics is about attitude as well as institutional structure, and theorizing about public life requires attention to the animating spirit of the polity as much as to the institutional structure of government. Practical liberalism offers distinctive conceptions of fairness and civility as key elements of the animating spirit of the liberal polity. Important as these elements will become, they may not be sufficient to satisfy republican and liberal critics. But it is a longstanding feature of liberalism to suppose that civil life is not entirely constitutive of a good life; and in this, practical liberalism again follows liberal tradition. It is worth exploring the nature and strength of the civil bonds that unite the liberal polity, however, and this is the task of the final chapter. The discussion there will conclude matters by considering why the state, under practical liberalism, remains, and should remain, a vital and viable political instrument in the lives of its citizenry and whether this justifies thinking that practical liberalism is yet another version of liberal nationalism.

It will no doubt be noticed that the argument to follow is silent on questions of distributive justice, questions that have come to seem of the first importance to a great many liberals.[26] Any argument that presumes to inspire reflection on standards of social justice should, from this point of view, pay some attention to the way money, wealth, other material goods, and the necessities of a good life should be distributed throughout the polity. Additionally, Marxists along with many liberals may object to the fact that my account of intergroup hostility and animus does not explain conflict in economic terms. By way of an apology for what might seem like an important oversight or straightforward socio-economic confusion, it seems to me that a focus on concerns of distributive justice are premature at this point because an economic interpretation of social conflict is not likely to receive universal acclaim from all groups that my inquiry must address.

The sociological presumption that backgrounds the discussion of practical liberalism imagines a social setting that teeters between the chaos of intergroup warfare (one extreme) and the deafening stillness of dominant-group oppression (the other extreme). Built into the presumption is the belief that groups have reason(s) to dislike one another that are lodged in group worldviews and moral theories of the human good. These reasons could be variously described as ethical, religious, or ideological, and they may or may not be linked to intergroup economic rivalries. This will seem wrongheaded to Marxist and neo-Marxist theorists who critique all manner of social conflict in terms of economic relationships. While Marxists tend to characterize social conflict in terms of class struggle and antagonism, I will locate this conflict in intergroup hostility. I do so, moreover, without first building a comprehensive social theory, and defend this apparent omission simply by pointing to the obvious reality of group demands for greater independence and autonomy, on the one hand, and the equally obvious presence of intergroup hatreds (as evidenced by hate crimes for example), on the other. It is not necessary to decide here whether or not these hatreds are caused by economic conditions, but it would be an error of the first importance to suppose that they do not matter in their own right to groups that believe they have moral, religious, or ideological reasons for objecting to (certain) others.

There are other reasons why the vision of practical liberalism that follows is bereft of any developed theory of distributive justice. This absence is not intended to suggest that a comprehensive theory of practical liberalism would not take some stand on the distribution of economic goods—the distribution of wealth and the things that money can and should be allowed to buy. As we shall see, this is not the case at all; practical liberalism demands not only toleration but also deference toward others, that is, a commitment to the principled resolution of conflicts over social space, resources, and time. But liberal worries about the distribution of economic goods are sometimes based upon the presumption that there are some basic goods that anyone will need or want in order to live a good life. This presumption seems to me questionable at best and may prove to be quite misleading if not largely false. My sense at present is that questions about economic goods and their just distribution are subject to important and various qualifications as one takes account of the worldview and moral theory of the human good that characterizes any given group. Group norms may have significant implications for how the members of the group view money, the accumulation of wealth, desirable work, and so forth, and tolerating these groups will surely involve respecting group efforts to cultivate their views on these matters.[27] Distributional considerations that proceed without first exploring the nature of group diversity present in the polity and crafting a theory of group toleration would thus seem to be premature, and for this reason they play only an ancillary role in the theory of practical liberalism to follow.

# 1
# A Prolegomenon to Political Thought

It is not possible to build castles in the sky; neither is it possible to theorize about politics without making some initial presumptions. Buildings cannot stand in thin air, and political theories must stand upon the foundation of what is given, what is taken as granted, what is simply understood without any great need for comment. And just as buildings can endure only if the ground they are built upon is capable of supporting them, so too political theories have value and pertinence only if the foundation supplied by what is initially presumed remains granted without worry or concern. So when it comes to political philosophy, the question of how to begin is answered only by thinking about where to begin: What presumptions should we build upon? What features of life should we consider given and indisputable?

These questions introduce problems that cause a small measure of embarrassment for those who want to take seriously the enterprise of theorizing about politics. Political philosophy, as I understand it, is a confrontation with social pathology. The inspiration to theorize about politics, if inspiration it is, seems invariably powered by the conviction that there is something amiss with the way human beings happen to be living together in some generally recognizable place and in some moment in time. This something, moreover, must be understandable in terms of a distinctive political failing, and it must be supposed, by anyone who is inspired to theorize about politics, that the social wrongs and deep conflicts that trouble him or her can and should be addressed, at least in some measure or to some degree, as theoretical problems. Implicit in this conception of political inquiry is the reasonable hope that theoretical reflection can actually do some good, that the pictures of a better way of living together that it produces really are compelling and really will (or at least can) be recognized as such by anyone willing to reflect upon the matter. The underlying purpose of political inquiry, this is to say, is practical. Its aim is to provide a vision or blueprint of a form of civil association free from the scars and travails of social pathology.

All this might seem simple enough, but it is prelude to some troubled waters. If political philosophy is to matter practically, two conditions must be met. First, there must really be some kind of social pathology that troubles the polity, and correspondingly, there must be some general appreciation of this fact. Machiavelli worried greatly and famously about the plight of his beloved Renaissance Italy; he felt her shame and suffered for her predicament. These worries inspired him to theorize in his own way about how things might be made better for Italy. But few listened, and most of those who did were far from convinced that things were as bad for Italy as Machiavelli believed. When times are good and people reasonably happy, there is not much inspiration to take up political philosophy and arguably even less reason to pay much attention to those who do so anyway, perhaps for reasons that should best, and most kindly, be considered idiosyncratic. When times are indeed quiet, political philosophy usually recedes from prominence and becomes little more than an academic exercise—in the worst sense of this term. This introduces what I will call the problem of pertinence. To matter much, theorizing about politics should best begin by exposing and identifying the social pathology that troubles the political environment the theorist intends to address. It should encourage citizens to recognize this pathology, and it should demonstrate why there is reason to think that something should be done about it.

Second, if political inquiry is to have the desired therapeutic results, it needs to display a force of reason and power of argument that speaks, and speaks importantly, to all audiences in the polity. This introduces the problem of audience that invariably accompanies the problem of pertinence. All members of the polity should be able to recognize both the strength and the importance of the arguments presented, and all should be invited to agree or find fault with the reasoning that supports the theorist's recommendations for how best to address and eliminate the pathology that inspires theoretical inquiry. Critics may object that this merely introduces to the theoretical project a controversial presumption in favor of democratic egalitarianism. But the objection is unnecessarily harsh; as we shall see, there are important practical reasons why theoretical argument should speak with force to all members of the state. For the moment, however, a less elaborate response to this objection must suffice. Theorizing about politics differs significantly from political activism in one important way. Both, I think, have a practical agenda; both hope to address social pathology in an effective manner. But those who sit to theorize about politics suppose that reason needs to guide action, that those deep fissures in the polity that inspire political theorizing require studied reflection, careful analysis, and thoughtful argument in order to direct action toward an appropriate remedy. Implicit in this conviction is the complementary belief that building for citizens a well-reasoned vision of how civil association should go is an integral step toward the desired therapy.

The inclination to theorize, in this sense, is inevitably democratic. It supposes that reflection, discourse, and argument are the necessary ingredients of political development and that all elements of the polity should be involved in the process. It makes little sense to theorize only for the rich or the poor, the bright or the desperately bored, or the disenchanted or disgruntled. Reasoned discourse is intended to speak to everyone and to have something to say to everyone, regardless of the beliefs, ideals, or worldviews that inform one's understanding of things. Theorizing about politics makes sense only if one accepts the view that the pathology troubling a polity is treatable with reasoned insight and studied reflection. And it can have practical importance only if it proceeds in light of the democratic spirit. To matter, political philosophy must speak with force to everyone in the polity, insofar and to the extent that this is possible, regardless of worldview and moral vision of the good; otherwise it cannot command and, I want to say, should not command much of an audience.

How can we be assured of the practical efficacy of political inquiry? That is, how can the theorist be sure that he or she has identified a social pathology in need of theoretical examination and not simply read his or her own idiosyncratic nervousness into public life? And how can we be confident that our arguments will matter if we suppose the polity in question is composed of a diverse audience whose members hold wildly disparate worldviews and moral theories of the human good? It is probably impossible to be very confident in any answer the theorist might give to the first of these questions. We really cannot know if we have identified a serious pathology, for this depends, in large measure, on whether the things the theorist asserts as pathological are similarly recognized throughout the polity. This might suggest that political theorists should begin with a bit of sociological inquiry. Perhaps the theorist should start by doing some survey research and asking questions of fellow citizens about the problems that concern them, or perhaps the theorist should spend more time in taverns or at baseball games eavesdropping on the conversations of fellow citizens in hopes of catching a glimpse of the pathologies that concern them. But there is little reason to suppose that the citizens themselves are aware of or sensitive to the pathology in need of theoretical therapy. Identifying the problem that troubles is a theoretical challenge in its own right, and consequently, the initial step in the theoretical project must be to present a strong case for the pathological character of some social condition. The success of the theoretical project hangs, in large measure, on the theorist's effectiveness in demonstrating that there really is a genuine need for the theoretical project.

If this is right, then initial presumptions about the nature of the theorist's audience are of the first importance. At this point, the theoretical project folds back upon itself. We encounter the state as it is; it constitutes the raw data of the theoretical project. There are states and then there are states, of course; different states display different pathologies. Some states qualify as such in name only; their pathologies seem overwhelming and intractable. It is hard to imagine that theory will matter much where order and security are fleeting moments that give way quickly to unsettled political chaos. Seventeenth-century England may have been unsettled by almost any standard of measure, but it was at least sufficiently stable to afford the luxury of a Hobbes. Other states seem reasonably settled, relatively just, and rightly ordered. Seen from sufficient distance, it is difficult to imagine that such states have much need for political theory, and the theorists who live and work there must seem at times like disgruntled malcontents who should spend more time marveling at how good things are and less time trifling over the details. Accordingly, there may be something to the idea that nineteenth-century Germany and England were sufficiently stable, orderly, and just to afford a Marx.

But viewed more closely, it may become apparent that even reasonably stable, relatively just, and rightly ordered states exhibit pathologies in need of theoretical confrontation; indeed, it might just be that theoretical confrontation is possible, not to mention profitable, only under such circumstances. But even though such states may be able to afford and sustain the luxury of reasoned discourse, their theorists must still confront the problem of audience. If the citizenry happens to be relatively homogeneous, this problem may not trouble all that much. Homogeneity introduces the possibility of a common denominator that can anchor theoretical insight by providing a suppositional *terra firma* to support the theoretical project. Homogeneity of this sort, on the other hand, seems to be a luxury enjoyed by few, if any, modern states. Sometimes it is said that the world has gotten smaller, but this of course is silly. The world is about the same size it has always been, but in many places it is more populous than it once was. This is not necessarily a cause of trouble in and of itself, to be sure, but it raises difficulties when the mixing, blending, and mushrooming of populations involves at the same time a corresponding expansion in normative viewpoints, ideological convictions, religious commitments, cultural and ethnic practices, racial variations, and economic divisions. These differences are the source of social friction and the spark of intergroup conflict. The greater the social differences in the state, the more pluralist it becomes. So, the more pluralist the state, the more likely it will face intergroup problems that threaten to spiral out of control and press in the direction of chaos. As pluralism increases, then, the more likely it is that the stability and integrity of the state will be threatened. It follows that pluralism—the fact of deep normative and ontological difference and disagreement—is a possible and even likely source of social pathology.

This is the source of the theoretical embarrassment mentioned earlier. If we suppose that pluralism is the source of the pathology in need of theoretical remedy, and if we suppose that the theorist must speak with equal force to all elements of the polity, the fact of pluralism both invites theoretical inquiry and at the same time introduces the greatest barrier to the theoretical project. If it is difference and the instability generated by difference that is the problem, how is it possible to construct a common language capable of meeting the challenges introduced by the problems of audience and pertinence? Before political theorizing can profitably begin, it is necessary to put an answer to this question. That is, before theorizing about politics can really get going, it is necessary to put forward clearly the precise nature of the pathology to be addressed and to explore how to guarantee that all elements of the state can both appreciate this pathology for what it is and understand and support the theoretical remedy recommended.

These comments set the challenge and identify the purpose of this chapter. I shall begin, then, by identifying the specific pathology I believe needs theoretical treatment and in so doing expose, explain, and defend the pertinence of the argument to follow. But I also want to emphasize the difficulties created by the problem of audience and indicate how these difficulties shape and direct the flow of the argument that does follow.

## Political argument and the demands of audience

Political philosophers have developed several strategies to get their projects going that might seem like just the thing to deal with the problem of audience. We might, for one thing, proceed to craft a political theory from presumptions widely shared by a great many elements of the state in question but not all, thinking perhaps that such total comprehensiveness simply is not possible. This strategy commits itself to the most capacious accommodationism possible while conceding that the problem of audience cannot be entirely overcome. It is possible to recognize something like this move in Locke's political thought. Unlike Hobbes, Locke does not attempt to base his political thought on the foundations of what we might call scientific certainty. He offers no empirical argument for his basic claim that human beings possess certain natural rights that are to be safeguarded and nurtured through civil association. Instead, he bases his argument upon an imaginative but decidedly arbitrary theory of property acquisition and a distinctively Protestant construction of Christian religious belief. God has given the world and all its bounty to human beings in common and in turn humankind is expected to work God's gift and turn this raw potential into wealth. One's labor, Locke insisted, is the source of ownership; that which one creates rightly becomes one's own. And since God is our creator, we are His property and our rights to life and liberty follow as a matter of course.[1]

This is an argument that is guaranteed to play rather well with Protestant groups able to accept Locke's rather modest recourse to Christian theology. Atheists, however, pose something of a problem, and given their doctrinal differences, Catholics may do so as well. It hardly seems remarkable, then, that both these groups fell beyond the reach of Locke's rather modest tolerance.[2] These characters are anathema in Locke's polity; they are not to be trusted. But of course they would also almost surely reject

Locke's argument for the foundation of civil association, and so their exclusion becomes essential. From Locke's point of view, they are a source of instability and political uncertainty. Consequently, they should be carefully watched, if not banished from the state altogether. They are a threat to the state, a source of pathology that should be carefully monitored in order to guarantee they remain politically impotent.

Nor is Locke the only thinker to have written for a majority in the polity and crafted an argument that has the practical effect of identifying certain groups as social pariahs and moving them to the social margins—if not inspiring their complete removal from the body politic. More recently, John Rawls has offered an argument about how stability can be assured in a just state that also moves in this direction. Rawls fabricates a theory of liberal justice that begins from decidedly liberal presumptions and not surprisingly reaches decidedly liberal conclusions.[3] When he stops to reflect upon how such a polity might come into being, and how it might conceivably endure through time, he both candidly and admirably wants to leave great room for diverse worldviews and moral outlooks, or comprehensive theories of the good as he puts it. Not only is Rawls clearly mindful of social diversity, he wants to accommodate it as fully as he thinks possible. He does not want anyone to be denied the basic rights, liberties, opportunities, and offices that should be open and available to everyone in the state simply because of who they are or what they happen to believe. Perhaps more importantly, he also hopes to address the problem of audience by supposing, in his more lyrical moments, that his defense of liberal justice is capable of gaining the allegiance of all elements of society. But his ability to accommodate diversity and welcome social pluralism has distinct and frankly troubling boundaries.

These boundaries are forged by Rawls's sense of reasonableness, which approximates a moral inclination on the part of 'reasonable' groups to accept the political standards of liberal justice.[4] Rawls feels no particular need to pose an argument to reasonable groups regarding why they should embrace the ideals of liberal justice. The members of groups holding disparate worldviews and/or moral theories of the good may not be swayed by such argument; this is an apparently necessary concession given the fact of pluralism that makes political stability into a problem. The value pluralism that Rawls supposes to exist in modern states makes the possibility of identifying a single comprehensive argument capable of enlisting the allegiance of all diverse groups extremely unlikely. But Rawls does suppose that a state can sustain the ideals of liberal justice only if the great preponderance of the groups constitutive of the citizenry happen to be reasonable, and they will prove to be reasonable if they have, internal to their own group beliefs, moral reasons to accept the standards of liberal justice.[5] On the other hand, Rawls acknowledges that not all groups in the polity are likely to be reasonable in this sense. Some may prove to be quite unreasonable—zealots and ideologues following a cause inconsistent with liberal justice. Rawls has nothing to say to these people and seems even to suppose that there is nothing reasoned argument can say to them. He hopes only that their numbers do not grow, that their ideology does not catch on, and that their influence (and presence) in the polity remains minimal and modest.[6]

Insofar as liberal theorists hope to offer a theory of civil association capable of enlisting the allegiance of everyone subject to political authority, this strategy of argument should have limited appeal. Liberal concerns for the justification of political authority and the legitimacy of the state incline at least some liberal theorists to desire something more, namely, a theory that reaches all, and not merely a great many (perhaps even a preponderant majority), of those subject to the authority of the state. But illiberals will surely reject liberal arguments if they are premised upon the moral views characteristic of liberal thought that they happen to reject; therefore, liberal argument that proceeds from such premises cannot hope to reach them. So liberals may admit the need to settle for a strategy of argument that reaches the greatest possible number of those subject to political authority, accepting, in effect, the concessions wisely made by Locke and Rawls. On the other hand, liberals need not, and sometimes do not, feel the need to advance a fully accommodationist argument. Those liberal theorists with great confidence in their moral viewpoint may have little concern for the illiberals in their midst. These are people, we can suppose, who generally show little respect for certain others or care little about the autonomy of others and who consequently hold normative convictions quite at odds with foundational liberal premises. From the viewpoint supplied by liberal morality, there is absolutely no reason to tolerate such people or to worry about their ability to live their lives as they wish. Liberal accommodationism need not, and some will certainly insist should not, include illiberals whose moral views are anathema from the liberal point of view.[7] So, some (and no doubt a great many) liberals have moral reasons not to worry particularly about the limitations of reach of liberal argument; and therefore, these liberals have moral reason to be entirely satisfied with Lockean and Rawlsian efforts to advance justificatory arguments that speak only to the *reasonable* elements of society.

There are, however, practical reasons to be unhappy with this strategy of argument. A politics based upon broadly majoritarian argument remains exclusionary. Some people are left to live within a state that operates upon basic political premises they may have reason to reject. As a result, it seems difficult at best to imagine the cultivation of a shared political vocabulary that will enable them to participate in the political affairs of the state. If and when the state intrudes upon their interests, they will no doubt work to defend themselves, perhaps by employing the political rhetoric of the state in their defense or perhaps by more activist or revolutionary means. But they will probably have a sorry political reputation among the social majority, and they will likely be branded as social pariahs and moved (or willingly relocate) to the margins of the political and social life of the state. They may, in extreme situations, go underground or otherwise hide themselves and their practices from the prying eyes of the government, the press, and the political majority more generally.

Yet, even if illiberals in the midst of the liberal state remove themselves to the social margin, they will still remain a political presence, and if it is not possible to reason with them, it will fall to the coercive mechanism of the state to assure that they do not bother citizens with more distinctly liberal inclinations. The state can guarantee that they are kept in line and that their illiberal practices do not compromise the autonomy and opportunity of others. Liberals need not blush at this of course; liberal argument legitimates efforts by the liberal state to guarantee the fundamentals of liberal morality for all citizens. From the standpoint of those liberals who have great confidence in their moral viewpoint, this is how things should be; this is how politics should go.

If some liberals happen to be content with this, grudgingly or otherwise, others will sense some uneasiness. Liberals like to think that the coercive efforts of the state need justification, and the required justification should reach all those subject to the state's coercive might. This, in turn, is why the illiberal are the cause of such theoretical consternation. If we cannot reason with them, if, that is, they are simply impervious to liberal argument, justification seems a practical impossibility, and there is nothing left but brute coercion to keep the illiberal in line. At the moment, however, I am less concerned with the theoretical troubles the illiberal cause liberal spirits and more concerned with the practical challenges they raise for historically or traditionally liberal states. The charge of oppression, as a practical matter, usually depends upon whose ox is getting gored. If at least some liberals see nothing oppressive about state efforts to enforce the standards of liberal morality against illiberal influences, those illiberals subject to the coercive pressure of the liberal state likely will. For practical purposes, it does not matter whether the liberal state really is oppressing the illiberal under the scenario I am imagining. All that matters is that the illiberal will *understand* things in terms of oppression and will accordingly have reason to reject the legitimacy of the state. We are left with a potentially dangerous and politically destabilizing cycle. Illiberal groups will see the state as a coercive oppressor, and they will likely take steps to defend themselves against its oppression. The state, unable to reason with the illiberal, sees this resistance as a threat to itself and an affront to liberal morality; therefore, it proceeds coercively to deal with illiberal groups. This inspires further fears in the illiberal that the state is an instrument of oppression, and they take steps to defend themselves—and so forth.[8] The histories of most, if not all, liberal polities are sprinkled with examples of this phenomenon, and they frequently lead to tragic results if they do not generate ongoing social unrest and instability.

The result is a social conflict that jeopardizes the very legitimacy of the state and further estranges at least some of the people living under its authority. This conflict may never reach the extremes that lead to disastrous results, to pervasive state oppression or to widespread social chaos, but it remains problematic just the same. It could reach such extremes of course, even in reasonably settled and stable states; it is not possible to fathom the forces at work with sufficient clarity to guarantee that such conflict can be kept within a reasonable balance. But it is problematic even if it does not reach such extremes, for it is a source of hostility, political struggle, and possible violence that anyone desiring a stable and secure political environment should want to do without. It remains a source of political instability and ongoing conflict even if it also remains at the margins of an otherwise stable political system. It is a social pathology produced by what I will call the fact of pluralism—the presence in society of differing, contradictory, and even incommensurable moral viewpoints and ontological outlooks. This is a pathology that should be addressed; it introduces a political problem that can (and I think should) legitimately inspire theoretical inquiry in the hope of identifying the possibility of a more accommodationist politics.

If we take the presence of the illiberal seriously, a broadly majoritarian liberal strategy of argument for the legitimacy of the state is not terribly helpful because it flounders upon the problem of audience. By supposing that a fully accommodationist argument is not possible, it begs the question at the center of the problem of audience. Much liberal theory proceeds this way, and as a result, illiberals simply fade from view and their presence in the state is diminished by liberal argument. This may have the practical consequence of further estranging and isolating illiberal groups, but it will not make them go away. If they fade from theoretical view, they are still a political presence and a source of instability. They remain an irritating sore upon the body politic. Recognition of this fact should do something to help suggest an answer to the problem of pertinence, but since broadly majoritarian argument cannot help us with the problem of audience, we had best look for another way to deal with the social pathology generated by the fact of pluralism.

A second way to deal with the problem of audience is to suppose that social pathology is the result of ignorance, either moral or epistemological. If human beings could only gain the proper knowledge about how they are supposed to live together, it should become a relatively simple matter to develop strategies for implementing our knowledge and building in theory at least an image of the ideal state. Perhaps, then, our theorizing about politics should be considered a search for moral truth or epistemological insight that can serve as the foundation for political certainty. Once we have managed the necessary insight, the problems of public life should dissipate. To establish social peace and maintain social justice we would only need to build and manage the state according to the dictates of moral and epistemological truth. This too has been a popular strategy in the history of western political thought. It calls to mind the spirit of Enlightenment thinking and the rationalist faith that the practical problems of living together are really problems of knowledge to be resolved by recourse to theoretical inquiry into the laws that govern the relations of human beings. This, of course, is the heart of the natural-law tradition that has inspired much modern political thought.

Postmodernist writers have cast considerable doubt upon the rationalist faith that typifies Enlightenment optimism. In the wake of the assault against reason—or rather the assault against knowledge—it might seem naïve to have much hope for this approach to political theory. But we can just as easily put postmodernist quibbling aside since we do not need to become so thoroughly skeptical about the power of reason to reject this approach to the problem of audience. Even if there was something approaching moral or epistemic truth that could serve as a foundation for political thought, even if we could build a political theory upon such a solid foundation, we still face an imposing practical problem. How might we get all the groups in the polity to recognize our truths as true? This problem goes to the heart of the practical challenge faced by anyone who feels the need to confront social pathology by taking up political theory.

To repeat what is quickly becoming the *leitmotiv* of this chapter, it is the diversity of heartfelt beliefs, and hence the fact of pluralism, that is the source of what I want to claim is the pathology that invites theoretical inquiry. The moral and ontological diversity characteristic of pluralism goes all the way down, we can suppose. While groups may agree on some things, they may well disagree, and disagree greatly, on many things that they happen to think matter. Is it possible, given the depth of the moral and ontological disagreement we have reason to anticipate, to suppose that groups, whose members cling to beliefs that modern science or modern moral philosophy consider false, will concede their errors and when confronted with something the rest of us consider conclusive evidence, abandon their beliefs and change their ways? Who could suppose that groups possessing their own epistemological standards of truth and their own moral convictions about right belief would be willing to abandon their most basic understanding of things when confronted with conclusions premised upon epistemological standards and moral beliefs they happen to reject? These deep moral and epistemological divides are the source of what I will call group incommensurability.[9] By this I mean that there is simply no metric, no common denominator, that can serve as the source of an initial agreement by which to measure the relative merits of the moral and ontological viewpoints that may be the source of intergroup conflict. Given the potential depth of the religious, moral, ideological, and ontological difference that exists under the fact of pluralism, it is simply fanciful to suppose that a foundationalist argument can suffice as an effective method for addressing the problem of audience.

A third possible strategy for dealing with the problem of audience is to suppose that we should forego the search for acceptable political standards or principles upon which to anchor political understanding and focus instead upon political process. This move, favored in particular by deliberative democrats of various stripes, recommends developing processes through which diverse and even conflicting groups can forge agreements and settle disputes.[10] The mechanisms of participatory democracy would seem to be particularly useful in this regard. They require groups to move to the bargaining table, so to speak, to discuss differences, debate problems, and address concerns with the hope of constructing some generally acceptable course of conduct that will work for them. This is the politics of compromise and participation. Groups are to find ways to get along in spite of all that separates them. It is also the politics of democratic activism and democratic egalitarianism. All groups are invited to the table and voting on policy proposals matters a good deal less than engagement in public discourse and deliberation. Discourse cultivates understanding and recognition and facilitates consensus building, even, it would seem, if the process remains deeply agonistic at heart. It is the process that matters, and defenders of this strategy place apparently great faith in the idea that process will yield positive results.

Yet one might plausibly wonder if this faith in the talismanic force of deliberation is in any sense justified. Why should we suppose that groups, whose members might be generally hostile to one another, will be willing to sit together and engage in democratic deliberation? Perhaps we can presume at this point that these groups share an overriding patriotism for their state, although this seems less than compelling. If group members share a sense of solidarity among themselves, and regard non-members as outsiders and hold them in suspicion accordingly, why should we think that some extra-group ties will incline them to sit with their adversaries and discuss common strategies for living together? For this to be possible, the extra-group ties must be forged, and it is difficult to see how they will be forged by means of a discourse that conflicting and competing groups are disinclined to enter. Before participatory democracy begins to make much sense, the members of the disparate groups that make up the state will need to have some sense of themselves as members of a common polity. Otherwise, the fact of pluralism would seem to encourage defection from the state and dissociation with groups considered hostile or unsavory. Group diversity, that is, may very possibly generate momentum for group independence and the consequent defection from association with other groups. In the absence of some countervailing force, pluralist states composed of possibly hostile groups are in danger of flying apart, ripped asunder by their own internal tensions.

Deliberative democrats may not consider this an insurmountable problem. Perhaps it only introduces the need to advance prudential reasons that counsel in favor of intergroup association. External pressures on a collection of groups sharing a common social space, and perhaps interwoven histories, may recommend pooling resources in order to provide for their mutual security. Or groups may face large-scale coordination problems in need of centralized management that is best supplied by the modern state. Such arguments may not appeal to all groups, of course, and some might want to defect from the state in hopes of benefiting from the association of the remaining groups and thus getting a free ride. But not all groups can hope for a free ride; if some do not agree to hold together, the external needs of these groups—needs to be met by means of civil association—will go unfulfilled. So, perhaps participatory democracy can address the social pathology caused by the fact of pluralism once the conditions specifying the need for the state are established and made clear.

But I see little reason to be optimistic on this score. Participatory democracy pays little heed to the actual nature of the divisions that separate groups and throw them into potential conflict. It presumes that groups will be willing to discourse with one another and that group members will welcome compromise in order to sustain the much-needed machinery of the state. Yet it is difficult to see how such an optimistic presumption can be defended given the very real and very deep danger of intergroup conflict. Some controversial issues simply go to the soul, and group members will likely find little reason to compromise on them. Imagine Catholic or certain fundamentalist religious communities engaging in open public discourse on the justifiability of abortion with members of pro-life feminist groups. Is it reasonable to hope for compromise here? Should we really expect these diverse groups to work through their differences and reach a mutually agreeable compromise? Is it feasible to think that minority groups will accept majoritarian decisions on such matters if they are put to a public vote? Or might it not make more sense to suppose that discourse will more likely move things in the direction of evermore hostility and discord rather than toward mutual understanding and appreciation for the position of the other?

The potential for conflict and hostility is exacerbated by the very real possibility that there are some matters, about which some people happen to feel strongly, that people with differing moral views and epistemic orientations simply cannot talk about. Their horizons of understanding may simply not intersect at any point that would make common discourse possible. In this event, people are likely to see these apparently strange others as moral demons or devils, as misguided fundamentalists, confused bigots, and so forth. Such conceptualizations are prelude not to democratic deliberation, but to increased intergroup conflict and animosity.

Sometimes, deliberative democrats suggest that these problems can be surmounted by the proper organization or control of the terms of political discourse. Some modes of argument may be prohibited, for example, because they are biased or fail to meet the proper standards of neutral discourse.[11] But such recommendations merely finesse the problem of audience by ignoring it. Why should groups bracket from argument those things that matter to them and play by the rules of discourse proposed by the democratic theorist? This either ignores or grossly underestimates the convictions of the groups likely to be involved in the deliberative process and presumes that groups have antecedent reasons for participating in democratic deliberation that might incline them to put aside those viewpoints excluded from deliberative discussion. Controlling the terms of discourse is likely to be considered biased in its own right by groups whose viewpoints are silenced. Consequently, they will have no reason to play by the terms introduced by the democratic theorist and will have reasons for not doing so based upon the moral and ontological viewpoints that matter to them.

It seems, then, that recourse to the processes of participatory democracy is not a sufficient strategy with which to approach the social pathology introduced by the fact of pluralism. It underestimates the nature of the problem, in effect, by underestimating the probable and likely depth and degree of intergroup conflict and hostility introduced by the fact of pluralism. Put in the terms that frame my discussion, appeals to process in order to deal with the challenges to the state posed by the fact of pluralism underestimate the problem of pertinence by under-appreciating the problem of audience. For democracy to work, a foundation of political unity—a common vocabulary of political life—must first be established. This requires, if nothing else, an accommodationist strategy capable of fashioning political unity in the presence of exceptional social, ethnic, religious, moral, and ideological diversity.

It seems, then, that none of the strategies commonly used to initiate a theoretical inquiry into the possibility of civil association manages to overcome the problem of audience, but their failings are instructive. Since the fact of pluralism introduces the pathology that inspires theoretical inquiry (or at least the inquiry undertaken here), a satisfactory response must take the problem of audience seriously and endeavor to present a theoretical defense of civil association calculated to be compelling to all worldviews and moral theories of the human good present in the state. This requires the construction of a thoroughly accommodationist politics, and it introduces, as the purpose of the theoretical inquiry to follow, the need to imagine in theory what I will call a politics of unity—a civil arrangement in which all citizens accept and share a common understanding of how their common social setting is to be managed or governed. Accordingly, I will reserve the term 'polity' for civil arrangements that satisfy the requirements of a politics of unity. If such a thing can be imagined in theory and the problem of audience can be satisfied, then a politics of unity is in principle possible, and this is about all that theorizing about politics can hope to accomplish.

A politics of unity, I want to say, is also and necessarily a politics of principle. An adequately accommodationist argument can succeed only if it derives and defends some principle (or set of principles) capable of acceptance by all elements of the polity. Such a principle, if indeed one can be satisfactorily articulated, becomes the focal point of political unity and the *grundlage* that galvanizes the state into a coherent polity. It works, if indeed it works at all, to direct members of the polity in their search for the proper boundaries of the public that is the polity, boundaries that define the realm of political authority and distinguish it from those non-civil, but public nonetheless, realms that are the seat of group autonomy and independence. A principle of this sort will introduce significant elements of the normative considerations pertinent to public discourse; it is the compass citizens use in order to push in the direction of social justice. The unity achieved by the articulation of an acceptable principle (or set of principles) will no doubt involve some general agreement on what the principle means and what it requires of citizens. The theoretical articulation and defense of such a principle must necessarily point in this direction. It is likely, of course, that this agreement will hold only at a rather high level of generality and lack clarity in specific instances. Nevertheless, this agreement establishes the basis upon which deeper or more specific justice claims are to rest. When conflict arises as a result of intergroup hostility or animosity, a politics of principle requires group members to advance their concerns and articulate their position in terms of the standards of justice established as a matter of principle. In short, a politics of principle inspires political unity by introducing the common ground for public deliberation as well as the common denominator against which conflicting concerns and interests are to be measured. By charting the parameters of political authority, it also charts the parameters of the group autonomy to be respected by all citizens as a matter of justice.

## Conflict, compromise, and the politics of interests

A politics of principle takes seriously the problem of audience. The theoretical project it inspires promises to seek and employ argumentation that should be compelling to all groups in the polity it seeks to constitute regardless of the moral viewpoint or ontological outlook they happen to accept and by which they happen to live. This may seem like tough duty, but if the pathology that inspires political theorizing is produced by the fact of pluralism, this is a promise theoretical inquiry must honor. I will endeavor to honor it as fully as possible in the argument of the chapters to follow, but I want now to say something more about the problem of pertinence. To do so, it is necessary to say a bit more about the social pathology introduced by the fact of pluralism.

Let me begin by imagining a condition I will call a politics of interests. In sociological terms, the jurisdictional boundaries of states are extremely arbitrary. Pluralist states are by their nature composed of groups with differing histories, traditions and customs, religions, beliefs, ideologies, languages, practices, and so forth. These are the conditions of difference and a (not necessarily *the*) source of great conflict. In the presence of such conflict (a conflict obviously generated by the fact of pluralism), states typically become the locus of intergroup struggle. I will say a politics of interests is present in states where political authorities take sides in the process of struggle, allowing or enabling some groups to prevail in their struggles with others. The state need not and, in states with liberal political histories, probably will not always side with the same groups (or sets of groups) as it referees inter-group conflict. Instead, the state reacts or responds favorably to those groups that are the most successful in marshalling political resources and applying them to their cause at any specific point in time. In the process, more dominant groups (i.e., groups with a preponderance of political resources) are likely to prove winners in the disputes in which they are involved, but these groups are not always or necessarily party to all the conflicts the state must referee. But under a politics of interests, there are always winners and losers; stronger groups (i.e., groups with superior political capital) will gener-ally gain the allegiance of the state, depending upon the amount of political capital they wish to expend on any given issue, and prevail in their struggles with weaker groups. Weaker groups, if they are to continue the fight, are left to find new allies, reconfigure themselves, amass new political resources, and if successful, return to the battle another day.

A politics of interests is invariably politically unstable. State legitimacy is often imperiled under such conditions, and there is always the possibility that things will decay into civil war or chaos if the issues that are the source of contention are of sufficient magnitude and the competing groups suffi-ciently intransigent.[12] Faced with the prospects of future defeat, however, dominant groups can be expected to cultivate their own political resources and work to control or overwhelm their political competitors. This tend-ency suggests that things could also swing in the other direction, away from chaos and civil war and toward what I will call a politics of dominance. This results in the event that some group (or alliance of groups) manages to amass sufficient power to capture the state and coercively impose its will upon its competitors. So, at least in principle, a politics of interests always teeters between the extremes of chaos and oppression. Sometimes oppression can be made to stick, but a politics of dominance is frequently unstable in its own right. Groups typically continue to struggle against oppression, and with time the power of dominant groups may wear thin, perhaps because of internal dissension within the ranks of the dominant groups, perhaps because oppressed groups have gained greater political clout, or perhaps because of external intervention on behalf of dominated groups. This sets the stage for ongoing and perhaps bloody political travail where the polit-ical pendulum swings wildly between the Scylla of chaos and the Charybdis of domination. This unfortunate predicament is familiar enough as the historic troubles in Northern Ireland and the seemingly eternal conflict in the Balkans (to cite only a couple of the more obvious examples) aptly illus-trate. The tragic saga of conflict, oppression, struggle, rebellion, and disorder, leading perhaps back to conflict and oppression, is all too familiar in human history. It represents a politics of interests at its worst.

In many states, of course, the politics of interests does not take on such terrible dimensions; the pendulum of conflict does not range between crude oppression and civil chaos and disorder. Some states boast long periods of (relative) political stability due in large measure to a system of politics that presumably permits all groups to participate in the process by which social policy is shaped. When viewed against the background of the terrible political injustices evident in human history, these states seem like pillars of decency and civility. Because a good many of these states have liberal democratic pedigrees, liberals sometimes share among themselves some self-satisfied winks, confident that there is something right or noble about their preferred form of civil association. But the winks are usually premature, for the pathology introduced by the politics of interests can corrode even the most exemplary liberal democracies. Political theory struggles mightily against the flux and *fortuna* of history, and modern liberal democracies are relative newcomers on the block. If places like the United States have managed a degree of political stability (and it is surely possible to overestimate this by fashioning a rather myopic view of American political history), it may be more the result of luck than good management. Liberal democracies too are subject to the ravages of history and the corrosive character of the politics of interests.

These ruminations suggest something of the eternal nature of theorizing about civil association and also something about its particularity and situatedness. On the side of the eternal, the central challenge of working toward a satisfactory vision of a politics of unity is and will likely remain constant. This seems invariably to be at the heart of political theorizing. Plato hoped to achieve unity in his republic by transforming the city into something like a family unit. Machiavelli hoped to achieve the desired unity of Italy by building a sense of civic virtue and encouraging political participation in public life. And Hegel, for his part, hoped to persuade his audience of the underlying rationality on display in a life dedicated to the ends of the state.

Strategies for achieving a politics of unity vary greatly from thinker to thinker, but the end remains much the same. Historical conditions and social circumstances demand that theorists think about new ways to overcome the politics of interests, and liberal thinkers are not the only ones to have engaged this issue. If Plato could imagine a city held together by a manufactured homogeneity, this vision offers little solace to contemporary thinkers worrying about the politics of interests in the terribly diverse and exceptionally complicated states of the twenty-first century. In the face of such remarkable pluralism, a politics of unity seems to depend, as I have suggested, upon the successful articulation of a politics of principle. But the effort at articulation—the project of theoretical inquiry—must be sensitive to the requirements of particularity. If the principle(s) that sets the foundation for political unity can reasonably serve those diverse states hoping to overcome the travail of the politics of interests, its practical demands will have to vary in order to accommodate and address the particular nature of the group conflict in evidence in specific states. A politics of principle will make demands upon the citizenry; this is simply unavoidable. But the demands it makes will depend on the political vicissitudes of the particular state in question. So, theorizing about politics is invariably time and place bound. It is a response to the particular manifestation that the pathology of a politics of interests has in any given polity. It follows that a politics of principle must satisfy a condition of practicality; it must suit the needs of a particular state as that state exists at some specific moment in time.

To satisfy the practicality condition, theorists need to have some sense of the way the politics of interests manifests itself in the particular state of concern to them. The need to be mindful of particularities localizes the task of theorizing about public life. As a practical matter, theoretical reflection must be considered time and place bound; it is only the effort to envision a politics of unity that remains eternal. This follows naturally from the therapeutic character of political inquiry. This is because the appropriate therapy depends upon the exact nature of the social pathology, as it manifests itself at a given moment and place in time, that is the cause for concern and the inspiration for political theorizing. So, it is necessary for me to situate my discussion in the political life of the United States at the dawn of the twenty-first century. This is not only the state to which I belong and the one with which I am the most familiar, it is also one that I think has a particular use for a theoretical vision of a politics of principle. To explicate the problem of pertinence, it is necessary to make good on this claim, and this requires a brief look at the politics of interests American style.

Americans typically like to think that the United States is a paragon of justice and a shining example to the remainder of the planet on how civil association should go. If Americans admit that things could be better—that some injustices still lurk across the land—they usually think things are at least in pretty good theoretical shape. American ideals, this commonplace view goes, are on the right track; there is just some unseemly foot-dragging that keeps the United States from fulfilling its moral manifest destiny. Political optimists in the country suppose that it is just a matter of time before the inexorable march of political enlightenment will prevail.[13] Those pockets of backward souls who seem, for whatever reason, to fail to embrace the standards of justice upon which the polity is founded will eventually fade from the social landscape, and civic peace, justice, and social tranquility will eventually prevail.[14] The pessimists in the land, on the other hand, are less confident of America's political future. They worry that human frailty poses an unconquerable barrier to social progress. The ideal of justice suffers when it encounters the sad fact of human greed. The grand goal of peace and justice is further compromised because of the intractable reality of social hatreds. And the enchanting vision of civic brotherhood is sullied by the stains of distrust and suspicion that seem to be the inescapable feature of a diverse and eclectic state. Yet there is nothing in this cynicism that questions the elegance of core American political values. The ideals of liberty and equality, believed to be at the center of American political culture, are embraced by optimists and pessimists alike as the primary stuff of civic life, and both champion a politics devoted to these noble norms. If the reality of politics in America is something less than it should be, it is because we have yet to get all the kinks out of ourselves, our political system, or perhaps both. In any case, the problems with which Americans continue to wrestle are presumed to be largely practical.[15] They are not considered to be the sort of thing that inspires theorizing about politics because, it is supposed, there just is not much serious social pathology present in America. Instead, America suffers only in the details of value implementation. It lacks only the dogged cultural dedication to the ends of social justice required by its own political ideals, perhaps because it suffers too much from what Hume called the 'confin'd generosity of men.'[16] In short, it will seem to many that the groundwork for a politics of principle is already present in the United States, and so there is no great need for political inquiry. The theoretical work would thus seem to be done, taken care of by the 'founding fathers' during the constitutional convention, and there is accordingly little reason to question the practical results of Enlightenment wisdom as it manifests itself in contemporary American politics. Thanks to their inheritance, Americans have no need for theory; they need only continue the struggle to bring their ideals to life in the daily workings of the state.

I think this view of American politics is unacceptably flattering. The United States is hardly closer to a politics of unity than many other states. But Americans have become adept at ignoring their dirty political linen and viewing their political landscape through the rosy lens provided by mythic beliefs about 'the land of the free and the home of the brave.' John Higham, among others, has done much to bring this dirty linen into plain view by calling attention to the ugly realities of nativist activity in American history.[17] Nativists see themselves as quintessentially American, and they see outsiders, immigrants, and others not like them in crucial cultural or ideological ways as distinctive threats to the American way of life. In the process, they interpret, or reinterpret, America—her values, customs, ideals, and practices—in terms of *their* values, customs, ideals, and practices.[18] Groups that are not like them are not just different; they are a threat to them and their way of life, and hence to America itself. This, as should be apparent, introduces the specter of intergroup conflict. More recently, and following in the tradition of Higham, Rogers Smith has documented the historic presence of the recurring theme of 'ascriptive Americanism' that fans the fires of nativism and continues to generate intergroup conflict in America.[19]

Nativist activity, and the responses it engenders in its targets, is but one example of the type of intergroup conflict prevalent, and *historically* prevalent, in America. There are others. Yet, American apologists may still want to insist that these misguided patriots constitute little more than a lunatic fringe to the American political landscape. And we have ways of dealing with them. Whatever hatred, animosity, or uneasiness these unsavory characters generate is easily managed by having recourse to the fundamental political ideals ensconced within and emanating from the American Constitution. If and when nativists get out of hand, if and when some groups attempt to prey upon or dominate others, the state is there to defend the rights of the threatened and the courts are there to articulate and assert the ideals of justice to which we are committed as a society. This hints, to be sure, at a politics of principle, and displays a remarkable confidence in the ability of core American political beliefs to harness, control, and eventually domesticate misguided or confused political zealots.

Appearances, however, are frequently deceiving, and this is the case when the politics of interests plays itself out within the context of American constitutional architecture, as it frequently does. Rights and liberties are traditionally viewed as ideals to be respected, a sentiment presumably shared throughout the United States. But rights and liberties are also the contemporary weapons of the politics of interests as it now manifests itself in the American political landscape.[20] By way of illustration, consider the legal and political controversy that recently swirled around the latest explosion of so-called hate speech in the late 1980s and early to mid-1990s. As the purveyors of hateful ideas grew more bold during this period, public officials responded, often at the behest of the unhappy targets of these views, by drafting and implementing regulations intended to control the way certain racist, sexist, homophobic, and religious views could legitimately be expressed. Groups officially wishing to articulate their racist, sexist, homophobic, and religious ideas took exception to these regulations; and sensing that they were defending a minority view, these groups quickly couched their concerns in the rhetoric of political legitimacy by insisting such regulation infringed upon their constitutionally guaranteed right of free speech. They were soon joined by free-speech patrons who also worried about all this and considered the city ordinances and college conduct codes to be a content restriction on speech—just the sort of thing that seems inconsistent with the American ideal of free speech.[21] Proponents of the regulations countered by arguing that the codes and ordinances at issue were permissible because they prohibited only 'fighting words,' a classification of speech the Supreme Court has long held to be subject to state regulation. Nonetheless, the struggle characteristic of the politics of interests was under way. The political agendas of diverse and hostile groups had come into conflict, and the apparent losers in the legislative arena began to conceptualize their concerns in legal terms.

At the heart of the politics of interests American style, one finds a struggle over conceptualizations; groups fight to have their sense of things—their construction of socio-political life—control the public understandings and thus dominate public belief. At one point in American history, the unequal treatment of African-Americans was basically considered consistent with American ideals about liberty. At a later date, there was great disagreement about and conflict over this very issue.[22] Today there is little disagreement; the pervasive view condemns racial inequality as anathema to the American ideals of liberty and equality, although pockets of racist sentiment remain. Similarly, the dominant public view in America today seems to condemn some more blatant forms of sexist and homophobic behavior. Accordingly, if the politics of interests in its crudest possible form worked its will, there would be no problem suppressing speech if its content failed the current litmus test of 'political correctness.' But there is still the matter of free speech; there is still the question of whether anti-bias prohibitions pass legal inspection under the 'fighting words' doctrine or whether they offend our principled commitment to free speech.

Free-speech activists, along with those purveyors of certain forms of group hatred, were predictably ecstatic when the Supreme Court took their side on the issue and struck down a St Paul anti-bias ordinance on the grounds that it improperly burdened the free-speech rights of Robert Viktora and several other teenagers who had burned a cross on the lawn of a black family in the early morning hours of 21, June 1990.[23] This looks on its face like a triumph of principle over political interest. While the majority of Americans may not like what some people have to say, a commitment to free speech entitles them to have their say. If we choose not to listen, that is our business, but we cannot silence the messenger just because the majority happens, for whatever reason, to dislike the message.

But this is little more than constitutional posturing, a rhetorical flourish (and a familiar one at that) serving only to obscure the workings of the politics of interests. If the purveyors of so-called hatred carried the day, it was because they managed to wrap their activities around one of America's most holy of icons: the right of free speech. Liberty, it seemed, was on their side, or at least they managed to convince a majority of Supreme Court justices of this. Even though we do not like what they have to say, we cannot silence them because what they have to say is protected speech. *Libertas vicat omni*. But the story is just beginning. The Court's work in this little area of jurisprudence hardly settled the issue—judicial decisions settle cases, not controversies. Instead, it transformed the controversy in a way that moved it from a crude to a considerably more subtle version of the politics of interests. To illustrate, consider Richard Delgado's impassioned response to the Supreme Court's dismissal of anti-bias ordinances:

> Racism and racial stigmatization harm not only the victim and the perpet-
> rator of individual racist acts but also society as a whole. Racism is a breach
> of the ideal of egalitarianism, that 'all men are created equal' and that
> each person is an equal moral agent, an ideal that is a cornerstone of the

American moral and legal system. A society in which some members regularly are subjected to degradation because of their race hardly exemplifies this ideal.[24]

This seemingly straightforward yet powerful comment advances a number of important claims. First, it asserts that racist speech is harmful, not just to those minorities subjected to it, but to the 'society as a whole.' The harm, presumably, is that racist speech chews away at the 'cornerstone' of American law, and more importantly at American morals, by challenging the 'ideal of egalitarianism.' Second, it supposes that equality is a fundamental—if not *the* fundamental—ideal of American politics. Of more modest interest are the claims that the idea of equality in America involves seeing each person as an 'equal moral agent' (presumably an oblique appeal to the Kantian view of persons as beings of incomparable worth) and that acts of hateful speech that submit some to degradation 'because of their race' offend this ideal of egalitarianism.

Taken together, these claims constitute a powerful counter-attack within the politics of interests. They challenge the principled high ground assumed by those who hoped to have the conflict understood in terms of a political intrusion into the realm of liberty. They do so, moreover, by attempting to identify and occupy even higher principled ground. 'Here,' they say, 'is an instance where the purported right of free speech should yield because it is in conflict with a more basic American ideal, with a more fundamental principle of American justice.' The interest certain minority groups have in social inclusion, along with the interest the dominant culture would appear to have in eliminating the stigma of oppression and exclusion these groups have been forced to suffer and endure, is reinterpreted to be something more than a plank in the political agenda of these groups and a policy objective for the dominant culture more generally. It has principled roots that run even deeper than any concern for free speech, and so adherence to principle should demand that the hate-speech controversy be settled in their favor. This is a politics of interests made subtle indeed. Policy objectives and group interests have been reinterpreted and articulated in terms of political principles. These interests have not been transformed in the process, but the contest of interests is now fought out on a decidedly different front.

This, to be sure, is a form of Orwellian politics. It involves a struggle over the proper conceptualization of the issue. Both sides to the conflict seek to control the outcome by giving the content that favors them to the otherwise 'empty vessels' of American political ideals—the key worship words of American politics. While these worship words resonate in the American conscience and operate as symbols of political legitimacy, they have no clear, generally accepted, and reasonably certain meaning in the absence of a politics of principle. Their meaning and importance depends upon what competing groups can pour into and make of them. The politics of interests continues in the United States because these worship words are up for grabs, and groups that can control their meaning will be able to realize their political ends. Groups that lose in this struggle, accordingly, will be relegated to the role of social outcast and become pariah groups whose beliefs and practices are shunned as un-American. It is, in other words, the emptiness or abstractness of American political concepts and ideals that sets the stage for the politics of interests as it is played out in the political culture of the United States. While it seems Americans are constantly being reminded of their historic commitment to liberty and equality, they rarely stop to ponder just how they should honor this commitment. In the absence of some attention to this issue, it is little wonder that a politics of interests, confused at times with a politics of principle, flourishes. We are left with a political environment where the political battlegrounds are shaped and controlled by constitutional vagaries and where the victors prevail because they are the most successful in capturing and controlling the meaning of key political concepts and ideals, thus 'remaking' American justice in the form that suits their particular political ends.

There is irony here that becomes visible if we stop to consider an apparently inescapable consequence of Delgado's impassioned defense of equality. His argument, in effect, tends to erode the very ideal—the ideal of egalitarianism—that he purports to defend. As the politics of interests moves in the direction of controlling the meaning/content of American worship words (the content of the normative ideals of the state, if one wants to see the point in more general and less localized ways), winning groups or collectives succeed in re-creating (or re-inventing) political ideals in the terms suitable to their own political agendas. Conversely, losing groups risk demonization by being identified as un-American or opposed to the basic values and ideals of American public life. Whether Delgado intends this to be his message or not, if his claims succeed in giving content to the otherwise rather ethereal American ideal of equality, racists and others who might want to endorse certain kinds of elitism (thereby reconfiguring the ideal of egalitarianism) based upon racial classifications are dismissed as un-American. They fail to accept and endorse the 'cornerstone' of American law and morality (viz., that 'each person is an equal moral agent') because they hold and espouse racist views. So, according to this reading of American ideals, racists, and others who reject the view that all persons are equal moral agents, are rightfully the subject of scorn and contempt. Living up to our own ideals, then, legitimates silencing these scoundrels at least insofar as they would direct their venom toward specific historically disadvantaged minorities.

But this is curiously inegalitarian, albeit in a sense at odds with Delgado's view of equality. Delgado's strong defense of minority interests and minority sensitivities has the curious consequence of marginalizing the racists he wants to defend certain minorities against. By identifying them as un-American, we can suppose they are made to feel like they do not matter at least politically. They are out of step with the rest of the land; their views are inconsistent with good morals and right belief. They should be ashamed of themselves; they are a blot upon the land, an ugly sore in the body politic, a source of national embarrassment. It is easy, then, to see them as targets of scorn and ridicule; victims—at the risk of hyperbole—of a form of hate speech in their own right. And here the politics of interests is again on display. Why is some speech considered hateful and therefore objectionable? Why is racist speech hateful but speech that derogates racists not hateful? (Think here about the success some groups have in getting some types of speech recognized as *hateful* in the first place!)

Once again we confront the Orwellian control of language and the consequent control of understanding. But we might now ask if those racists who have been dismissed as moral reprobates have received proper recognition as moral agents. Is the marginalization they are made to suffer because they emerge as losers in the politics of interests consistent with American ideals of equality? Is this a fate we should want to see imposed upon any element of the population regardless of how noxious we might think their views to be?

I suppose there are a great many Americans who will want to answer these questions affirmatively. They may want to insist that in fact the racists in our midst really are un-American and really are out of touch with fundamental American ideals. They are out of step with basic standards of American justice, and consequently they should be marginalized if that means denying them the right to put their hateful beliefs into practice. This, in any event, is the dominant way of seeing things, and it may not matter to those who hold this dominant view that it is a product of the politics of interests, that we see justice the way we do because of the struggle of political forces working to control the meaning of justice itself. It is to see things from the inside, so to speak, and to be content with doing so. But these pariah groups have not gone away, and given their historic tenacity, it seems unlikely that they will ever go away. The verbal flurry set off by the latest wave of hate-speech activity is but just the latest round of the politics of interests, and if today's construction of political correctness has tended to go against the 'purveyors of hatred' we cannot know what tomorrow's construction of political correctness will look like. This, I should think, is reason for all groups party to the dispute to want to put the politics of interests behind them and look for a more principled remedy to this pathology.

The hate-speech controversy, of course, is but one example of the politics of interests American style; there are many others that could be identified to supplement my claim about the social pathology that presently (and historically) characterizes American politics, in the event that doubters think I am exaggerating the pathology I wish to identify. Consider, for example, the ongoing dispute over abortion in the United States, and the conflict it has generated. It is hardly necessary here to document the militancy displayed by the members of some groups who seem to feel they have lost the upper hand in this continuing political struggle. Of greater interest, perhaps, is the clash of conceptualizations as both sides to the conflict seek to put their preferred linguistic spin on the issue and place it within the context of American political legitimacy. Thus, those groups favoring the legalization of abortion press their case in terms of a 'right to choose,' while groups favoring the criminalization of abortion put the matter in terms of the 'right to life.' Both 'pro-life' and 'pro-choice' advocates press their cause in the language of American political legitimacy, and both insist that the other side live up to the fundamental ideals of American justice. No doubt few Americans would want to consider themselves either 'anti-life' or 'anti-choice'—both seem decidedly un-American—but even fewer Americans seem inclined to see the conflict as a dispute about divergent group views on the morality of the practice of abortion and to sever this intergroup conflict from the ideals of American politics. Here again the politics of interests is at work, and its workings tend to shroud from view the actual character of the conflict at issue.

Nor does the politics of interests necessarily or invariably play itself out only on the national stage or in front of the Supreme Court. It dominates disparate local venues as well, and only sometimes bubbles up to national prominence. As I write, for example, several American jurisdictions are faced with a controversy about the legitimacy of gay marriage. In one local jurisdiction, Multnomah County, Oregon, this issue came into prominence when county commissioners declared that Oregon law did not prohibit homosexual marriage and permitted the County to issue marriage certificates to gay couples. Opposition to the decision quickly materialized, and the politics of interests came into plain view.[25] As the issue took shape in Multnomah County, opponents to gay marriage sought to carry the day by controlling the meaning of the concept of marriage. Marriage, opponents have insisted, is possible only between a man and a woman; therefore same-sex couples cannot marry.[26] Granted marriage is not ordinarily viewed as an American worship word, but opponents to gay marriage in Oregon now seem intent on modifying this slightly by pressing for a state initiative that would amend the Oregon Constitution to stipulate that marriage is only possible between a man and a woman.[27]

The gay marriage issue is only now unfolding, and it is difficult to see how the politics of interests will play itself out in this instance. At present, both sides seem intent on controlling the definition of marriage, with one side wanting to ensconce its account of marriage in the official law of the land, thus bestowing legal legitimacy on their understanding of the issue. If this seems both unfortunate and just a little bit foolish, it is probably because the meaning of marriage is not the real issue local jurisdictions should be concerned with. In its present form, the politics of interests masks the ongoing intergroup conflict between homosexual groups and the more fundamentalist groups spearheading local opposition to gay marriage. The controversy raises some important questions about the ability of certain groups to control their own affairs and receive support for their own ways from the state without interference from the outgroups around them. That is, the controversy raises serious questions about how best to manage intergroup conflict. The politics of interests is unable to answer this question; in fact, it is unable to isolate the question itself and recognize its pertinence to the issue at hand. Instead, the question is lost within the context of group efforts to identify their interests with the true and binding beliefs of the land. Under the politics of interests, intergroup conflict is shrouded amidst the efforts groups make to control the conceptualization of the controversy in matters favorable to their preferred understanding of things.

## Ideals, interests, and the politics of principle

There are reasons, however, why we should not be content with the vicissitudes of a politics of interests. For one thing, it seems unfortunate to sustain a political struggle that produces only winners and losers. Depending upon how one chooses to understand notions like equality or marriage, there may be something objectionable about a political process that continues to isolate, marginalize, oppress, dismiss, or demonize certain elements of the citizenry. I do not mean to suggest by this that I am worried about the poor racists in our midst or any other illiberal sorts that might suffer because they have been unable to control the conceptualization of American politics. I am, however, modestly concerned about the dilemma of oppression the politics of interests feeds. Liberal sentiments turn against themselves on this score. Liberals sometimes insist that others, regardless of whether or not they qualify as liberal, should be allowed to live as they wish, but they have a hard time making good on this claim when they confront illiberals who would live in ways inconsistent with liberal morality. We have noticed already that this does not necessarily catch liberalism in a contradiction, but, as we shall see, contradiction can be avoided only by making one of two moves. Either the liberal can champion his or her moral convictions and feel justified in condemning and not tolerating illiberals, or she or he can search for alternative political strategies that might find a place for illiberals even in societies dominated by liberal morality. Anyone who is even a bit uncertain about the outright moral dismissal of illiberals will have reason to explore this second option.

Still, moral objections to the politics of interests will play best for those groups whose worldviews or moral theories of the human good are not in great favor with the dominant elements of society. These are the groups that will feel the sting of what they might consider unfair and unequal treatment at the hands of the politically dominant groups. These dominant elements, on the other hand, have moral reasons of their own to prefer a politics of interests as long as they can manage to control the language of politics and interpret it according to their own moral predilections. But dominant elements should be mindful of the fundamental instability of a politics of interests. It occupies a shaky and uncertain space between chaos and dominance. If they have succeeded today in capturing and interpreting the empty ideals of American political morality to their liking, they may be on the losing end tomorrow. The infighting is sure to continue, and today's winners may turn out to be tomorrow's losers. At the very least, the infighting will continue to smolder, and it may erupt from time to time and from place to place in violence or open hostility. By way of support for this claim, it would be easy to list numerous tales of racial, ethnic, religious, homophobic, and intergroup violence in recent American history, but such tales are so legion and so commonplace on the American political landscape that this hardly seems necessary. Suffice it to say that the threat to social peace and tranquility created by these intergroup conflicts and tensions is its own independent cause for concern. If this is reason to be unhappy with the politics of interests as it is on display in American politics, as I think it is, the problem of pertinence should be satisfied.

Faced with the insecure reality of a politics of interests, groups can secure their political presence in the body politic in either of two ways. They can either work toward achieving a politics of dominance or they can settle for a politics of principle. There is some reason to think that a politics of dominance would be the most desirable alternative to those groups that are currently politically ascendant: it would assure their most desirable socio-political condition by guaranteeing them ongoing political control. It remains an open question and an empirical matter, on the other hand, whether dominant groups are really likely to prefer dominance over a politics of interests. But in any case, the realization of a politics of dominance is also likely to be the most difficult achievable solution to the instability problem introduced by the politics of interests. We can suppose that all groups existing under the conditions I have associated with a politics of interests will have some interest in working toward a politics of dominance, and here we find further evidence that a politics of interests is a condition best characterized by ongoing struggle. Marginalized groups will fight against domination just as more dominant groups will fight for it. This is surely the most compelling reason to want to transcend such a condition, and it holds even if one belongs to a group that is currently dominant in the state. Once we appreciate the dynamics of a politics of interests, dominance will begin to seem like a fleeting and precarious social condition, a point to which I shall return in the chapter to follow.

Still, there are other reasons why groups might elect not to pursue a politics of principle. For one thing, there is reason to be suspicious about the very possibility of such a politics. If the social setting is characterized by a degree of normative diversity, or by a variety of moral, religious, and ideological views, it is hard to imagine how anyone could hope to discover or construct some principled view of political association that all members of the state could endorse. The possibility of crafting an argument capable of persuading such a diverse audience would seem to be so remote that committing to a politics of principle could be considered a waste of time. There is a bit of irony here. It is likely that the best response to the social pathology introduced by the politics of interests is to pursue the possibility of a politics of principle. And yet, the more diverse the state, the greater the normative and ontological pluralism on display there, the more difficult the challenge of constructing a viable politics of principle—bringing us back to the problem of audience with a vengeance. But it is just in settings of this sort that the need for a politics of principle is the greatest, for the politics of interests is all the more insidious in such places.

Perhaps the best way to meet this problem is to forge ahead with theoretical inquiry and consider whether the possibility of a politics of principle can be imagined in theory. It might not be possible to imagine such a politics even in theory; but since we cannot know this until we try, this problem can be understood to pose a significant challenge to the theoretical project but not a reason to abandon the project before it is even begun. On the other hand, even if it is possible to imagine in theory a politics of principle, groups may still have reason to reject it as a desirable mode of civil association. Such a politics, we can suppose, comes with considerable moral costs; in order to achieve its accommodationist agenda, it will almost certainly ask a great many, if not all, groups in the state to limit or control those activities inconsistent with the principled limits it imposes upon intergroup activity. Seen from the inside, the interests that groups have and the normative convictions that in all probability power them are of the first importance to their members. If a politics of principle requires that these interests be compromised or deferred, it might be preferable to live with a politics of interests and take one's chances. If a politics of principle demands that groups put up with what they consider the immoral or unjust behavior of others, they may object on the grounds that this encourages bad moral faith.

But this too provides little reason to abandon the theoretical project before it gets under way, and it might also be taken to offer some insight into the challenges that an inquiry into a viable politics of principle must confront. When faced with the fact that a politics of principle may require at least some groups to forego acting upon moral convictions in ways they feel they should, the case for such a politics becomes something of a hard sell, even to liberals who have a historical commitment to something of this sort. The sell, however, is part of the challenge, part of the theoretical project. Keeping the problem of audience firmly in mind, we need to proceed to construct a case for a politics of principle that all elements of the state can understand and accept, regardless of the normative and ontological views that characterize them. We need to see if such a politics is desirable and to explore the conditions under which it would seem to be possible; this is about all we can expect from theoretical inquiry. In the process, we must demonstrate what a politics of principle involves in practice and indicate the demands it makes upon all elements of the polity. Finally, we must explain why these costs do not outweigh the benefits to be gained by securing the stability and tranquility a politics of principle has to offer. But we must also be mindful of the fact that theoretical inquiry is basically a philosophical endeavor. As such, it operates upon a basic presumption that can only be taken as a given. It supposes that reasoned argument and thoughtful analysis can get the attention and gain the allegiance of anyone possessing a sliver of rationality.

The search for a politics of principle must therefore proceed against the background belief that there is a realm of rational insight that holds independently of any normative or ontological viewpoints that might characterize someone's worldview. If the problem of audience is to be overcome, it is necessary to presume that it is at least possible to speak to all elements of the polity in terms they can reasonably comprehend and understand. Political inquiry, like all forms of theoretical endeavor, must presume some dimension of rational understanding; otherwise the theoretical project is simply not possible. It may prove to be the case that there are limits to what we can do with theoretical inquiry and that the problem of audience is too intractable to be fully met. But this possibility need not deter us from trying to fashion a politics of principle and may in the end signal only a modest limitation to what theoretical inquiry can achieve. Nonetheless, this presumption may seem to cause trouble because it looks like an epistemological claim in its own right and should therefore be ruled out of order at the outset. At the very least, this notion needs an element of justification, and justification will be forthcoming in the argument to follow. For now, it will suffice to notice that theorizing about politics must presume there is *something* people share in common that will enable them to approach and understand one another no matter how extraordinary or capacious the differences that separate them. Hobbes supposed this something to be prudence, not morality, and he might just have been right.

There is no guarantee, of course, that a politics of principle, if one can be imagined or possibly established in the American political context, will put an end to intergroup conflict and violence and remedy the social pathology displayed by the politics of interests. But it might, and in any case, it should be clear that continuing along with a politics of interests will only keep intergroup conflict going and invite and facilitate the dangers associated with it. This too supports an effort at therapeutic political inquiry.

# 2
# A Politics of Principle

The appropriate remedy for a politics of interests involves working toward the practical development of political unity and thereby transforming the state into a polity. The first step in such a process is to see if political unity is even conceivable given the fact of pluralism. This is first and foremost a philosophical problem that invites theoretical inquiry into the logic of civil association. So far, I have suggested that political unity is possible only if we can imagine a principled basis for civil association that all elements of the state can accept and endorse regardless of their worldview and moral theory of the human good. Insofar as the strategies of argument discussed in the previous chapter are unable to overcome the challenge posed by the problem of audience, they are unable to direct an inquiry dedicated to the construction of a politics of principle. Accordingly, there is little reason to worry further about them. But the problem of audience is still with us. The fact of pluralism that produces it effectively guarantees that there is no pre-existent common ground to which one can appeal in the process of exploring the possibility of a politics of principle. Nonetheless, the possibility of a politics of principle must presume that some reasons (or cluster of reasons) for accepting political unity—reasons that speak and speak forcefully to all elements of the state—can be given. This chapter takes up the challenge of searching for such reasons and in the process presents what I will call a thin theory of political unity.

## Manufacturing unity: Practical argument and social diversity

How should we begin to search for reasons to accept a principled politics in spite of whatever social diversity we might encounter in the state? One rather popular way is to imagine some initial or basic condition—a state of nature, for example—that sets the social baseline against which the desirability of some form of civil association is to be measured. Moves of this sort sometimes work to illustrate the problem of pertinence, or to dramatize the social pathology a theorist hopes to expose and help remedy. Since the issue of pertinence has already been discussed, we do not need to employ such a device for this reason. But state-of-nature arguments also work at times as ontological or normative filters that control contingent features of human life and expose basic or fundamental facts (moral or ontological) that support and direct theory articulation. They are employed in order to expose or highlight certain fundamental truths (again moral or ontological) that enable people to imagine the kind of civil condition suitable to or appropriate for them. This is the keystone of foundationalist argument. But it is best to forego foundationalist arguments for reasons already encountered. Even if such arguments qualified as true in some (murky) objectivist or realist sense, they inevitably flounder on the problem of audience. There is no reason to suppose that everyone in the state could recognize their truth or would even be open to doing so. The fact of pluralism works against this very possibility. In fact, the fact of pluralism requires us to work in the opposite direction and forsake efforts of theory construction premised upon foundationalist or universalist moral claims. The fact of pluralism suggests not only that there is no reason to suppose that some fundamental moral claim (or set of claims) could be recognized as true by all elements of the polity, but also (and more importantly) that there is reason to suppose that no such claim (or set of claims) would be recognized as true by all elements of the polity.

Of course, we might also hypothesize some baseline social condition, like a state of nature, in order to pursue what I will call a blindfold strategy of argument. Suppose, for example, we blind ourselves to certain (allegedly) contingent features of our lives that burden or obfuscate the theoretical project. By shrouding these aspects of our being from view, they cannot cloud the theoretical project, and we can proceed to consider only those principles or rules that reason (untarnished by the contingencies of faith, ideology, mysticism, or belief) recommends for the governance of civil association. This, I think, is the role played by Rawls's duly famous notion of an original position. He imagined a condition where rational agents in the original position stand behind a veil of ignorance designed to factor out specific information and details about the nature of one's own being, thus assuring a modicum of impartiality within the rational-choice project he constructed.[1] The difficulty with using blindfold devices of this sort, however, is that we need reasons to put the blindfold on. Why would anyone bother to begin the theoretical project by blinkering out normative and ontological viewpoints and understandings that determine and characterize how they see and value things? Philosophical fantasies of this sort will surely be rejected as inappropriate or nefarious by groups whose members hold dear to the views about the way the world is, and what matters in the world, that they are asked to bracket off as contingencies of their being. Such moves seem sensible only from within the context of some given normative or ontological orientation, but seen from outside this condition they are both arbitrary and objectionable.

Further, the blindfold device is hardly neutral between competing worldviews and moral theories of the human good. Before use of the blindfold makes sense, there must be some prior determination of what should be filtered from view and what should be seen. The judgments required to make these determinations are likely to be controversial in their own right under conditions of pluralism. Rawls, for example, crafted his blindfold in order to guarantee a strictly egalitarian condition behind the veil of ignorance, but this in itself is reason for racists and elitists to be suspicious of such moves. If it is not possible to craft a blindfold that is neutral between competing worldviews and moral theories of the human good—and it seems unlikely that this is possible—then at least some groups in the social setting will have reason to object to the exercise on the grounds that some imagined blindfold is biased against their particular vision of the good and perhaps in favor of such a vision held by others.

Blindfold arguments get off to a bad start immediately; they address the problem of audience by asking us to suppose it really does not exist. Admitting the problem of audience at the outset means that we need to keep the fact of pluralism in front of us at all times and not pretend to hide it from view. Rather than imagine some mythical condition that masks the contingencies of being, it is best to give the fact of pluralism its due and find ways to enlist the diversity it introduces positively in the theoretical project. Political unity, in effect, is possible only if it is manufactured, so to speak, in the presence of the diversity that makes it both difficult and important to achieve.

Manufacturing political unity requires building an argument, to be presented to all elements of the state, for the acceptance of first-order political ideals that are to govern the relations of groups holding disparate, conflicting, and perhaps incommensurable worldviews. Such an argument must avoid claims of epistemological or moral truth; in the presence of the fact of pluralism, such matters are thrown into inevitable and irreconcilable dispute. To succeed, the argument must ideally speak to all groups in the state in a fashion they can understand and respect regardless of the worldview and moral theory of the human good they may happen to hold. Unity can be achieved only if our argument can win the allegiance of everyone in the state. By advancing such an argument, we invite all ethnic, cultural, religious, and ideological groups in the state to consider, analyze, and if possible find fault with it. If they cannot find fault with it, the practical ground is established for a politics of unity.

We can anticipate that no one will be terribly happy with such an argument, if in fact one can be pressed. Groups possessing their own ontological and normative viewpoints will have, internal to these viewpoints, reasons to think that they know how things should go politically. Comprehensive worldviews, we can suppose, will dictate to those who hold them what the social and political world should look like, and there is no reason to think that the political ideals supported by an argument for political unity will mirror any of these political or social visions. So, groups will most likely have their own internal moral or epistemic reasons for rejecting any effort to manufacture political unity in a way that attempts to accommodate all elements of the state. The practical test of a manufactured political unity, then, depends upon advancing arguments strong enough to recommend a principled politics in spite of the fact that groups will have internal moral reasons to object to the political ideals demanded by such a politics. Political unity can be manufactured, in other words, only if we can demonstrate that a principled political unity is worth its price even for those groups asked to adhere to political ideals that at times conflict with their most treasured normative convictions.

Strange as it may seem, the realization and acknowledgment that groups will likely have their own independent and disparate views about how things should work politically is a good point of departure for crafting an argument supportive of a move toward a politics of unity. The normative diversity and disagreement likely displayed by differing visions of how civil life should go according to various groups is solid evidence of the intractable problems posed by the fact of pluralism. Exposing and highlighting the challenges raised by these problems should do much to illustrate the need to hit upon civil mechanisms to control them. If theory building is fundamentally a response to social pathology, the necessary first step in constructing an effective response is to understand the social condition that houses the pathology at issue. It is important not only that this condition be accurately and adequately conceptualized, but also that the conceptualization that emerges be grasped and accepted as legitimate by all groups to whom the argument for political unity must be addressed. If groups recognize the nature of the problem, and if they also notice that the costs associated with moving beyond the problem by establishing political unity are not as great as living with the problem, they will have reason to prefer political unity to the political status quo, and the theoretical foundation for manufacturing political unity will have been established.

Since I have already situated my theoretical project within the political context of the United States and explored the way a politics of interests manifests itself in American political culture, it might seem that the place to begin with would be a careful empirical examination of group differences that exist in America under conditions of pluralism. This, of course, would be a considerable—and invariably contentious—chore in its own right and may prove to be unhelpful in any event. Others may disagree with the picture of the elephant that I happen to draw, and they may find reason to think that this flaw taints the entire theoretical project. However, it is unnecessary to engage in a protracted and, no doubt, somewhat tedious sociological description of American pluralism in order to set in place the background conditions that situate the theoretical project. All we need to do is imagine the most dramatic impediments to political unity possible given the fact of pluralism. And to do this, we need only hypothesize a social environment that extrapolates loosely from the socio-political conditions that background the theoretical project, and in so doing, dramatize the challenges introduced by exceptional ontological and normative diversity. The circumstances to be imagined, this is to say, should be inspired by and also mirror the conditions characteristic of the politics of interests in the American context.

If the pathology that puts theoretical inquiry in motion is the intergroup conflict generated under the fact of pluralism, then an elaboration of the socio-political conditions that give rise to this pathology is fundamental to the process of dramatization. Given the fact of pluralism, we must presume that the social environment to be imagined displays a variety of disparate, conflicting, and possibly incommensurate worldviews and moral theories of the human good that are the sources of social conflict. A fuller elaboration of the nature of this environment must involve only naïve and practically compelling generalities that stop at the boundary of simple description. This is a requirement of the problem of audience, and accordingly, it is necessary to avoid descriptions of the social environment that depend or rest upon underlying epistemological or scientific claims about the nature of humankind or society, the human condition, human psychology, or the like. While the insights and scientific presumptions of the social scientist may be acceptable to some (and perhaps even a great many) individuals and groups in the socio-political setting that backgrounds the theoretical project, they need not be, and likely will not be, acceptable or compelling to everyone in this social environment. So it is best to avoid them in favor (if this is possible) of simple and reasonably straightforward descriptions of the nature of social conflict that will likely, if not inevitably, arise under conditions of pluralism.

The need for a neutral and naïve description of the social environment that houses the pathology requiring theoretical remedy is not an easy condition to meet by any means, and I may seem to violate this condition in the process of dramatizing the social environment troubled by intergroup conflict. But the building blocks for such a description are already in place since they derive rather straightforwardly from the problematic nature of the politics of interests described above. Under a politics of interests, groups stand in opposition to one another, and for a variety of reasons that need to be put in some sort of conceptual order. They struggle to realize their desired interests and ends at the expense of the interests and ends of their rivals. But victory, if it can be achieved, remains a precarious and fleeting thing, for the rivalry with opposing groups does not go away unless the opposing groups do.

The first aspect of this scenario, in need of development, is introduced by the fact that groups are the central players on the political stage. Accordingly, human beings should be supposed to have group attachments that matter to them and provide them with ontological and normative viewpoints about the world and social life in general. This is a modest departure from the traditional liberal view, inherited from Enlightenment thinking, in which the solitary, independent individual, complete with natural wants and desires and capable of authoring and developing her or his own life by virtue of the capacity to reason, was taken as the primary unit of theoretical concern. Because we are familiar with this mode of theorizing, because, that is, the independent individual is a commonplace of the theoretical market that students encounter when they begin to explore the history of theorizing about civil association, this focus of inquiry raises few philosophical problems or puzzles. Students are not inclined to ask what an individual person is, for example, for we rather suppose we can recognize persons when we see them and have a good inkling about what they are like, and so forth. (Marxist and neo-Marxist theorizing introduces an important qualification to this, of course, by shifting focus from the individual to classes understood primarily in economic terms. But we are also accustomed to thinking about social life in terms of class divisions—although there is little agreement on where to draw the line between classes—and thus again there is little incentive to ask what a class is.)

Spurred on by emerging multiculturalist concerns and the rise of the politics of identity, however, liberal thinkers have begun to recognize the place and importance of groups for theorizing about civil life. But as focus shifts from independent individuals to groups, certain conceptual difficulties arise. What is to count as a group for purposes of analysis anyway? Further, is it possible to offer an account of a group that is sufficiently neutral and inoffensive that all the various groups inhabiting the social setting can accept it? The notion of a group seems so nebulous and vague that making it the primary unit of theoretical focus is likely to flounder on self-inflicted ambiguities. Clarifying the notion of a group would require a full theoretical inquiry in its own right, and the result might still generate such controversy that it would fail to satisfy the demands of the problem of audience. While I am mindful of these problems, I shall suppose, for present purposes, that we should understand groups—as distinct from other forms of human associations—as communities of persons that fix the epistemic, ontological, and normative horizons of their members.

Thus understood, groups provide their members with more than just the 'context of choice,' to borrow from Kymlicka, within which group members operate.[2] They also orient their members in the world and provide their members with the conceptual apparatus that enables them to formulate some understanding of the world. That is, groups supply their members with a sense of meaningfulness that not only enables them to make choices and decisions about how their lives should go, but also provides them with the criteria by which they make such choices and decisions. In more descriptive terms, groups help fix membership identities by enabling them to understand who they are and who they are not in terms of the beliefs and ideals they take from the group.[3] They generate for their members both a sense of who they are and an understanding of what the world is (and thus is like). That is, they provide the normative, epistemological, and ontological data that renders William James's 'bloomin' buzzin' confusion' intelligible *for them*.

But this account of a group needs to be supplemented with a more practical view of the matter: that the understandings and self-awareness one inherits from groups are inevitably sharpened by those outside groups that are also present in a given group's social space. Awareness of one's sense of self, and one's sense of group identity is magnified by the presence of others belonging to different groups and thus holding different understandings of the world and views about what matters. The realities of intergroup politics are driven by the variety of distinct, and perhaps hostile, groups facing the shared problem of managing to live in each other's company.[4] Consequently, groups may be further understood practically in terms of the political conflict that exists between their respective members, conflict that is driven by some ethnic, religious, moral, or ideological outlook considered dear to some and anathema to others. Seen from this perspective, groups are representative agencies that promote and protect particularly important and formative shared beliefs and ideals that determine who belongs to the group and who does not. There is, to be sure, more to the nature of a group than this, and the need to be clear—or clearer—on this nature is of more than just passing theoretical concern. As we shall see, there are additional practical reasons for sharpening our understanding of a group that surface when we begin to develop a viable theory of group autonomy. But it may be best to put this issue aside for the moment and return to it again when it surfaces once more in the flow of the argument.

In spite of any ambiguity that still surrounds the notion of a group (as this notion is used here), one thing should be clear. Groups must be considered the primary focus of theoretical concern under practical liberalism. This follows naturally from the fact that the social conflict that worries practical liberals is driven by group concerns and group activities. By bringing groups into the foreground, practical liberalism necessarily removes the solitary individual to the background of the discussion. In fact, the solitary individual is transformed under practical liberalism into a group member whose identity is fixed and given by his membership in certain key groups. Persons can no longer be considered abstractly as beings with specific interests and brute desires who come into conflict with each other when these interests and desires clash—for they also share with certain others certain beliefs and ideals that place them in conflict with those who happen to hold differing and conflicting beliefs and ideals. This is the source of the conflict that the politics of interests brings into the foreground and inspires the pathology that drives this particular theoretical inquiry.

Perhaps this underestimates the significant role liberal individualism now plays in American political culture, but this seems unlikely. The Marlboro Man may really be out there prowling the prairies and streets of America, but he is not alone—and he is certainly not the force driving the social pathology at issue here. There are also group-centered beings out there holding, advocating, and transferring worldviews and moral theories of the human good that stand in stark opposition to one another. These are the people it is necessary to focus upon and bring into clear view, for these are the people that drive the politics of interests. If this focus blurs the view of those hearty individuals so prevalent in American mythology, it is because these are not characters associated with the problem underlying my theoretical project. And their presence in the social environment—if in fact they are present—does not alter the nature of the social pathology that concerns practical liberals.

This does not mean, however, that we ought not recognize the presence of independently minded individuals within groups. Such individuals do exist, of course, and it is important to appreciate the way distinct individuals generate group transformation and social change. This feature of individualism—the individual finding herself or himself within the larger group context that configures much but not all of her or his life—should be kept in plain view. These are the characters that drive group transformation and generate changes that destabilize group life. As we shall see, group members must also be understood as reflective individuals who raise questions, promulgate doubts, and generate disagreements about the worldviews and moral theories of the human good constitutive of distinct groups. In the process, they transform the nature of groups themselves in unpredictable and probably unpreventable ways.

Similarly, it is also important to appreciate the fact that individuals can, and probably will, belong to more than one group. Some groups may determine the normative and ontological horizons of their members more exhaustively than others, and some groups may even desire to be the sole determiner of these horizons, to control completely the worldview of their members. But it is always possible for even these viewpoints to be supplemented with additional (perhaps even alternative) normative and ontological factors provided by and constitutive of other group identifications, even if more comprehensive groups are resistant to this possibility. I will have more to say about this shortly, but for the moment I want only to emphasize that viewing persons as group-centered beings does not mean that individual identity is given entirely and unalterably by one's membership in one and only one formative group. Though this may be the case in some circumstances, this is probably a rather rare condition. It seems more likely that individual identities are layered by memberships in a variety of formative groups. In some cases, this may generate contradictions and confusion in an individual's belief system, and in others it may cause some individuals to amend or qualify some beliefs or ideals associated with their membership in a given group in order to reconcile this element of their identity with the beliefs and ideals they hold by virtue of their membership in other groups.

As we shall see, the ability of individuals *qua* group members to adapt the beliefs and ideals they hold by virtue of their membership in one group in order to reconcile this identity with their membership in other groups is crucial in the theoretical argument for manufacturing political unity.

## The sociology of liberal politics

Once the group as the primary focus of theoretical attention is in place, the process of dramatization must attempt to bring some conceptual order to the problem of intergroup conflict. There are sure to be many varied types of social conflict present in the social setting, each driven by different forces and concerns. We can begin to bring some order to all this, however, by supposing that normative and ontological difference, and the corresponding likelihood of intergroup incomprehensibility, introduces the background condition that permits us to speculate on certain features of intergroup conflict and opposition. Difference and incomprehensibility, when coupled with the fact of social proximity, are to be considered possible and even likely sources of intergroup hostility and conflict. For reasons to be explored shortly, we should suppose that disparate groups holding conflicting and possibly incommensurate worldviews may well dislike one another, and some may even find reason to pursue strategies designed to disadvantage the targets of their animus, including fanatical strategies intended to eradicate, eliminate, segregate, isolate, or assimilate them.[5] Although some may think that this presumption is unnecessarily bleak and pessimistic, it is necessary in order to dramatize the extreme conditions that are conceivably associated with, or lying behind, a politics of interests that troubles real polities and inspires the pursuit of a politics of unity.

There is no lack of sociological and psychological accounts of the sources and nature of intergroup conflict; nor is there a lack of sophisticated explanations about why groups adopt strategies designed or intended to eliminate, segregate, or assimilate group outsiders.[6] Once again, however, there is no reason to review this material here; it brings with it considerable epistemological, psychological, and sociological baggage that may be rejected by groups that concede little merit to sociological or psychological thinking. Still, it is important to have some account of intergroup conflict in order to impress all elements of the polity that such conflict poses a real and tenacious problem. The required account need not, and probably should not, attempt a comprehensive explanation for this conflict, but it does need to bring clarity to intergroup conflict in ways that will be recognizable and acceptable to all elements of the polity. The more straightforward and intuitively plausible the account of intergroup conflict the better, and toward this end, I will say that sometimes intergroup conflict is understandable in terms of the presence of allocational (i.e., economic or distributional) rivals and sometimes it is understandable in terms of the presence of normative (i.e., ideological, moral, or religious) rivals.

Conflicts produced by the clash of allocational rivals give rise to what I will call coordination problems. To resolve or mediate problems of this sort, decisions must be made about how social goods should be distributed within the social environment.[7] Needless to say, it is necessary, in the face of allocational rivalries, for those groups sharing a common social setting to coalesce and converge upon some standards, procedures, or principles to govern distributional issues, since the alternative is ongoing and possibly devastating intergroup hostility. By itself, however, the understood need to mediate and resolve coordination problems is not sufficient incentive to inspire groups to work toward a politics of unity, for normative rivalries may be so great, and the resultant intergroup animosity so entrenched, that unity for the sake of creating standards for the just distribution of social resources may not be considered worth the effort. But the need to manage coordination problems does introduce a reason for pursuing political unity that must be factored into any equation designed to balance the desirability of a politics of unity against the alternatives.

Conflicts produced by the clash of normative rivalries, on the other hand, introduce into the social environment what I will call tolerance problems. These conflicts arise when the value scheme or belief system of some group (or groups) inclines or requires its members to condemn (some) outgroups because the members of these outgroups are considered to be mistaken or misguided in their beliefs, or damned and/or disgusting because of their beliefs or simply because of who or what they are. From the standpoint of a group's worldview, the judgment that (some) outgroups are not to be tolerated because of who they are or what they happen to believe may well justify or even require adopting social policies designed and intended to eliminate, segregate, or assimilate them. Intolerance of this sort is an obvious source of tolerance problems. Sometimes, groups struggle to defend their group identity and group autonomy against what they perceive to be external threats. They seek to preserve their own ethnic, cultural, linguistic, ideological, religious, or moral identity and enable their members to live their lives as they wish without intrusion or pollution from outside forces. When outsiders push in upon them in a way they find unacceptable or frightening, when they fear that their way of life or the things that they value are threatened by outsiders, they may adopt defensive policies that commit them to the elimination, segregation, or assimilation of their rivals. At other times, groups will want to expand their control of the social environment and impose their ways upon others, perhaps because they do not think that false beliefs or disgusting and immoral ways of life should be allowed to exist. In either case, the nature of group moralities, the presence of external group pressures, and the confined condition of the social environment under the fact of pluralism all but guarantee that groups will have or develop social agendas which generate normative rivalries and introduce tolerance problems.

Historically, religious conflict has provided an obvious and salient example of normative rivalry, and of course, the effort to develop a modicum of peace and toleration among the fragmented faiths of Christianity became the historic inspiration for the emergence of what we now regard as the liberal tradition of political thought.[8] But normative rivalries now range well beyond religious divisions. Those theorists who take multicultural concerns seriously have noted, among other things, that the ways of some (perhaps dominant) groups threaten the integrity of other cultural groups, perhaps even to the point of extinction. When cultures clash in this way—as they almost inevitably do—conflict is sure to arise. The inability of distinct cultural groups to coexist within a common social setting raises coordination problems of the first order, problems that have come under careful scrutiny in the literature on multiculturalism. But multicultural concerns are often blind or insensitive to ideological groups—groups that may fail to qualify as cultural or ethnic units—that also generate normative rivalries, just as they too often ignore the tolerance problems raised by the clash of disparate normative and ontological viewpoints. By bringing these additional variables to light, practical liberalism presents a picture of the modern pluralist state as a place where a host of ethnic, cultural, racial, religious, and ideological rivalries generate both coordination and tolerance problems. Nor is it easy to classify normative rivalries as, say, either distinctively ethnic or clearly religious, for the nature of the rivalry is shaped fundamentally by the various understandings of the rivals and may well include ethnic, religious, racial, and/or ideological dimensions that are difficult to disentangle for purposes of antiseptic classifications.

Although it may further complicate matters, intergroup conflict resulting from normative rivalries is also to be understood to take place against a background of group flux and transformation. Groups should not be regarded as stable and enduring units that reproduce themselves through time. To be sure, groups do reproduce themselves as members pass their beliefs and traditions on to future generations. But groups also disappear occasionally if the normative boundaries a group has defended for purposes of self-identification erode or are transformed by outside forces or pressures, and sometimes groups fragment as internal political pressures generate schisms within the group or as outside pressures invade group politics and set members against one another.[9] Of course, new groups also come into existence as some worldview gains increased following, as people rediscover aspects of their being that become salient features of their sense of self, and as social attitudes evolve and develop in the process of the exploration of the manifold features of human life. Consequently, intergroup conflict should not be considered a static or predictable condition; instead, it unfolds in a chaotic and uncertain fashion that makes the social environment that houses this dynamic a kaleidoscope of intergroup relations, hostilities, and alliances. If we recall the reflective individuals mentioned above, we can begin to appreciate the dynamic interplay between reflective individuals and the groups to which they belong. Such individuals are transformative forces that are one source of group change and one reason why groups are always and invariably in states of flux with memberships that ebb and flow with time and circumstance.

It is probably not possible to provide an exhaustive listing of the possible sources of the flux and uncertainty of group life in pluralist societies, but it is also unnecessary for present purposes to do so. Yet some sense of how the fact of flux, if I may call it that, affects intergroup conflict is certainly desirable. It is important, for example, to appreciate the presence and uncertain nature of intragroup politics. Group coherence is often fragile and rests upon convictions or beliefs that are themselves subject to dispute and disagreement among group members. Sometimes groups splinter when doctrinal differences emerge between group members and two (or more) groups emerge where before there was only one. At other times intragroup differences are not sufficient to divide the group, although it is always possible that some external group presence may introduce an additional variable that does cause the group to divide. But these internal divisions remain a source of group instability that can threaten group solidarity in the event pressures or influences in the social environment external to the group happen to change. Additionally, changes in the external social environment may also cause groups to solidify and might even facilitate the enlistment of new members or encourage a greater allegiance on the part of weak or tertiary identifiers. In the United States, for example, the growth and increased self-confidence of so-called alternative lifestyles and the accompanying emergent views about the good life has added to the overt presence of group diversity.[10] This has introduced new sources of normative conflict into the social environment as new or suddenly more vocal groups press beyond the frontiers of what other (often more dominant) groups consider socially acceptable or tolerable. As homosexuals have come out of their closets to insist upon social recognition and respect, religious fundamentalists have come out of their own closets to challenge homosexual lifestyles. As feminists coalesce and formulate a group consciousness that takes its place in the social fabric, traditionalists—perhaps fearing that their ideals are directly challenged by all this—coalesce for purposes of articulating and defending values they hold dear, values they consider threatened by a social movement they consider anathema to all they believe.

Given the nature of intragroup politics and struggle and the corresponding impact new, emergent, or revitalized groups may have upon other groups, the fact of flux introduces an uncertain variable into the social environment that should be kept firmly in mind. The change produced by the process of flux is uncertain and unpredictable making group integrity and group status within the society questionable and tenuous at any point in time. This is reason to suppose that normative rivalries will change over time although they still continue to be an ongoing difficulty in pluralist states. In order to guarantee that we do not underestimate the difficulties in producing a politics of unity introduced by these rivalries, I want to mention two conditions that we should presume to be characteristic of normative rivalries in general.

We should suppose, first, that normative diversity and ontological difference might be, and very likely are, sources of what can be called a righteous 'hatred' for the targets of group animus. This hatred need not manifest itself in the form of a loathing accompanied by a strong desire to see the targets of group animus die, suffer, or be removed from the social environment, although it surely can (and frequently does) take this form. It may also take the form of pity or disdain for outgroups because they seem desperately confused, misguided, or mistaken by virtue of what they believe, or inadequate, inferior, or incompetent because of who they are. Nonetheless, this hatred has two important aspects. First, it is considered valid or justified by the groups whose members hold such views. The basic elements of their worldview and their moral vision of the human good incline them to see (certain) outsiders as proper and even necessary targets of their animus. Thus these groups believe they are altogether justified in their 'hatred' of (certain) outgroups and do not believe there is anything wrong or objectionable about these beliefs. In fact, they consider it wrong or objectionable to countenance the alternative (and liberal) view that they should love or at least respect others no matter how different or how misguided they might be. Second, it sets the group's agenda for how to deal with the targets of group animus. Because group members despise or disdain (certain) outgroups, they feel justified in giving expression to their hatred by adopting and practicing strategies designed and intended to bring about their elimination, segregation, or assimilation. So, the conditions of righteous hatred exclude the possibility that a politics of unity can be achieved by finding a common normative ground that could serve as the basis for the development of intergroup understanding or agreement. The fact of righteous hatred—the consequence of deep and conflicting normative and ontological difference and disagreement—eliminates this optimistic possibility.

We should also suppose that the worldviews that constitute and define distinct groups under the fact of pluralism are self-validating and internally coherent when seen from the inside. Group members have their own internally valid reasons to think that truth is on their side, and the standards of truth and falsity group members use to validate claims about the way the world is, and the way it ought to be, are internal to the conceptual scheme of the group itself. Sometimes faith and simple belief determine what one sees (and is able to see), and what one sees is not itself determinative of either faith or simple belief. In response to challenges to the truth or validity of a group's worldview, group members can point to some ideological outlook, religious conviction, sacred scroll, or moral belief that is considered to be authoritative within the group, and hence beyond question or equivocation. Similarly, the standards of truth or falsity a group holds may be lodged in such presumptively authoritative mechanisms as western science, western empiricism, eastern mysticism, faith and/or revelation, tradition or orthodoxy, or dogmatism. These distinctive and distinct 'conditions of understanding' power the characterization of what is to count as a credible claim within discrete worldviews, and where and when groups hold different conditions of understanding, the possibility of mutual understanding for purposes of fashioning a dialogue that may generate the development of political consensus simply does not exist. This sets the background that makes plausible claims about the incommensurability of group worldviews and moral theories of the human good. While the members of (some) different groups might share a common language and be able to converse politely and intelligently about some things, there may be other things they cannot begin even to talk about. Though it may sound strange, we must hold out the possibility that while disparate groups share a common social setting, there is also an important sense in which they actually live in very different worlds.

## Pluralism and political argument

Normative rivalries, as I have described them here, should be regarded as real, important, and generally irreconcilable. The political history of humankind should be sufficient to attest to this fact, as should the politics of interests, as described above, operating in the United States. Of course allocational rivalries can also drive the politics of interests, but they are unlikely to give rise to conflicts as unsettling and troubling as those that emerge from the clash of normative rivals. In fact, conceptualizing the more intractable forms of political conflict in terms of normative rivalries does much to explain the pertinence of the theoretical challenge posed by the politics of interests. The struggle to control the proper conceptualization of the matter at issue is itself a reflection of the fact that normative rivals really do conceptualize the problem differently, with each rival group seeing and understanding the matter from within the context provided by its worldview and moral theory of the human good. Consequently, the normative rivalries that arise amidst the fact of pluralism introduce the challenge to be met if a politics of unity is to be possible. How can these rivalries be resolved in a manner that all parties to the dispute can find acceptable and authoritative? The possibility of a politics of unity depends upon putting an effective answer to this question, but before turning to this matter it is necessary to consider some possible problems with my account of the fact of pluralism.

Dramatization though it might be, the social conditions inspired by fact of pluralism as described here should be sufficient to achieve its analytical purpose. The argument required to advance a politics of unity must be open ended in one crucial sense; it must support a politics of principle capable of promoting political unity under both present conditions (no matter how we conceive of them in practice) and all conceivable future circumstances. It is not possible to anticipate the types of religious, cultural, or ideological group that may emerge in the future or the beliefs and viewpoints that will characterize them. But they too must be included in the calculus that articulates the possibility of a politics of unity if we are to be confident that such a politics can endure into the future and remain stable in the face of the ebb and flow of group development and intergroup collision. Dramatizing the fact of pluralism supports this end by presuming the most extreme possible form of group diversity and intergroup conflict.

Perhaps, however, this dramatization actually overdoes it. If in fact the groups sharing a common social environment really are as opaque to one another and as normatively diverse as I have suggested, what conceivable hope is there that they will share enough in common to make the construction of a politics of unity possible? If hoping for the presence of an overlapping consensus seems naïve, then surely supposing that all groups in the state could find persuasive some basic argument for adhering to a political principle (or set of such principles) will also seem naïve. If groups really are as zealously devoted to their own normative scheme and vision of the good as I have imagined, why should we even bother to entertain the possibility that they would qualify their commitment to their group ends in order to embrace a politics of principle? Additionally, if the ontological diversity I have imagined really is as striking as I have supposed, why should we think that groups could recognize or comprehend the members of outgroups as fellows in any sense of the term or even be the least bit capable of communicating with them?

Some of the worries introduced by these questions are important and should be taken seriously; others are silly and can be summarily dismissed. Philosophical argument might push on the fact of pluralism in order to contend that the unique and incorrigible character of group worldviews means that in principle some group might be unable to recognize outgroup members as anything but incomprehensible creatures who fail to qualify as human—assuming they have something that approximates the concept of humanity—in any discernible way. Where and when such radical opacity occurs, politics is not possible, understanding is not possible, living together is not possible. But I want to resist this conclusion for practical reasons. While it is perhaps reasonably true that groups are sometimes deeply opaque to one another, the fact of intergroup animus and hatred is evidence enough that there is an element of 'recognition' on display here. It is the fact of intergroup conflict (reinforced by an appreciation for the depth of ontological and normative difference that animates it) that serves as the inspiration for my dramatization of a social setting characterized by the fact of pluralism. In practice, groups do understand others in the terms available to them thanks to their respective worldviews. Catholics see Protestants as apostates, Muslims see Christians as infidels, black Muslims see whites as devils, white supremacists see blacks as 'mud people,' liberals see racists as misguided souls, and so forth. Under the fact of pluralism we are to suppose that groups do not see or understand outsiders in the way these outsiders see and understand themselves and that such an insider understanding is not possible for outsiders, but it would be a mistake of a different sort to suppose that groups cannot recognize outsiders as outsiders, that is, as others in the sense that they differ from group members in normatively and ontologically important ways. As outsiders, others are present to group members chiefly in the terms the group's worldview and moral theory of the human good make available to them. But they are also present in a less conceptual and more logistical sense, they happen to share a common social setting. And if they are unable to understand one another fully or completely; they can still grasp the political problems created by this fact of proximity.

Concerns about the ability to find sufficient logical space for the construction of an argument that all elements of a state characterized by the fact of pluralism can endorse, on the other hand, are real and troubling. Why should we suppose all groups possess the ability and inclination to 'listen to reason' sufficiently to assure us that a manufactured political unity has a chance of success? Why should we believe that all (or any) groups would believe that their moral theory of the good should be trumped by argument encouraging the suspension of their beliefs and viewpoints in favor of a politics of principle? Why—to put the matter as starkly as possible—should we even believe that all (or any) groups in the social environment will be able to understand/comprehend an argument for a politics of principle?

I have introduced the problem posed by these questions already, but with the fact of pluralism now fully present to us, it is worth repeating my earlier qualification. There simply is no very good reason to think that these questions can be answered in a manner that provides assurances for the possibility of a politics of principle. The possibility of a politics of principle does suppose—indeed it must suppose—that some element of rationality is present in all groups in the social environment, no matter how zealous they might otherwise be. Kant supposed famously that even a collection of devils could learn to live together justly if only they were capable of understanding (*Verstand*).[11] These Kantian devils do not need the rationality Kant associated with moral insight in order to live together; they need only the ability to discern where their true interests lie. And I also want to say something like this—for the underlying conviction that powers, and must power, theoretical inquiry into the possibility of a politics of unity is the presumption that groups qualify as prudentially rational regardless of the worldview and moral theory of the human good that characterizes them. If groups are prudentially rational, they can learn to live together under a politics of principle, and theoretical inquiry can show how this is possible. Prudential rationality, then, must also be presumed to characterize groups sharing a common social setting typified by the fact of pluralism. If this presumption is rejected as false or foolish, there is no way for theoretical inquiry to proceed and no further point to philosophical argument. But fortunately, it is possible to accept this presumption and still honor most, but perhaps not all, of the deep ontological and normative diversity we should expect to be present in the social setting given the fact of pluralism.

Of course we should also suppose under practical liberalism that reflecting on and arguing about these matters makes sense, that theoretical inquiry has a point that can be grasped by anyone willing to engage this inquiry and regardless of worldview or moral theory of the good they happen to hold. This too is an initial presumption that must be accepted if theorizing about civil association is to have a point; if we do not think theoretical reflection might help in some way to show how social conflict and travail might be overcome, managed, or assuaged, there would be little philosophical (and even less practical) reason to bother with it. At this point, however, all we can do is hope and work to craft an argument that we think should persuade all elements of the social environment characterized by the fact of pluralism to endorse a politics of principle and thereby bring about political unity.

## The liberal principle

A politics of unity seeks to get everyone on the same side, so to speak, while at the same time honoring and preserving the greatest amount of group diversity possible.[12] To accomplish this, it is necessary to advance an argument stipulating why group members should converge upon and accept some principle (or set of such principles) that will serve as a unifying force and offer the opportunity to find principled solutions to intergroup conflict, solutions that all groups can therefore recognize as principled and just. And it is necessary to articulate the required principle(s) in a fashion faithful to the tremendous normative and ontological diversity dramatized in a manner intended to honor the problems posed by the fact of pluralism.

If any proposed principle is to realize the threshold condition of general group acceptability, it must meet three basic conditions. First, the principle(s) in question must be inclusive. No group can claim exemption from the principle, or claim privileged status under the principle, by virtue of its ideological convictions, religious beliefs, or moral point of view. Inclusiveness is easily expressed by articulating the principle in imperative form, thus structurally allowing for no exceptions, but it can be demonstrated only by supporting and defending the principle with argument sufficient to indicate that even the most illiberal, orthodox, and dogmatic groups have compelling reason to accept it when faced with the fact of pluralism. In short, inclusiveness demands that exemption claims be trumped at the outset as a condition of establishing the principle's general acceptability. The second condition derives logically from the first. Any principle suitable for a politics of unity must be egalitarian in structure. That is, it must hold with equal force for all social groups and distribute the burdens and benefits it introduces accordingly. Principles that privilege some groups over others will hardly be satisfactory to those groups disfavored by the principle. To satisfy this condition, a principle must not play favorites or accord some group(s) preferential treatment by virtue of its worldview. The egalitarian condition is met by presenting the principle in suitably general terms, that is, in terms that are blind to specific groups and their differences. Accordingly, the principle will require that all groups play by the same political and legal rules, enjoy the same rights and liberties, share the same obligations and responsibilities as citizens, and so forth. Sometimes liberals refer to something like this as a requirement of state neutrality, but this is both unhelpful and misleading.[13] Playing by the same rules does not require the strong—in fact, unmanageable—condition of state neutrality, as we shall see.

Finally, the principle must also be supportive. It needs to stipulate that the members of all groups living within the polity to be forged by acceptance of the principle have the right to live their lives as they wish, adhere to their worldview no matter how unacceptable or insane it might seem to others, and to pursue those activities and ways of life that are important to them when viewed from inside their worldview and moral theory of the human good. The stability and social peace promoted under a politics of principle will be desirable to groups only if they allow group members to live their lives as they wish, and this means allowing them to live according to the ways they value by virtue of their worldview and moral theory of the human good. But because the egalitarian condition establishes that a supportive principle must be equally supportive of all groups, there is an obvious limit to the supportiveness any one group can expect from the principle. The supportive condition defends the right of group members to live their lives and pursue their vision of the good up to the point where doing so intrudes upon the ability of the members of outgroups to do so as well. If the supportive condition permitted group members to live their lives entirely as they wished, it would not require any accommodation for the other, and we would be left with a politics of interests in its most extreme manifestation, namely, complete anarchy. So, the supportive condition mitigated by the egalitarian condition should be understood to defend the right of all groups to practice their way of life in a manner consistent with the equal right of all others to do so as well. In its starkest terms, this means that groups should not be allowed, under a principled politics, to pursue strategies designed and intended to eliminate, segregate, or assimilate their normative rivals.

A principled politics, then, is accommodationist in the strong sense that it brings together all elements of the social environment according to standards that enable the members of each group a maximum opportunity to live as they wish and pursue those things that matter to them compatible with a like opportunity for the members of all other groups present in the newly constituted polity to do so as well. If such a politics demands compromise from the groups to constitute the polity, as it must if it is to have any value at all, it demands only those compromises necessary to accommodate the presence of others. A principle that fails to meet these three conditions, then, will either be incapable of cohering a polity or unable to earn the acceptance of all groups in the social setting. Nor at this point is it difficult to imagine a principle that might be up to this challenge, for by stating the requirements of the principle in these terms, we all but articulate the principle itself. That is, if we give appropriate expression to the inclusive, egalitarian, and supportive conditions, one principle emerges automatically. Nor is there anything terribly startling or original about the principle that comes to mind here. Something like it is familiar enough, as one might expect, in the history of liberal political thought. Perhaps, then, there is some modest justification for referring to the principle anticipated here as the liberal principle or LP. According to LP,

> The members of each group present in the polity must be accorded a maximum amount of freedom to live according to their worldview and pursue the ideals associated with their moral vision of the human good compatible with the freedom necessary to assure that the members of all other groups in the polity can do so as well.[14]

In the most general terms, LP defends group autonomy by stipulating that the members of all groups should be accorded the maximum freedom to live their lives as they wish, to put into practice their moral theory of the human good, to hold and promulgate those beliefs fundamental to their worldview, and to practice the lifestyle they believe worthwhile. More succinctly, LP assures the members of all groups the right to pursue and live worthwhile lives *according to whatever standards define the notion of having and living a worthwhile life for group members.* But the right is limited in principle; it ends where its exercise would infringe upon the same right held by other groups. As should be evident, the inclusive, egalitarian, and supportive conditions follow from the underlying logic of a politics of unity coupled with a general appreciation for those conditions that any group in the state would likely support if it elected to imagine a workable politics of unity. The egalitarian condition assures that no group will be victimized by the mechanics associated with a politics of interests or a politics of dominance; the supportive condition guarantees all groups the maximum opportunity to live according to their beliefs and practice their ways consistent with a politics of unity; and the inclusive condition emphasizes that the conditions necessary for political unity obligate all elements of the polity equally.

It should be clear, then, why LP has the form and content it has; it is merely a reflection of the logical condition entailed by the idea of a politics of unity. But we might also wonder if there are other principles that might do duty here and supplement LP. It is no doubt possible to construct derivative principles articulating basic group rights that follow from LP within specific political contexts, but such principles depend for their validity upon the meaning and prior acceptance of LP. It should also be possible to derive from LP some principled structure for the resolution of allocational rivalries, thus providing at least the outline of a theory of distributive justice under a politics of unity. But these matters need not concern us at present. And while it may be possible to articulate the inclusive, egalitarian, and supportive conditions in a different manner, the resultant principle would be the logical equivalent of LP as constructed here and thus be, in effect, the same principle. Alternative or competing principles, on the other hand, must either contradict or reject one or more of the three conditions expressed by LP or add additional conditions to the list. Since, however, the inclusive, egalitarian, and supportive conditions seem to be the only conditions necessary and appropriate for a viable politics of unity, I will suppose that alternative or competing principles are inconsistent with the demands of such a politics. Thus LP, or something logically equivalent to it, is the only principle capable of supporting a politics of principle in a social environment characterized by the fact of pluralism.

Because LP protects against domination and oppression in general and throughout the polity, it may be regarded by some groups as dominant and oppressive in its own right. Groups whose members have religious, moral, or ideological reasons to pursue strategies designed and intended to eliminate, segregate, or assimilate outgroups will have internal reasons to object to the fact that they are not exempt from the inclusiveness condition. Such groups will likely see political association as an extension of the moral, religious, and/or ideological belief that motivates and legitimates their efforts to shape civil association according to their vision of the right or the good. As we have seen, under the fact of pluralism this includes virtually all groups in the state, for if group A views some practice associated with group B as immoral or wrong, it will have reason to intrude into the internal affairs of the members of B and require them to clean up their behavior. It follows that the defense of LP must provide all groups in the polity with persuasive reasons why they should commit to LP and accept principled limits upon how they can pursue their moral, religious, or ideological views. The articulation of the principle suitable to a politics of unity, in short, is a relatively simple matter compared to the challenge of crafting an argument that will demonstrate why the principle should be acceptable to all groups. While political unity requires the principled mediation of intergroup conflict, the real challenge of generating political unity involves explaining to groups that may have reason to think otherwise why this unity is a good idea in the first place.

## Prudence, persuasion, and practical argument

As we have seen, the type of argument that might be successfully employed to defend acceptance of LP is circumscribed by the fact of pluralism; consequently, we are unable to appeal here to traditional moral argument and claim that LP follows from some objective moral truth about the good or the right. Once again, the problem of audience blocks this strategy of argument at the outset. But we do have something to work with. Anticipating the social circumstances dramatized by the fact of pluralism, Brian Barry has discussed three strategies that might be used to defend logical convergence upon some principle or social good. He calls them the social peace argument, prudence argument, and inefficacy argument respectively.[15] The first imagines a social condition where conflict exists between two or more groups of roughly equal strength. Conditions being what they are, the only way these groups can achieve a modicum of good order and security is to adopt the terms appropriate to civil peace, perhaps by adopting LP or something like it.

Of course, Barry quickly and correctly notes that this is not much of an argument. It supposes that groups will prefer social peace to righteous conflict, and for this to be the case they must already be rather domesticated—something belied by the fact of group hostility itself.[16] It seems reasonable to think that groups will prefer social peace to righteous conflict, on the other hand, if the prospect of eternal intergroup conflict would frustrate the ability of group members to live decent and purposive lives as they understand such things given their worldview. They would prefer civil war to social peace only if their dominant-group commitment involved the elimination, segregation, or assimilation of their opponent at any cost, including their own elimination or assimilation. Groups whose members are so single-mindedly obsessive will not listen to reason, and therefore there is little point to arguing with them. Theoretical inquiry, therefore, must suppose that most groups are not like this, and consequently, groups do not need to have a prior disposition to social peace to appreciate the social peace argument. They need only have the ability to recognize that social peace may well be preferable to ongoing social conflict and the possible destruction of the group itself.

But there is a greater problem with this argument. We have little reason to suppose that the hostile groups present in the social environment really are of roughly equal strength. And groups sensing they have the upper hand in some conflict, or whose members think that they may be able to gain an upper hand, may prefer to gamble on their chances of achieving the desired domination rather than opting for peace. There is simply no reason provided by the social peace argument to explain why dominant groups should not press their advantage rather than opt for some kind of political compromise. It follows that the social peace argument cannot sustain a stable polity, even if it could bring one into being in the first place—something that seems unlikely given the uncertain demographics imagined under the fact of pluralism. The prudence argument again imagines a condition of general equality of strength in Barry's judgment. When this is the case, groups would find it in their best interest to settle for a civil peace rather than risk possible domination. Even though a group may think it has the upper hand or may suspect it will be able to gain the upper hand, it cannot be sure of this, particularly if it is unsure about the resources possessed by its adversaries. So from a prudential standpoint, it seems best to cut group losses and settle for peace rather than risk a vastly more unacceptable outcome. Once again, however, the argument rests upon a controversial claim about the relative equality of group strength. If this relative equality of strength is not the case, or if groups do not believe this to be the case, the maximin strategy of settling for peace will be less appealing than the maximax strategy of trying to achieve the desired social domination.

Finally, the inefficacy argument supposes that efforts to assimilate, dominate, or control outgroups are doomed to failure, and therefore conflicting groups should just as well settle for a brokered peace. This argument has its foundations in the Enlightenment conviction that one can torture another's body but not control her or his mind. Belief can only come about voluntarily, and if one cannot coerce another to see things their way, efforts at domination or assimilation are bound to fail. Therefore, it makes little sense to attempt to bring about such outcomes, and trying to do so anyway may simply make things worse by driving hated groups underground and reinforcing their resolve to defend their beliefs. In its present form, however, the inefficacy argument has limited reach and may even be quite false. It has limited reach because groups may prefer policies of segregation or elimination to the assimilation of outgroups, and this might be a more achievable objective. In the modern era the argument might also simply be false. With continued pressure through time, beliefs may be made to change. Committed and resourceful groups may well prove able to assimilate—and thereby destroy or eliminate—despised and detested outgroups through subtle or aggressive strategies of indoctrination. This is, in any event, an empirical matter, and given improved techniques in what might crudely be termed thought control, there is today far less reason to be sanguine about the integrity and inviolability of personal belief than there was in earlier periods.

Although each of these arguments has problems, they nevertheless point toward the possibility of a more successful effort. Since epistemic and moral reasons for accepting LP are excluded by virtue of the problem of audience, a successful defense of this principle must make appeal to something that matters, or should matter, to groups regardless of the worldview and/or moral theory of the human good that characterizes and defines them. Each of the arguments introduced by Barry pushes in this direction by introducing concerns about the costs and benefits of social peace to groups when measured against continued conflict. In fact, there is reason to think that there are really not three arguments here at all but three faces of a single argument that makes a strategic appeal to prudence. If we develop the counsel of prudence more forcefully and supplement the argument by recalling those sociological presumptions that follow from our understanding of the fact of pluralism, we may just be able to make a strong case for the acceptance of LP. If the case does turn out to be strong, I must hasten to add that it is not terribly original. Recourse to prudence is reasonably common in the endeavor of theorizing about political life, and I suppose the argument to follow will remind some of Hobbes, that notorious proto-liberal.[17] There is little reason to consider this an altogether bad thing unless, of course, one remains committed to a morally infused and driven theory of civil association. Since it should be reasonably clear by now that argument of this sort cannot hope to achieve political unity given the fact of pluralism, any attempt to demonstrate the theoretical possibility of political unity will need to be considerably more practical in its approach, and few arguments are more practical than appeals to prudence.[18]

Let me now introduce a two-pronged appeal to prudence in support of LP.[19] The first prong presents the more negative side of the argument while the second has a more positive aspect. Taken together, the two prongs of this argument from prudence will present what I will call the basic argument for LP. It is intended to provide us with an initial theoretical reason for thinking that all elements of the social setting have legitimate and powerful reasons for accepting LP, regardless of the worldview or moral theory of the human good that helps identify them. And it also introduces the more specific empirical conditions that need to be considered and analyzed in order to give the argument something more than *prima facie* credibility. To begin, it seems best to explore the notion of prudence itself in order to appreciate the way these two prongs draw from prudential reasoning.

Prudence is sometimes associated with the strategic pursuit of individual self-interest, and moral philosophers often juxtapose prudential reasons for acting (which thus assume a selfish or self-centered base) with (allegedly more noble) moral reasons for acting. The juxtaposition hardly works to the advantage of prudential reasoning, which is frequently dismissed as selfish and inconsiderate—flaws that moral reasoning is supposed to trump. But prudence is also, and perhaps more commonly, associated with sagacity and wisdom. The prudent individual pursues one's ends with care and foresight; does not act recklessly, fecklessly, or unreflectively; is careful, cautious, and inclined to avoid unnecessary or unreasonable risks; steers a steady, thoughtful, and determined course in the pursuit of those things the individual holds dear; and might be a dedicated egoist or a devoted altruist, or might fall somewhere between these extremes. While prudence does involve a concern for one's self-interest, it does not dictate how one is to understand or conceptualize this interest. It only promotes the discovery and adoption of the wisest (i.e., the safest, most secure, most reasonable) means or path for pursuing, promoting, and practicing one's self-interest as one comes to understand it. Prudence, in short, simply *is* the counsel of a strategically rational mind that understands and appreciates the importance of attacking one's ends thoughtfully and reflectively in order not to frustrate one's efforts to achieve them. As Sidgwick observed, 'Prudence may be said to be merely Wisdom made more definite by the acceptance of Self-interest as its sole ultimate end: the habit of calculating carefully the best means to the attainment of our own interests, and resisting all irrational impulses which may tend to perturb our calculations or prevent us from acting on them.'[20]

This view of prudence contains an ambiguity that is of some importance. On the one hand, we might understand prudence to involve promoting one's interests by putting oneself first and disregarding the interests of others. On the other hand, we might also understand prudence to involve the strategic use of reason, that is, of converging upon and pursuing strategies of action calculated to be the most efficient means for the achievement of one's interests. William Paley was attentive to this ambiguity, near the end of the eighteenth century, when he noticed that some moral thinkers take prudence to involve hitting upon the best strategies for the attainment of good or desired ends while other moral thinkers described prudence as simply attentiveness to our own interests without further concern for the interests of others.[21] If we take this ambiguity seriously, we may conclude that prudence may involve either of two possible forms of reasoning: Prudential reasoning could thus involve either (1) putting one's interests first in the calculation of personal ends (prudential reasoning) or (2) calculating and pursuing the most efficient and effective way to achieve one's chosen ends (strategic reasoning). I will suppose here that both forms of reasoning can legitimately be considered prudential; therefore, both persons and groups can be said to act prudently if they formulate their ends according to a primary and controlling concern for their own interests and well-being *and* if they reason strategically about how to best realize the ends they have chosen and maximize the interests they have identified. These two aspects of prudential reasoning merge in each of the prongs that constitute the basic argument for LP.

Imagine now a prudent person facing the following choice situation. Suppose X can pursue her ends by adopting either of two possible strategies. Strategy A would enable X to achieve her ends with a maximal result; that is, A would create the exact type of world X prefers. Strategy B, on the other hand, would not create exactly the type of world X prefers, but it would nonetheless permit X to live her life and pursue her vision of the good without meddling or interference from others. If X adopts B, she gives up some strategies she might use to make the world to her liking, but she remains free to argue for and defend her worldview and moral theory of the human good. So, B is only slightly worse than A for X, all things being equal. If all things really were equal, X would obviously opt for A over B, but X's problem is that all things are not equal. Suppose B can be chosen without risk; by committing to B, X does not run the risk of bringing about—or helping to bring about—condition Φ which is considerably worse than the condition she will bring about by opting for B. On the other hand, A is not risk-free and it is possible that if X opts for A, she will lose control of the situation and Φ will result. Imagine further that the chances of success, in the event X elects to pursue A, are indeterminate and undeterminable although there is some reason to think they are not very good. Finally, taking the gamble and opting for A risks something of great value to X, which X will lose in the possible and perhaps even likely event that Φ comes about.

Faced with such a choice, the prudent individual would no doubt elect to adopt B. It would be foolish to risk so much by opting for A when the chances of success are unknown, but perhaps not great, and when the outcome anticipated by the choice of the alternative strategy (B) is both all but guaranteed and only slightly worse than the best result one can hope for by opting for A. Even fanatics and zealots would need to concede as much, provided, of course, that they are also the least bit prudent. If this is right, then we need only ask whether this formalized choice predicament aptly describes the situation facing groups living amidst a politics of interests and reflecting upon the desirability of constructing a politics of principle, and thereby forming a polity.

It may be argued, however, that this scenario does not actually mimic the choice situation groups find themselves in given the social setting I have imagined. This situation is more closely approximated, it might be suggested, by thinking of it in terms of a rational-choice game with N players. If we think this is right, X's choice of B over A, accompanied let us say by a similar choice by Y, may incline Z to attempt a free ride by benefiting from the choices made by X and Y while still working toward her most desired social condition, say Φ, and thus not accepting B. In a game with N players, defection is always a possibility and even becomes likely in the event some group believes it can realize its most desirable social condition by defecting. If X realizes that B is an unstable condition by virtue of this free-riding possibility on the part of Z, she may be better off rejecting B and opting for A in the first place. If B is not a real possibility, X may just as well work for the realization of her most desired social condition, which is A. But the choice situation I have imagined is not easily modeled in terms of free-rider problems. Since all groups present in the social setting must accept B in order to assure social peace and stability, defection from B will hardly go unnoticed. Defection here involves Z working for Φ rather than accepting B, and doing so is destabilizing. But unlike free-rider situations, Z does not have the opportunity to get something for nothing by defecting from B. If Z defects by working strategically to bring about Φ, the stability brought about by the general acceptance of B will collapse if Z's action inspires X to work for A and Y to work for his most favored social condition. This will surely weaken and jeopardize Z's chances of realizing Φ. Of course, this may not happen, but sensing the danger posed to B by Z's refusal to accept it, X and Y may turn against Z and frustrate her ability to realize Φ. Since Z's actions will hardly go unnoticed, and since Z's pursuit of Φ will have negative repercussions when it is noticed, there is a strong, perhaps even compelling, reason for Z to endorse B if X and Y do so.

The phenomenon on display here is a product of the generalized character of social conflict. Social peace, under this scenario, certainly qualifies as a collective good, but it is only realizable if a sufficient number those groups that constitute the social setting opt for it. If enough groups do opt for it, defection will not permit a free ride; instead repercussions will follow as the other groups in the polity work to police defection and sustain social peace. Unless a given group is sufficiently dominant, it cannot hope to control the outcome resulting from its defection. So, while all groups in the polity may have reasons to defect, they also have reasons to hope that others do not. The only way to assure that others do not, on the other hand, is to not defect themselves. Solidarity in the face of randomized intergroup conflict is the best defense against group defection. This conditions holds if groups recognize the generalized character of intergroup conflict and if they understand that the benefits of cooperation far outweigh the alternative of intergroup warfare that results if all groups abandon their commitment to social peace.

So then, should groups living under a politics of interests think it prudent to abandon this condition in favor of one governed by LP? If group strength and group resources were basically equal, a politics of interests becomes terribly unstable and risks decaying into chaos and/or civil war. This is the condition that made Barry's social peace and prudence arguments seem attractive, and so it seems safe to conclude that under these conditions prudence would recommend acceptance of LP. But there is little reason to suppose relative group equality, and this has not been built into the dramatization of our social environment. Given the fact of flux, however, a politics of interests is inherently unstable regardless of group strength or relative group equality. A politics of interests will appear to be a politics of dominance to those groups whose members prove largely or generally unsuccessful in managing to control the political environment in desired ways (perhaps, for example, by being unable to put their desired spin on the sacred political concepts present in the social environment). Dominated outgroups—or outgroups who consider themselves dominated—may consequently resort to illegal methods to pursue their group agendas. They may become radicalized in the face of this felt oppression and work to terrorize, and hence destabilize, the political status quo. They may seek allies among other groups whose members also feel dominated (either historically or at the moment) in order to put together more powerful coalitions and erode the political control of dominating groups.[22] And as dominating groups pursue their own strategies, they may generate new normative (or even allocational) rivals and thus expand the possibility that outgroups will find willing allies in the struggle for political control.

Further, there is no way of knowing how the ebb and flow of political decision-making will affect the political landscape. Dominant groups never know when their own numbers will fragment and reconfigure their ability to influence and control sacred political symbols. If Catholics stood united, they might be able to bring about a change in American law regarding the practice of abortion, but Church efforts to bring this about might actually drive many Catholics (and not just female Catholics) away from the Church and perhaps toward feminist groups advocating the importance of freedom of choice, thus weakening both the Church itself and its political clout. The internal politics of a group does not remain static, and internal group struggle may weaken group integrity thus diminishing the group's ability to sustain political control of sacred symbols; new or suddenly salient social or economic issues may bring about group realignment and weaken the position of dominant groups; outgroups may find new allies and thereby pose a more serious threat to dominant groups; immigration and emigration may impact relative group strengths; and socio-economic changes in the social environment may bring some groups into greater prominence and diminish the numbers in others or alter the distribution of existing political resources. In short, a group's (or an alliance of groups) ability to maintain political control under a politics of interests seems both uncertain and unmanageable. The problem of managing *fortuna* that Machiavelli understood to plague political stability is still very much with us under the social demographics inspired by the fact of pluralism and characterized by the fact of flux.

When faced with the inevitable instability associated with a politics of interests, groups may adopt one of three possible strategies; these, I think, exhaust the actual choice situations groups face in the American political context. First, they may elect to continue with a politics of interests, gamble on their ability to control the political worship symbols common to the social environment, and be resigned to taking their political lumps in the event they lose control of the situation. At best, this choice will yield a continuation of political struggle and intergroup conflict filtered through the mechanisms of political legitimacy operative in the environment; at worst it will result in the decay of this struggle which may (again) ultimately reach the extreme level of civil war.

Second, dominant groups may seek to press their advantage and solidify their political control by moving toward a politics of dominance. This choice inevitably requires dominant groups to practice strategies intended to eliminate, segregate, or assimilate their political rivals. Under a domination strategy, the vicissitudes of group conflict can be eliminated only if dominant groups succeed in overpowering their rivals and making their social environment politically and socially homogeneous. Needless to say, domination strategies have had a long, if not horribly storied history, but their logic commits the 'oppressors' to an ongoing practice of oppression in the name of political stability. The move to a domination strategy forsakes a politics of interests and abandons the shaky balance associated with efforts to control, say, political worship symbols—the concepts of political legitimacy. With this veneer of legitimacy forsaken, groups face one another as hostile, warring camps, and the likely success of domination is correspondingly minimized. As domination strategies increasingly require more dominant groups to rely upon naked power and brute force to control the social environment, rival groups will invariably work to develop and pursue their own survival strategies. In the face of brutal elimination strategies, rivals will likely go underground, remove themselves to safe havens, adopt familiar guerilla strategies against the dominant group(s), seek allies from outside the social environment, and find ways to fight back. If segregation is attempted, the segregated may organize, build alliances among themselves and develop their collective strength, go underground and continue to practice their group ways, and find ways to fight back. If assimilation is attempted, it will be opposed. Rival groups will again go underground to practice their group ways and retain their beliefs; they will endure; and they will find ways to fight back. This is the lesson of a history of intergroup struggles for domination, and while there is little reason to document this history in great detail here, it is still a history that normative rivals would do well to keep in front of them.

Yet, even if a domination strategy manages to eliminate all group rivals in one way or another and establishes a pervasively homogeneous social environment, the need for continued dominance remains in place. This is because now, intragroup differences—the stuff of group politics—effectively divide the environment, creating new outgroups and setting the demands of dominance back into motion once again. When dominant groups can no longer find normative rivals to prey upon, it is altogether likely that they will begin to prey upon themselves.

Until and unless dominance can become as thorough and as dedicated as Orwell imagines in his little distopia of *1984*, domination strategies will remain uncertain and unstable, and the vicissitudes of intergroup conflict will continue to haunt the social environment, pushing in the direction of greater domination, on the one hand, or civil war on the other. An Orwellian outcome is of course possible; dominance might finally be achieved. But if Orwell is right, it will come at an extraordinary cost to the victor as well as the victimized. This is because domination is successful, in Orwell's tale, only because it becomes and end in itself—the desire to oppress is all that drives Orwell's oppressors. Here domination has become its own objective, and the struggle that put the pursuit of domination into motion is long lost. Underlying Orwell's story is his fear/belief that the struggle for domination has a transformative power all its own. As domination becomes its own end, the group itself atrophies, and little is left of it but the desire for domination for its own sake. If this is the price of successful domination (and can we readily suppose that it is not?) it is too great for any group to want to pay. The end to be realized by means of domination is lost and the only end that remains is domination itself.

The third alternative, of course, is to opt for a politics of principle (and hence a politics of unity) by endorsing LP. Initially, this might seem like a distasteful course of action; it requires groups to learn to get along with their normative rivals—hardly a desirable situation. Nevertheless (and if my account of life under a politics of interests and a politics of dominance is reasonably accurate), the alternatives are not terribly tasteful either. Therefore, groups have reason to consider seriously the acceptance of LP. This, once again, becomes the prudent choice if the three conditions introduced above are realized: (1) accepting LP means that group interests and commitments are only slightly compromised compared to the best possible alternative situation, (2) the possibility of achieving acceptance of LP throughout the polity is more probable than a group's realizing its most desired alternative condition, and (3) the likelihood of things going wrong (and hence realizing an unacceptable outcome) is less in the case of LP than the possible alternatives. At this point, however, it is not clear that endorsing LP is a good choice because we have not considered the costs associated with making this move. The basic argument must therefore be fleshed out with a consideration of what groups commit to—what costs they assume—if they do elect to accept LP and move to a politics of principle.

Nonetheless, the force behind the negative prong of the prudence argument depends upon the underlying presumption that groups care greatly about group autonomy. Groups, that is, can be presumed to value control over their own affairs, to live according to their worldview, and to practice their moral theory of the human good free from outside interference or intrusion more than anything else. Regardless of whatever else matters to groups by virtue of their moral theory of the human good, the autonomy and well-being of the group is their primary concern. If group autonomy is lost, everything else that matters to the group is threatened. Group autonomy is uncertain and unstable under a politics of interests; it is a gamble under a politics of dominance that does not seem to be winnable. It is maximally assured only under a politics of principle that accepts LP, though the corresponding costs associated with this choice have yet to be assessed. Unless these costs are surprisingly great and require a great sacrifice of group autonomy, it would seem that the acceptance of LP is a safe bet.

This brings me to the positive prong of the prudence argument. The dramatized vision of the social environment that exists under conditions of pluralism should not be confused with a state of nature. Instead, it is best modeled as a social environment that has in place political mechanisms for the management of large-scale social problems and for the maintenance of social order in spite of the intergroup hostility and animus present there. The politics of interests, that is, presumes a precarious social order challenged and destabilized by the presence of normative and allocational group rivalries. Nevertheless, groups can be generally supposed to profit from the presence of outgroups, and this prong of the prudence argument calls to mind the importance of this fact for group well-being. It has three basic steps. First, it illustrates the advantages to be gained from a peaceful and commodious association of groups. Second, it emphasizes the importance of a well-theorized understanding of political authority for managing the welfare of this commodious association of groups. And finally, it indicates that converging on LP is the best method for configuring this political authority and realizing the benefits to be gained from a group's political association with others, including their normative rivals. The argument remains prudential, of course, because its focus is on the best strategy for promoting and enhancing group interests.

Some groups strive to be self-sustaining and independent. Survivalists, for example, think they can take care of themselves without any need, or any appreciable need, for others, and the Old Order Amish are mostly content to go their own way and ignore the larger world around them. But claims of self-sustenance and independence are largely mythic; if some groups in the United States tend to go their own way successfully, it is largely because authorities in the United States underwrite their efforts to do so and protect them from the outside invasion to which they would otherwise be vulnerable. The vast majority of disparate religious, ethnic, cultural, ideological, and racial groups in the United States make no pretence of going their own way, on the other hand, and their members can readily acknowledge the fact of group interdependence. Although such groups set the primary identity of their members and provide them with an ontological focus and a normative orientation, they remain only partial communities.[23] They fall rather short of qualifying as units capable of meeting all the needs and providing all the services their members require or desire.

The potential benefits to be gained by groups from the support and social contributions of group outsiders may be quite exceptional. Sometimes the goods and services from which one benefits are supplied by outgroups as such, and at other times the goods and services received are more public in character and just happen to be provided by individuals belonging to outgroups. The benefits will range from certain necessities that groups cannot supply for themselves (or cannot do so in a cost-effective manner) to superfluities that happen to enrich and embellish the lives of group members in desirable ways. In part, this point involves the acknowledgment that our lives do not orbit entirely around those fundamental groups that happen to set our primary identities, and it calls to mind the fact of interconnectedness that typifies the complicated modern states of today.

While some benefits might seem inconsequential to particularly imperialistic groups, or while the members of such groups might be willing to do without the superfluities provided them by those outgroups that they regard as normative rivals, the fact of interconnectedness indicates that groups simply do not exist in a social vacuum. The presence of others introduces numerous organizational and coordination problems that need to be addressed if groups are to be able to practice their way of life without obstruction and frustration. Political organization provides the structural and managerial mechanisms necessary to coordinate group and individual association in a mutually acceptable, if not entirely desirable, fashion. By coming together and accepting political authority, groups can pool resources to provide for the common defense of their social environment, establish institutions for the management of coordination (including collective action) problems and thereby facilitate the ability of group members to go about their business without interference from outsiders, maintain a general level of lawfulness, and organize the scientific, technological, and social expertise necessary to manage the large-scale social problems that will inevitably arise as great numbers of groups and individuals pursue their lives and their sense of the good within the confines of a given social environment.[24]

In short, even if no basic religious, moral, or ideological differences were present in the social environment to generate normative rivalries, some form of civil association would still be necessary in order to guarantee the organization necessary to enable disparate groups to go their own way and practice their moral theory of the human good without bumping into one another, and to assure that unforeseen problems do not arise that jeopardize group well-being as a result of the unintended consequences of life in the region. There simply can be no viable social life without organization. Introducing the positive need for government, however, simply lends poignancy to the traditional problem posed by this need. If government is necessary, it is also necessary to determine the constraints that should define and limit its power.

Within the context controlled by government, groups contribute to each other's well-being both directly (by providing materials or services that enrich the lives of outgroup members) and indirectly (by acknowledging and adhering to managerial and organizational rules and institutions that make the pursuit of group ends viable in a crowded social environment). In order to secure the ends of mutual contribution, there is reason to adopt political arrangements that all groups present in the social environment can accept. Domination strategies frustrate this end, as we have seen, by introducing intergroup hostility into the region and destabilizing intergroup relations. But a politics of interests is also less desirable in this regard than a politics of principle since it too is a considerably more unstable and uncertain condition. Groups whose members sense that they are continual losers under a politics of interests may elect to defect from the process and abandon cooperative practices. The politics of interests is likely to foster and encourage a sense of intergroup estrangement that frustrates or impedes intergroup cooperation and coordination. If, however, groups can converge upon a political principle for the regulation of group life that does not overly burden the ability of group members to live their lives as they wish and pursue their moral theory of the human good, things will go much better. Once again, then, prudence, understood in terms of the strategic pursuit of group interests, recommends the acceptance of LP if this principle does not impose upon groups a burden considered to be greater than the dangers encountered under a politics of interests or a politics of dominance.

## Stability, civility, and the politics of principle

To summarize, the two prongs of the prudence argument indicate that a politics of principle is superior to the political alternatives *if* the burdens LP imposes on groups is slight, *if* the dangers to group life and group well-being under the political alternatives are considerable (thus outweighing any burdens imposed under a politics of principle), and *if* the chances of these dangers being realized are either great or indeterminate. If these conditions are satisfied, prudence suggests that groups should endorse a politics of principle over the political alternatives. So far, I have argued only that there are *prima facie* reasons to think that groups would be better off under a politics of principle (and regardless of their worldview or moral theory of the human good) because they have much to gain from a stable and well-organized political order and much to lose from political instability, and because LP satisfies the important conditions of inclusiveness, egalitarianism, and supportiveness. We are still unclear, however, on the exact nature of the burdens LP would impose on the polity, and the prudence argument can be made compelling only by exploring and considering these burdens. If the prudent group members perceive the burdens as too great, they may well prefer to run the risks associated with a politics of interests or attempt a politics of dominance and face the consequences, rather than endorse LP.

I will discuss the apparent burdens groups face under LP in the following two chapters and thus develop and supplement the basic argument for the acceptance of LP. First, however, I want to consider two familiar objections to the prudence argument. Some groups might accept the argument in general but still insist that some group (or groups) is so evil, damned, disgusting, or misguided that the polity would be better off without it. The fact, say, that some group(s) is pervasively perceived by others as a pariah group may seem like sufficient reason to eliminate, segregate, or assimilate it in spite of LP. Perhaps its mere presence in the polity even threatens political stability, and perhaps too it contributes absolutely nothing to other groups. Under such conditions, it might be argued, pariah groups should abandon the polity or face justified assimilation efforts by the citizenry. This argument, as should be apparent, is exceptionalist in nature, and as such it violates the inclusiveness condition. If it gains acceptance, it introduces and legitimizes something like majority tyranny, and under these conditions a politics of unity is impossible.

More dominant groups may be inclined to defend an exceptionalist position anyway, however, and suppose that if only they can do away with pariah groups, they (and the remainder of society) can live happily ever after. But once again it is important to notice that normative rivalries are likely to be widespread and volatile. Perhaps the As hate the Bs while the Cs hate the Ds, and so forth. It is unlikely that there will be any single pariah group at any given time; different groups will identify their own normative rivals and insist that these particular rivals are the ones that should go. Under such a scenario, things quickly decay and we are left with the politics of dominance or the politics of interests—both conditions we have hoped to avoid. Given the social dynamics associated with the fact of pluralism, then, exceptionalist claims defeat a politics of principle and return us to a condition of political instability.

Still, this response to the exceptionalist argument might seem to fail where and when there really is only one pariah group (or a small set of such groups). Under these circumstances, exceptionalist logic might seem to make sense. Yet even if there is but one pariah group present in the polity at a given point in time, exceptionalist logic still fails to appreciate the shifting and uncertain nature of normative rivalries. Perhaps all other groups in the polity hate the Crazy Betas, and as a result, they may wish to rid themselves of these people. But the Crazy Betas will likely adopt the kind of survival strategies we have already encountered, strategies that tend to destabilize the political status quo. They may look for allies external to the region, go underground and fight back, alter their views so as to align themselves with other groups and reconfigure normative differences, find ways to exploit fissures that separate currently allied groups, and so forth. And they may succeed.

But even if the Crazy Betas fail, the precedent established by exceptionalist logic is dangerous. Given the ebb and flow of group belief anticipated by the fact of flux, some other group in the region may now come under attack, and one can never anticipate which group (or set of groups) this might be. With the elimination or assimilation of the Crazy Betas, once overlooked intergroup differences might be magnified and new normative rivalries might emerge. Groups who formed an alliance against the Crazy Betas may now begin to question the practices of their former allies since they no longer have the Crazy Betas to worry about. Immigration may bring new groups into the region and shift political attitudes, and now other groups may again come under attack. In short, the uncertainty and instability of group life under the fact of pluralism makes exceptionalist logic a dangerous thing. The only viable way to avoid these dangers is to stick with the inclusiveness condition and reject exceptionalist claims.

Suppose now we imagine that LP is adopted for the reasons associated with the prudence argument. The result is a polity that takes the form of a *modus vivendi*, that is, a way of living together made possible by the happy convergence of the particular interests of the groups sharing a common social setting.[25] It might be argued, however, that such arrangements are fatally unstable, and thus a polity forged by the logic of a *modus vivendi* is unlikely to endure. The argument supposes that *modus vivendi* arrangements will be acceptable to groups only as a compromise, given the inability of any particular group, or coalition of groups, to dominate their state and thereby realize their most desired social condition. They are presumed to depend, then, on social demographics that establish a rough balance of power among rivals. But demographics can and do change, and the resultant changes may favor a particular group or coalition of groups inclining them to abandon the *modus vivendi* in favor, perhaps, of a domination strategy. Absent more principled reasons to adhere to the arrangement brought into being by the *modus vivendi*, the liberal polity must remain fragile and precarious.[26] This argument, in effect, turns the fact of flux against the basic argument, whereas I have supposed that it actually works to support the basic argument for LP.

I will have more to say about this concern and the problems that are often claimed to haunt *modi vivendi* arrangements in Chapter 5, but enough has been said already to suggest that a *modus vivendi* arrangement need not be considered all that unstable. Social demographics certainly do change, and they change in unforeseeable and unpredictable ways; there is simply no way to escape the uncertainties introduced by the fact of flux. While some changes may greatly increase a group's ability to dominate its social environment, future changes may work against the group and push it toward obscurity. Nor can groups easily anticipate how defections from the *modus vivendi* will affect social demographics. Recourse to a domination strategy may trigger a backlash against the group that erodes its strategic advantage and places it at risk of elimination, segregation, or assimilation. So it seems that groups will defect from the *modus vivendi* only at great risk; doing so is at best short sighted and at worst fatally imprudent. No matter how dominant a particular group may be in a state, its future under a politics of dominance is hardly guaranteed unless its members prove to be awfully good at domination, and the cost of failure may turn out to be high indeed.[27] There is, then, no reason (at present) to suppose that the fact of flux must work against the type of *modus vivendi* arrangement imagined by practical liberalism instead of working for it, and some reason to suppose that it will work for it after all.

In the face of an uncertain future and the largely uncontrollable nature of the fact of social flux, and if the cost of adhering to LP is reasonably modest and the price of failing to succeed in a domination strategy possibly great, a *modus vivendi* arrangement is likely to provide about all the political stability we can hope for. If normative rivalries are deep and entrenched and if social demographics dramatically favor some groups over others, prudential argument may not carry the day. This is an obvious and inevitable risk. But of course, prudential argument may not carry the day anyway. All political theorizing can do is craft the argument for a politics of principle and thereby construct the case for manufacturing political unity; it cannot manufacture such a politics by itself or bring it into being. What matters here is the theoretical accuracy in imagining the social condition for which and in which one theorizes. In the face of the fact of pluralism, there are no grounds other than prudential ones upon which to construct a politics of principle. This is hardly problematic in itself; prudential argument need not be any less compelling than more morally infused argument.

But fortunately, we do not need to leave things at this. Political stability can be greatly enhanced by the cultivation of a political culture supportive of a politics of principle, and in Chapter 6 we will have occasion to consider the type of political culture to be promoted under the auspices of LP. Of course, the cultivation of such a culture will also likely impose certain costs on groups, and these costs introduce additional reasons for groups to reject LP. Once again, then, it will be necessary to explore and assess these costs in order to determine if the benefits to be gained under a politics of principle should be worth the costs that groups are asked to pay. This too is a necessary aspect of a thorough exploration of the possibility of a politics of unity. Perhaps ironically, the more theoretical inquiry develops and explores the conditions required to solidify the liberal polity, the more costs it introduces into the choice equation. But there is no reason to conclude at this point that these added costs jeopardize favoring a politics of unity over the alternatives.

# 3
# Freedom and Toleration

If we presume that people are prudent, regardless of what they believe or how driven they are by their moral theory of the human good, the basic argument for accepting LP and embracing a politics of principle seems reasonably strong. It needs further development, however, and this can be accomplished only by exploring the costs and benefits associated with the choice situation that groups pondering the acceptance of LP necessarily face. If groups think that the sacrifices required by the acceptance of LP are too great, or cut too deeply into their ability to pursue their vision of the good as they understand it, they may prefer a politics of interests (or even a politics of dominance). It is necessary, then, to explore the basic obligations groups assume once they accept LP and correspondingly to consider the benefits they can expect from adherence to a politics of principle.

Put in the most general of terms, LP demands two things of all members of the polity. First, it demands acceptance and loyalty. Regardless of their group affiliations, people will need to devote themselves to the ends required by LP, practice its demands, and recognize it as the primary norm for the management of intergroup relations within the polity. This we can think of as the spirit of citizenship; to be a good citizen is to be faithful to LP and to put its demands into practice in the course of living one's life and pursuing one's sense of the good. Being a good citizen may, and probably does, require more of a person than this, of course, but it involves at least this much. Given the place of primacy and importance that one's moral theory of the human good must invariably play in a person's life, this is both a considerable and a controversial condition. This is because the responsibility of good citizenship requires that persons *qua* group members come to identify and understand themselves as members of the group that is the polity and learn to practice an allegiance to this group that occasionally overrides the lifestyle requirements of other more primary groups to which they belong. This introduces both costs and benefits associated with a politics of principle that will be explored more thoroughly in the concluding chapter.

Second, adherence to LP establishes the jurisdictional primacy of LP as the focal mechanism for settling intergroup disputes. The acceptance of LP cannot and should not be understood to end intergroup conflict in either its allocational or normative aspects; instead it institutionalizes and redirects this conflict by introducing principled considerations that govern intergroup disputes and control their authoritative resolution. The liberal polity will be required to call upon its political and legal mechanisms to bring the demands of LP alive in the process of mediating and resolving those intergroup disputes that happen to arise. These systems introduce the institutional structures responsible for putting the requirements of LP into practical effect. It is both necessary and important for the polity as a whole to have some inkling of what this involves. That is, it is important for citizens to have a reasonable understanding of what LP requires; how it is to be applied for purposes of settling intergroup disputes; and the kinds of political and legal judgments it requires in order to bring the justice it mandates alive within the polity. This introduces further costs and benefits associated with a politics of principle that will be examined in this chapter and the one to follow.

It would be a mistake to suppose that resolutions to intergroup disputes can be deductively derived from LP, and it would be just as mistaken to think that the requirements of liberal justice mandated by LP can be grasped in detail by philosophical guardians and implemented by them on behalf of the polity. As we shall see, a politics of principle does not transcend politics by transforming it into a matter of rational insight. But it does focus political controversy and the management of intergroup conflict upon specific norms that need to be clearly understood by all citizens (and particularly by group elites in more oligarchical groups), and it requires that all citizens have a shared understanding of the norms at issue. This is the precondition for political debate and controversy where conflicting parties can put their case in terms of shared political ideals. In order to guarantee that things do not reduce to a politics of interests, however, citizens need to appreciate the common core meaning of the requirements of LP. It is this core meaning that they accept when they agree to embrace LP, and it is this core meaning that guides the resolution of intergroup conflict and sets the parameters of legitimate political discussion and debate. To borrow a phrase from William James, this is the 'cash-value' of the cost of accepting LP.[1]

## Toleration

What then is the common core meaning of LP? Recall first that the principle defends *group* freedom rather than the freedom or independence of the individual. Put the other way around, LP provides maximum protection for group autonomy against external intrusion or invasion. Group outsiders are justified in coercively interfering with intragroup activities only to encourage respect for LP and to ensure that its requirements are honored by all group members. In practical terms, LP holds that groups are free to live by their worldviews and moral theories of the human good until and unless doing so involves compromising the ability of the members of other groups to enjoy the same freedom. As should be evident, LP does not require group members to respect, love, or embrace group outsiders; instead, it leaves plenty of room for intergroup hatred and animosity. But it does require groups to put up with outsiders even though they may loathe these people because of who they are or what they believe. In short, LP introduces jurisdictional boundaries. It prohibits outsider interference with group ways, but it also requires the priority of state ways when these come into conflict with group ways. This means, in effect, that LP introduces standards of toleration into the polity. It does so in two ways that correspond to the twin demands that LP makes of citizens. First, it requires citizens to practice toleration or to put up with those they might consider, by virtue of their group identifications, damned, disgusting, or misguided because of who they are or what they believe. Second, it requires the government to adjudicate intergroup disputes that take the form of tolerance problems, and it expects citizens to understand and accept the results of this adjudication, provided of course that it is defensible when measured against the core meaning of LP. Both demands necessitate an appreciation for what toleration, as mandated by LP, involves, and it is now time to say something about this.

In traditional liberal discourse, tolerating something means simply not prohibiting it by law.[2] Thus understood, a tolerant polity is one where the legal machinery of the state is unavailable to groups desiring to use its coercive power to prohibit certain modes of behavior they consider unacceptable for some reason. This is, however, a fairly cramped understanding of toleration, and there are those who would prefer a more robust view of the matter. Mieczyslaw Maneli, for example, thinks toleration should be understood to have two aspects, one negative and the other more positive. The negative side requires only forbearance; to practice toleration in this sense is simply to put up with those one has reason to consider damned, disgusting, repugnant, or misguided. The positive side, according to Maneli, requires a tolerant person to value and appreciate the contributions that diversity can make to a robust and valuable social life.[3] Here toleration would require people to look favorably upon those who are otherwise viewed with disgust and loathing because the differences they introduce into the polity add dimension and texture to social life.

But it seems difficult if not impossible to make much sense out of the claim that toleration has a positive dimension. As Maneli admits, it makes little sense to say one tolerates something one agrees with or is indifferent to.[4] Toleration simply does not work this way. Toleration is paradoxical precisely because it requires one to practice forbearance toward persons and activities that one finds repugnant, loathsome, or morally objectionable.[5] If it required us to abandon such judgments and embrace those persons or activities we would otherwise regard with disdain, it would be transformed into something else: acceptance, appreciation, or esteem. If people have what they regard as legitimate reasons to consider others damned, disgusting, repugnant, or misguided by virtue of who they are or what they believe, it asks a great deal of them to change their minds and alter their beliefs on the grounds that the differences these others introduce actually enrich their lives. Since those who believe they have good reason to find certain others loathsome and disgusting will surely hold such judgments by virtue of the differences they sense in these others, it will be a hard sell to convince them that this difference is really a source of social enrichment. But toleration does not ask this of us; nor does it have any magical or transformative power to change loathing into appreciation or esteem. It seems best, then, to rest content with the negative aspect of toleration. To tolerate others is merely to put up with them and not to regard those one loathes as a social benefit by virtue of their loathsome qualities or ways.

Unfortunately, dismissing the positive dimension of toleration does little more than make the paradoxical character of the concept all the more explicit. While it looks like toleration should qualify as a moral requirement of some sort and while it is frequently supposed to work in just this way, it seems largely inconsistent with dedicated moral belief.[6] From a moral point of view, it makes sense only to tolerate those things about which we are morally indifferent; those things that seem morally wrong or reprehensible ought not be tolerated.[7] What kind of a moral notion would require us to put up with something we consider morally objectionable? If this is what toleration asks of us, what possible moral grounds could there be for thinking it good, morally speaking, to practice toleration at all?[8] If we consider toleration a moral virtue, it would presumably introduce moral reasons to tolerate things that we have moral reasons not to tolerate, and this brings our moral beliefs into conflict with one another.

We can avoid this conclusion and reach some modest accord with toleration as a moral virtue by supposing that toleration requires people to put up with things they consider tacky, rude, tasteless, or unpleasant but not morally wrong. That is, toleration might be viewed as a virtue of benign neglect that encourages us to put up with bad manners or disgusting personal habits but not the transgression of moral duties and obligations. But although it makes sense to speak of things like tolerating bad manners, limiting toleration to such contexts robs the notion of much of its apparent importance. For one thing, a non-moral account of toleration rather trivializes the notion. Does putting up with the disgust we might experience when witnessing someone spit in one's soup reach the level of insufferability we generally associate with tolerating something? We may think such behavior boorish and yet not think it so disgusting that we feel compelled to take action against it. Curiously, it often seems that it is just where we feel the need to take such action that toleration seems to matter, for it works as a check against doing what we have moral reason to think we should do. Moreover, this point is of some importance, for it suggests that we can at times recognize reasons for putting up with people and/or activities we find morally objectionable that trump the moral reasons we have for not doing so. Developing such reasons is fundamental to the articulation of a political morality supportive of political unity.

There is another, more practical problem that arises if we think of toleration as a virtue embedded within some moral theory of the human good. Understood chiefly as a moral notion, toleration is easily transformed into its opposite and may well become mired in a politics of interests or worse. It becomes caught up in a politics of interests, for example, if it takes on the role of a political worship word whose practical meaning is up for grabs. Thus in the United States, some groups look with disfavor upon the normative convictions of other groups and condemn them for being intolerant of their normative rivals. Many Americans who wish to identify with a liberal political viewpoint consider racists, who want to practice segregation, intolerant, and they characteristically condemn them accordingly.[9] Confident in their own convictions (and perhaps rightly so), they do not consider themselves intolerant when they condemn racists for their racism and block them from practicing segregation. Instead, their own moral convictions persuade them that they are on the side of the righteous and are merely checking the intolerance of the racists, whose moral scruples are in serious doubt. But racists might be equally convinced of the moral integrity of their views and may regard liberal efforts to restrain them as little more than an insidious form of intolerance. As a weapon of moral righteousness, toleration is easily confused with assimilationism and lost within a politics of interests. This occurs when the moral convictions of dominant groups in society are imposed upon others and advertised as the proper social standard to be used to distinguish between what should and what should not be tolerated.

A polity governed by a commitment to LP would not allow such intolerance masked in the guise of toleration. To avoid the problem, however, it is necessary to decouple toleration from the moral theories held by the groups constitutive of the polity. Toleration, as required by LP, stands independent of these normative theories and works as a governor to check their potential for exacerbating normative rivalries and as a mechanism of adjudication to manage and resolve some of the more intransigent forms of intergroup conflicts that happen to arise. (This is not to say that a group's normative theory might not endorse in its own right a theory of liberal toleration of the sort mandated by a commitment to LP.) As we have seen, groups have prudential reasons to accept LP regardless of the moral viewpoint and worldview to which they adhere. Yet, insofar as their moral theories of the human good prescribe moral conduct inconsistent with the demands of toleration under LP, they also have reason to reject LP. The case for LP must be strengthened, then, by demonstrating that the burden imposed upon them by practicing liberal toleration is still preferable to a politics of interests (or worse), and this is best achieved by considering what toleration requires of them in practice.

Unhinged from a particular moral theory, toleration as a political virtue introduces a normative scheme that can profitably be regarded as a component of a political morality that trumps group beliefs about how they should treat the members of outgroups with whom they share a common social setting. That is, toleration now becomes a primary virtue of the political morality inspired by LP, and it introduces a central cost of accepting the principled politics mandated by LP. This does not mean, and should not be understood to suggest, that the requirements of toleration are in some sense morally superior to the normative convictions associated with the moral theories of the human good present in the polity. Acceptance of LP, and the accompanying recognition of the need to practice toleration, does not demand any alteration in a group's moral belief; it requires only that group members act upon these beliefs in ways consistent with the demands of toleration. This, I think, makes toleration valuable as a distinctive political virtue, and it also indicates that the only feasible way to make sense of toleration is to think of it as a political, rather than a moral, virtue. But to make LP palatable to groups existing under conditions of pluralism, it is necessary to make explicit the fact that liberal toleration does not impose a cost upon their moral convictions greater than the benefits gained by the political stability and security it brings into being. Toleration can be acknowledged as a political *virtue* only if this latter point can be established. If the point cannot be established, on the other hand, it would seem that toleration must cease to be a virtue of any sort.

As a first step toward articulating a reasonably serviceable theory of liberal toleration, I want to consider further the distinction between tolerance problems (caused by the presence of normative rivals in the polity) and coordination problems (caused by the presence of allocational rivals) introduced in the previous chapter. Sometimes, A's doing X interferes with B's ability to do Y simply because X and Y are mutually exclusive actions. The National Socialist Party of America cannot hold a political rally at the same time and in the same place that the NAACP is holding a freedom march. More generally, where and when resources are rendered scarce because competing groups enter claims against them greater than the amount of the resource available, where and when competing claims are advanced against some indivisible good, where and when group practices create burdens for outsiders or generate collective action problems, and/or where and when groups plan mutually exclusive activities, allocational rivalries come into being and questions of distributive justice arise.

All groups in the polity are potentially, if not actually, allocational rivals. When specific distributive conflicts arise between allocational rivals, these groups—and the polity as a whole—face a coordination problem. Although allocational rivalries can turn into normative rivalries, they need not do so. The As might generally get along famously with the Bs and vice versa, or the As and Bs might simply be indifferent to one another, but they might still find themselves adversaries in a coordination problem. Coordination problems are the standard stuff of politics, requiring a measure of social organization and coordination in order to give all groups in the polity a fair and reasonable chance to realize their ends in a manner they consider suitable and acceptable.[10]

Coordination problems raise some intractable difficulties in their own right, but they differ from tolerance problems that arise because of the often more intractable conflict between normative rivals. Tolerance problems emerge when groups have reason to practice intolerance or to act upon their moral theory of the human good in a way intended and designed to eliminate, segregate, or assimilate other groups and deny those members the opportunity to live their lives in accordance with their worldview and moral theory of the human good. It is easy enough to call to mind familiar and frightening illustrations of the more crude and obvious examples of such intolerance; things like slavery, genocide, ethnic cleansing, and imposed segregation come readily to mind here. Liberal spirits, of course, are quick to condemn such practices and to look for ways to bring them to an end. If asked why, say, ethnic cleansing is objectionable, moral liberals will insist that the practice is immoral; people do not deserve to be rousted from their homes and way of life and segregated, deported, or killed simply because of who they are or what they happen to believe. This is a crude violation of the equal concern and respect persons as such deserve from one another. But if this is the best moral liberals can do, if this is all they can say here, their arguments would seem to turn back against them. Why cannot ethnic cleansers insist that they are the victims of liberal intolerance in the event liberals intervene in their lives and prevent them from pursuing their sense of the good as they understand it?

Liberals, following a lead suggested by Kant, might insist at this point that ethnic cleansing qualifies as intolerance because it disrupts the lives of its victims, and it is not intolerance to prohibit the practice of intolerance.[11] Moral liberals cannot tolerate everything, and if their views are to be coherent, they ought not tolerate intolerance. This, however, will not appease the ethnic cleansers; nor should it. They can respond, both reasonably and plausibly, by arguing that this liberal sense of intolerance follows from the particular morality that makes liberals liberal and not from any more fundamental moral sense that they should accept. Thus by intruding into their lives and forcing them to abide by liberal ways, they are required to conform to a moral view they do not hold and have reason to reject. This, as should be apparent, looks like a form of intolerance, and it will surely be regarded as such by the ethnic cleansers.

At issue in all this is a sense of intolerance that needs to be exposed; and once exposed, rejected. Intolerance is frequently and popularly associated with prejudice, bigotry, and hatred. These are things that, from the viewpoint of modern moral liberalism, ought not be tolerated; or rather, actions motivated and inspired by such sorry attitudes as these ought not be tolerated. These are not the only sources of intolerance, of course; at times intolerance is motivated by more benign concerns (religious missionaries come to mind here), although some might question whether missionary zeal is properly described as intolerant. But prejudice, bigotry, and hatred are frequently regarded as the chief reasons why the members of one group seek to intrude upon the way of life of others. Like religious proselytizing, judgments about the hatred or prejudice of others are made from within a particular moral perspective; they emanate from and are powered by one's distinctive moral theory of the human good.[12] Thus hatred is considered a moral wrong by liberals, and liberals look with disdain upon those they think happen to prejudge others. Yet the others in question are motivated by their own moral agenda. They may, and probably will, insist that they do not necessarily hate the objects of their moral animus; or if they do concede their hatred, they may claim that it is altogether justified. Correspondingly, they may argue that they are not prejudging the targets of their animus any more than religious missionaries prejudge the heathens they are intent to bring to their God. They may even suppose that it is the liberal who prejudges them by failing to see and understand things with the clarity that their own moral perspective affords them.

If intolerance judgments remain lodged entirely within specific moral theories of the human good, they will invariably fuel the very politics of interests that practical liberalism attempts to overcome. Though this may sound odd, such judgments create the very tolerance problems that a politics of principle seeks to mediate. The appropriate remedy, or the remedy appropriate for a politics of principle, is to remove judgments about what is tolerable and what is intolerable from group-specific moral theories of the human good and to premise them instead upon the principled grounds introduced by LP. This means that tolerance problems arise when group conflict results from incompatible group efforts to pursue their respective moral theories of the human good as they see fit. In short, a tolerance problem emerges when group A claims that LP protects its right to do X while group B contends that the A's doing X interferes with its members' freedom to do Y, thus violating LP where both X and Y are perceived, by the groups committed to them, as valid activities according to their respective worldviews and moral theories of the human good.

Consequently, tolerance problems must be understood to arise under the strictures of LP, for it is LP, and not the moral theory of the human good of any given group, that establishes the normative context from which tolerance judgments emerge. The concerns of toleration thus reconfigure the intergroup conflict that emerges between normative rivals and set the evaluative context within which these conflicts are to be adjudicated. There are some obvious group activities that are clearly inconsistent with LP—and again, ethnic cleansing is one obvious example. Because, say, ethnic cleansing so obviously encroaches upon the freedom of members of the targeted group to live as they wish according to their worldview and to practice their moral theory of the human good, it is hard to imagine that any group wanting to practice ethnic cleansing while also willing to abide by the demands of LP could possibly insist upon the right to do so. Such activities do not pose significant tolerance problems, for problems of this sort presume that the conflicting groups can make legitimate claims under LP that the burden of toleration is on their side. Some of the costs of toleration under LP are obvious enough, even to groups with a history of implementing policies designed and intended to eliminate, segregate, or assimilate their normative rivals. Tolerance problems become practically problematic, on the other hand, when it is less clear where the burden of toleration goes, that is, when it is not certain which group is required to tolerate the other.

Tolerance problems are theoretically interesting because they pose a practical challenge to the workings of the liberal toleration required by LP. A politics of principle requires the articulation of theoretical standards appropriate for the resolution of such practical difficulties, and the exploration of these standards, in turn, is an important element of an argument intended to explain why groups would do well to endorse LP and accept a politics of principle rather than struggle with the alternatives. Yet the theoretical exploration of these standards cannot indicate in the abstract where the line between tolerance and intolerance is to be drawn or how all imaginable tolerance problems are to be resolved. It can only proceed by offering some inkling of what it means in practice to honor those spheres of control that are properly and entirely the province of group (or individual) control under LP. Correspondingly, we should be mindful of the fact that theoretical inquiry can only direct the resolution of tolerance problems by indicating the common core meaning of LP. It can only hope to get everyone on the same page, so to speak; it cannot presume to settle tolerance problems definitively. Its purpose is only to facilitate insight into the political morality generated by adherence to LP and perhaps to direct and inspire discussion about the nature and requirements of this morality. As a practical matter, the disagreements likely generated by tolerance problems when they emerge, and the possible disgruntlement created by institutional efforts to resolve them, probably will and probably should encourage ongoing public discourse over the nature of social justice under a politics of principle.

## A schematic of liberal toleration

One way to develop the theory of liberal toleration generated by LP is to articulate the demands of toleration in terms of a set of rights designed to implement the requirements of equal group freedom. If we pursue this path, the following liberties would surely make the list: freedom of conscience, belief and worship; freedom of expression; the right of group members to practice group ways and pursue group beliefs free from outside interference (something we might call the right of group privacy); freedom of association (understood as the right of individuals to associate with willing and like-minded others); and the right of group autonomy or self-governance with regard to internal group affairs. There is something, and perhaps a good deal, to be said for each of these rights, but there is also reason not to rely too heavily on the rhetoric of rights as we expand upon the notion of liberal toleration. Liberals traditionally suppose that rights adhere to individuals and only derivatively, if at all, to groups.[13] But practical liberalism, as we have seen, is concerned chiefly with group freedom or the freedom of group members to live their lives according to the worldview and moral theory of the human good that inspires and unites them.

Given the emphasis upon group autonomy mandated by LP, it is necessary to develop a theory of liberal toleration by conceptualizing matters in terms of jurisdictional group boundaries. Because liberal toleration requires recognition of and respect for these boundaries, a theory of liberal toleration has at its core an exploration of what this means, practically speaking, for intergroup relations. This, in turn, must involve an examination of the nature of those tolerance problems that are likely to arise in pluralist polities and a corresponding analysis of how they are to be resolved in a manner faithful to the theoretical requirements of liberal toleration.

Recall that liberal theory began to emerge in the seventeenth century as liberal thinkers worked to achieve a shaky peace between hostile (and primarily religious) groups by depoliticizing the normative issues that brought them into conflict. Faced with the intractable difficulties associated with mediating conflict over matters of fundamental belief, these thinkers supposed that the assimilationist strategies employed by more dominant religious groups would do little more than generate greater intergroup conflict and thereby exacerbate the problem of political stability. Accordingly, they countered religious intolerance and bigotry by arguing that such matters were terribly personal and should be left to the private discretion and deliberation of the individual.[14] This distinction introduced new political considerations (e.g., a defense of liberty in terms of a sphere of personal control) that served both to limit and to empower state authority. By depoliticizing key matters of belief and placing them in the realm of what we now think of as the private, principled limitations were placed upon the state's authority. The state was prohibited from intruding into this private realm and making matters of, say, personal belief a political—that is to say public—concern. In more contemporary liberal jargon, the state was to stay officially neutral with regard to private matters. But the state was also empowered to defend the realm of the private against intrusions by other citizens who might wish (for whatever reason) to make another's business their own. Thus, Locke supposed the chief responsibility of the state to be the policing of natural rights, while at the same time the state carried the obligation to respect these rights itself. A central *raison d'être* of the state, under emergent liberal theory, was to police those particular privacy rights that walled individuals off from one another and safeguarded matters considered outside the domain of the public.

The public/private distinction has now hardened into a commonplace of life within those states whose political cultures have been largely shaped by liberal influences.[15] The citizens of modern liberal states conceive of social life largely, if not exclusively, in terms of the twin realms of the public and the private, although they do not always agree on what activities go in which realm, a fact that does much to fuel the politics of interests since *this* conceptualization remains often informed by group conviction and belief. The distinction, however, is both too crude and too misleading to service the needs of practical liberalism. The group-centered understanding of social life under practical liberalism invites a more refined and nuanced group-sensitive distinction between the various publics actually present in pluralist societies, all of which have an authoritative political standing for those individuals who belong to them.

In keeping with the requirements of the problem of audience, groups are to be understood here as publics bounded by the worldviews and moral theories of the human good to which their members largely (though not necessarily entirely) subscribe. They can be presumed to vary greatly both in the nature and type of organization they display as well as in their size and general unity; and consequently, the range of associational identifications that qualify as groups, in the admittedly capacious sense the term carries here, can be presumed to be quite great. Some groups may be little more than a loosely connected collection of persons sharing similar or common worldviews and moral visions. The larger and more ethereal the group, the less formal, organized, and structured its internal authorities and group elites are likely to be. We can think of the liberal sentiments that constitute the political consciousness of many contemporary Americans, for example, as an illustration of one such large and nebulous group. Other groups, however, may be tightly knit communities possessing their own clear organizational structure, authoritative policy makers, and internal political machinery. Nonetheless, what matters for present purposes is the dual nature of the polity that emerges when we take groups to be its constituent members. On the one hand, the polity should be understood as a single political unit bounded together by a common commitment to LP; yet on the other hand, it is also a grouping of distinctive and possibly hostile groups (differentiated by worldview and moral theory of the human good)—a *communitas communitatum*, so to speak.[16] The aim of practical liberalism is to chart the legitimate domains of these dual jurisdictions, to define the authority of the public that is the polity, and distinguish it from the authority of the multitude of distinct publics that are the groups residing in the polity. As a discrete group in its own right (defined by and possessing its own governing political morality), the polity should be understood as a public with members to be viewed as fellow citizens and with its own distinctive political machinery and jurisdictional boundaries. From an external point of view, these boundaries are recognizable in both legal and territorial terms. Internally, however, the polity's jurisdiction is established primarily (though as we shall see not exclusively) by LP. Since LP, and the liberal toleration it mandates, involves a strong defense of group autonomy, the central challenge associated with explicating the practical demands of a politics of principle is to establish a reasonably clear understanding of those jurisdictional issues that are the province of the public that is the polity and distinguish them from those jurisdictional issues that belong to those publics that are the groups whose autonomy is protected—for these groups also qualify as publics in the sense that their business matters to all their members and is an authoritative influence in their lives. As we have seen, these groups will likely have their own internal politics premised upon whatever disagreements over group belief, dogma, jurisdiction, and policy happen to exist there. By defending group autonomy, practical liberalism leaves the politics of these publics to their members, and prohibits jurisdictional intrusion from the outside.

Internal group conflicts—the stuff of group politics—raise some curious problems for a liberalism that envisions the polity as a realm of publics, some of which will be discussed in the following chapter. For the most part, however, when groups face internal conflict, they must go it alone; dissenting group minorities have little in the way of recourse to the polity if they are searching for external support for their viewpoint. Not all Catholics are sold on the Church's stand on abortion. But from the standpoint of liberal toleration, it would be an unwarranted jurisdictional intrusion if pro-abortion Catholics asked the United States government to intervene on their behalf and, say, remove the Church's tax-exempt status in hopes of pressuring the Church to change its policy on abortion.

Internal group disputes of this sort frequently trouble because they are often triggered by group members with some allegiance to other groups with competing policies, norms, or visions. People can and frequently do belong to different groups, and therefore they may have moral views that hybridize the moral theories of the human good associated with their group identities. Hybridization may drive a desire for transformation that would bring these moral theories into closer alignment. A Catholic feminist (or for that matter a feminist Catholic) may well oppose the Church's policy on abortion. If group members who feel that group elites are wrong to insist upon moral ideas they consider repugnant remain in a minority, they are unlikely to affect significant change in group practices, as pro-choice

Catholics have discovered.[17] Under these circumstances, group minorities are likely to suffer from the vicissitudes of internal group politics in particularly distressful ways. But while such dilemmas are the source of personal tragedy and discomfort, they are not matters to be appealed to the polity. Here, liberal toleration leaves the individual to wrestle with his or her own conscience, for these are personal matters—or matters of personal moral struggle—that have no jurisdictional pertinence to the public that is the polity. Disgruntled minorities can always leave the group (a matter to be discussed shortly), or they can put aside their moral concerns and remain faithful to the group. Of course, they might also continue to remain associated with the group and continue to oppose those group ways to which they object. This too is a matter of personal conscience, but not one relevant to their status as citizen in the polity.

This will be objectionable, however, to group outsiders who think or fear that dissident group minorities are being oppressed by the majority or by group elites. These outsiders may think justice demands state intervention in internal group affairs in order to protect dissident minorities against group tyranny; and since practical liberalism would prohibit such interventions, this might seem like reason for dominant groups to reject LP. I will have a good deal to say in response to this objection as the discussion develops, but a brief response to the problem is in order here. In the American context, the problem arises in its most troubling form when illiberal groups appear to compromise rights and liberties that should be safeguarded for all persons according to the beliefs of the dominant liberal culture.

To illustrate, consider a much-discussed case involving the Pueblo nation in the southwest United States. The controversy developed as a result of efforts by the US Congress to extend civil liberty guarantees to Native-Americans. Members of the Pueblo nation requested an exemption from the resultant federal legislation arguing that the federal requirements are alien to the Pueblo nation and would endanger Pueblo culture.[18] Problems arose when minority elements within the Pueblo defended the extension of civil liberties to their nation and alleged that they had suffered serious injustices because of certain dissident views, including ostracism and exclusion from tribal affairs because some of the dissidents had converted to Protestant Christianity. Under practical liberalism, Congress would not be empowered to impose liberal ways upon a non-liberal minority in this fashion. Doing so anyway, of course, would cause no problems if the Pueblo simply ignored congressional action. But the realities of internal group politics suggest that dissident groups would seize upon federal guarantees in order to pursue their own interests against the group majority.

As Frances Svensson has emphasized, religion is a defining feature of the Pueblo and a fundamental aspect of community life. According to Pueblo belief, 'violation of religious norms is viewed as literally threatening the survival of the entire community.'[19] Enforcing liberal standards of religious independence would thus compromise the integrity of the tribe. It also seems reasonable to suppose that the complaints of intimidation and isolation raised by the religious dissidents in search of the First Amendment free-exercise protection can also be understood as traditional Pueblo practices for defending and sustaining the traditional religious beliefs integral to tribal existence. What seems like intimidation to the Pueblo minority is simply a legitimate method for policing group ways in the eyes of the Pueblo majority.

Interestingly, Will Kymlicka has supported the extension of religious liberty to the Pueblo arguing that it does not constitute an external intrusion into Pueblo affairs that will subvert or corrupt traditional tribal ways. Noting Svensson's concerns, Kymlicka still concludes that defending religious diversity among the Pueblo is permissible because it would give all members of the tribe the opportunity to practice and express their religious beliefs as they see fit. This extends an egalitarian ideal at home in liberal circles into a non-liberal community by guaranteeing that tribal elites or a tribal majority cannot impose their religious convictions upon dissident tribal members.[20] But Kymlicka does not think this threatens the cultural integrity of the Pueblo; instead it permits Protestant Pueblo to live alongside traditional Pueblo and participate in tribal affairs. The Protestant Pueblo, the argument goes, remain Pueblo and introduce new texture and new opportunities into the tribe. In good liberal fashion, Kymlicka supposes that this expands lifestyle opportunities and choices for all tribal members without threatening the coherence or integrity of the tribe itself.

Other liberals are less convinced that non-liberal groups like the Pueblo should be required by the dominant liberal culture to respect liberal ways. Chandran Kukathas, for example, believes that the imposition of liberal practices upon the Pueblo will have a corrosive effect on Pueblo culture. If liberalism wants to take cultural integrity seriously, it should not, according to Kukathas, chisel away at Pueblo practices in this fashion.[21] Practical liberalism, on the other hand, is not concerned with extending standards of liberal egalitarian morality to non-liberal groups; nor is it concerned with a moral defense of the integrity of minority cultures. It is concerned, instead, with identifying and articulating ways in which disparate religious, cultural, ethnic, racial, and ideological groups can manage to live together free from the uncertainties and instability introduced by the politics of interests. Toward this end, it supposes that groups facing the circumstances associated with the fact of pluralism and the fact of flux would think it best to opt for a political arrangement that accorded them the strongest support for group autonomy. Dominant groups might now object to this if respecting group autonomy means they must allow perceived injustices within minority groups to go unrequited. But it is just this sort of thing that dominant groups are required to tolerate under LP.

In the case of the Pueblo, the requirements of liberal toleration under practical liberalism must be based upon a clear understanding of the dispute between the tribe and its dissident elements. If the Protestant faction believed that in turning to Protestantism they had left the tribe and become a new group unto themselves, the claims of the new group to property or belongings that are also claimed by the tribe raises a coordination problem that the government of the polity can rightly adjudicate.[22] If, however, the dissident Protestants wanted to remain part of the tribe but practice their own religion, they would seem to be asking for a drastic revision of what it means to be Pueblo. They would be asking, in effect, for religion to be regarded as a contingent feature of Pueblo life rather than a necessary feature of Pueblo identity. The extension of religious liberties to the Pueblo would provide this dissident group with legal weaponry with which to press their interests against the dominant tribal views. Since such weaponry would lack practical importance if disputes of this sort were not subject to federal court jurisdiction, the extension of these liberties would effectively authorize the federal judiciary to resolve them and in the process determine what it means to be Pueblo.

While Kymlicka might not think that defending Pueblo freedom of religious belief would alter Pueblo culture, members of the tribe might reasonably disagree. And under practical liberalism, this is not Kymlicka's call to make; nor is it the federal judiciary's call to make. Such decisions are to reside with the Pueblo themselves, and if it becomes a matter of internal political conflict, the group will need to resolve it according to its internal political standards. If it makes sense to suppose that all groups would want to retain jurisdiction for themselves over such vital matters of group life and group identity, then group members can be presumed to welcome a strong defense of group autonomy of the sort displayed by LP. Once again, dominant groups will find this objectionable when specific instances of apparent injustice (as seen from the perspective of the dominant groups) are brought to their attention. But it would be unwise to make selective exceptions to the requirements of LP in order to address specific apparent injustices. If LP does not hold categorically, it cannot hold at all. Groups will be uncertain when dominant groups will think invasion in their ways is justified, and the politics of interests will break out once again. And the dominance currently enjoyed by some groups may atrophy as minority groups organize and pool their resources in opposition to dominant influences. Dominant groups may lose control of the terminology of justice, for example, and find that it is now their group ways that are jeopardized by the politics of interests. So even dominant groups have reason to support a strong defense of group autonomy.

Perhaps, however, this argument can be weakened by expanding the gravity of apparent injustice a majority population imposes upon its dissident minority. Suppose, for example, the Pueblo majority elect to torture or kill the dissident Protestant Pueblo in their midst, and suppose further that this practice is entirely consistent with traditional Pueblo ways. Now, one wants to say, surely the dominant culture has reason to step into the picture and stop this sort of thing. But practical liberalism would still not permit state intervention even at this point. The dissident Protestants would need to make some serious choices under these circumstances. They may now decide that they should disaffiliate from the tribe and establish themselves as an independent group. As we shall see, practical liberalism can support this move, and if this is the move the dissidents make, they would transform the issue into an intergroup dispute in the event the Pueblo majority continued to persecute them. Now the government could and should intervene in order to manage what becomes a fairly straightforward tolerance problem. If, however, the dissidents elect to remain within the tribe, the controversy would remain an intragroup affair and thus beyond governmental jurisdiction under practical liberalism. Dissidents will have to work to get the majority, or tribal elites, to change their ways or suffer the consequences as fixed by tribal custom and tribal authorities.

As we shall see, it is not possible under practical liberalism to insist that an injustice of some sort is on display here even if the Pueblo majority elected to kill its dissident elements. The moral sensitivities of some elements of the polity, even a dominant majority of these elements, do not fix the standards of social justice operative in the liberal polity. Instead, these standards are set by LP, and they leave internal group dynamics and internal group politics to the groups themselves. Liberal toleration requires us to put up with practices we do not approve of, regardless of how horrible or objectionable these practices might seem to be. The demands of LP require all elements of the polity to permit the various groups constitutive of the polity to live by their own ways, no matter how horrible outsiders might think them to be. The Catholic Church is free to practice excommunication and interdiction free from state interference even though these are horrible punishments when viewed from inside the Catholic faith and may spark a sense of injustice in religious outsiders. But the Church's authority is separate from the polity's authority, and each remain sovereign within their respective spheres. This is the logic that practical liberalism extends to all groups that have a home within the legal jurisdiction of the polity.

## Forbearance and non-interference

Let me turn now to the conflict sparked by intergroup normative rivalries, for this is the type of conflict that needs mediation under a politics of principle. It is the source of the tolerance problems that require a principled resolution from a theory of liberal toleration. The conflicts I have in mind here can take either of two distinct forms. They have a formal character when the government is an instigator of the conflict or if groups in the polity use or enlist the government on their behalf to invade the autonomy of a targeted group to segregate this group, eliminate it, or assimilate it, at least partially, by requiring it to change its ways and adopt practices more favorable to outgroups. Other conflicts will have a more informal character. These arise when some group (or set of groups) is informally targeted by an outgroup (or set of outgroups) that adopts and privately pursues strategies designed and intended to invade the target group and disrupt or compromise its autonomy by endeavoring to segregate, eliminate, or assimilate it either totally or partially.

Both formal and informal normative conflicts evidence intolerance and both are prohibited under practical liberalism. We have already noticed that LP introduces a spirit of citizenship that all elements of the polity are expected to respect and practice. It introduces the basic normative glue that bonds an otherwise eclectic collection of groups and individuals into a common polity. Ideally, a spirit of toleration will animate citizens and the cruder and more predatory aspects of intergroup normative rivalries will be forsaken. But while the cultivation of a spirit of toleration (and hence of good citizenship) can do much to put an end to the cruder and more predatory forms of intergroup intolerance, it cannot eliminate tolerance problems completely. Both formal and informal types of intergroup predation remain possible and even likely where intergroup animus runs high. Some groups may suppose that LP protects their freedom to protest against the presence of others, while the targets of such protest may believe their freedom to live as they wish is compromised by such acts. This, of course, gives rise to a tolerance problem. It falls to political authority, then, to anticipate these problems, to police informal intolerance strategies, and to avoid being implicated in formal strategies.

As should now be apparent, political authority, or more generally the government (the institution empowered to police the shared morality of the public that is the polity), has a dual responsibility in promoting the practice of liberal toleration. It must, first of all, police informal intolerance strategies and require the citizenry to live up to its responsibility under LP to forbear those groups (whose members are fellow citizens) they find disgusting, damned, misguided, or repugnant by virtue of who they are or what they believe. If, however, LP empowers the government to police forbearance, it also limits governmental authority by circumscribing the conditions under which government may involve itself in the internal life and politics of the groups constitutive of the polity. So, political authority is both empowered by a forbearance condition that requires the state to police informal intolerance practices and circumscribed by a non-interference condition that limits, but does not completely prohibit, state intrusion into internal group affairs. While government must respect group autonomy, it can settle or adjudicate internal group disputes if it is asked to do so by all the contending parties. We can think of this as a good-offices option for groups desiring mediation of internal group disputes.

The dual responsibilities of forbearance and non-interference define the parameters of governmental involvement in defusing and resolving tolerance problems. In the former case, the government is charged with the job of mediating intergroup normative conflicts that take the shape of tolerance problems, while in the latter case it is charged with adhering to the demands of tolerance itself and avoiding any unwitting or witting complicity in the practice of intolerance. Exploring these dual governmental responsibilities should do much to explain what a theory of liberal toleration demands of the liberal polity and its citizenry, and this is a crucial component of social justice under practical liberalism. Since the acceptance of LP can still be presumed to lie in the balance, there is reason to say something about what toleration requires in practice.

I will consider first the non-interference condition because it raises some immediate difficulties. Non-interference, I have said, limits but does not entirely preclude governmental involvement in intragroup affairs. Governmental involvement is permissible, and might even become necessary, under two conditions. The first arises when the intragroup activities of, say, group A affect in some way the ability of the members of group B to live their lives as they wish. Such problems are particularly apt to arise with regard to a group's recruitment and retention practices, and I will return to this issue shortly.

Governmental intervention is also permissible, on the other hand, if it is invited. We can suppose that intervention is invited when group members expect the government to use its police powers to enforce group norms and standards of behavior throughout the group. Groups may do this because they lack sufficient resources or sufficient will to police themselves or because they have come to regard the government as the group's authoritative political institution for purposes of policing compliance with group norms and adjudicating intragroup disputes. It is typically the case, for example, that large or dominant groups tend to regard government as a part of their own political/legal machinery, and they anticipate that government will function accordingly.

It is best to dwell on this point a moment, for it requires us to confront the state in its historical and sociological particularity. States are historical entities, and their politico-legal character is a product of this history. So it might not be too great an exaggeration to say that a state's legal codes, both civil and criminal, are a reflection of this particularity; they take the shape they do because they are a product both of the dominant worldviews and moral theories pervasive in the culture and the political struggle characteristic of cultural history. Understood practically and historically as a reflection of dominant cultural influences, state law will reflect the normative convictions of those groups whose histories align most intimately with the emergence and development of the state. The state, that is, should be practically understood as implicated in the life of these dominant and perhaps pervasive groups bound together by such things as a common (if nebulous) culture, common language, similar customs, shared ethnicity, ideological homogeneity, and so forth. It belongs, in a reasonably intimate sense, to these groups because it functions as the politico-legal component of their intragroup public life.

It would be a mistake for practical liberalism to ignore or deny the historical and sociological particularity of the state. This is yet another reason why theorizing about civil life should be considered both time and place specific. The state's historical particularity introduces not only the social pathology in need of theoretical scrutiny but also the practical socio-political condition that englobes theoretical possibility. Thus the nature of group life in the United States sets the sociological background that must guide reflection upon the proper parameters of the non-interference condition. Things would be different than they are, for example, if the United States had a long and established history of consociational group involvement.[23] But it does not have such a history; instead, it has a history of intergroup conflict in which groups struggle to capture the political rhetoric of the (historically and politically) dominant liberal tradition. But of course, these dominant liberal influences also expect the government to police and enforce whichever conceptualization of liberal ways and practices gains the upper hand in the struggle of a politics of interests. The intragroup disputes of the dominant liberal tradition are played out in the halls of government, and the prevailing norms of the liberal tradition are accordingly defended in the streets throughout the land.

In one sense, of course, it could hardly be otherwise. Liberal influences are sometimes supposed to be coterminous with the United States itself; and by defending liberal ways and beliefs, many liberal Americans will suppose that the government is merely defending the country as it is supposed to do. But under practical liberalism, the state must be more than the politico-legal vehicle of dominant groups; it must also respect the non-interference condition and avoid becoming a vehicle by which dominant groups impose their normative convictions, unwittingly or otherwise, upon less dominant outgroups. As we shall see in the chapter to follow, the temptation to ignore non-interference and impose dominant-group ways and beliefs upon outgroups is especially strong when dominant groups believe that outgroup practices are particularly immoral and unjust, but it is just here that toleration matters. Still, according to practical liberalism, government in the American context should be recognized to have a dual function. Its first and primary responsibility is to police forbearance and practice non-interference as required by LP, and in the American context this means the liberal polity must not confuse dominant cultural sentiments with the demands of social justice established by LP. Yet, as the political authority for dominant liberal influences, government must also police liberal ways and promote liberal beliefs within those broadly defined and admittedly rather nebulous groups that take their worldview and moral theory of the human good from the liberal tradition.

Tolerance problems arise under the non-interference condition when state responsibilities under LP conflict with state responsibilities to protect and police dominant-group norms and ways. Under a politics of principle, these responsibilities collide in a manner that invites a reconsideration of the traditional Anglo-American view of the government's police power. According to this traditional view, the government is ultimately responsible for insuring the health, safety, and morals of the citizenry. Viewed from the standpoint of historical and sociological particularity, the government's conception of what is required of it under the police power—literally what it means to promote health, assure safety, and maintain moral integrity—will correspond to, because it is informed by, the norms and beliefs of dominant groups. Under practical liberalism, however, the government's primary responsibility is to assure groups the autonomy necessary to determine and police the health, safety, and moral well-being of their own members, and to support and reinforce group efforts in this regard only when groups request or expect this from the government.

Tolerance problems, in the form of jurisdictional disputes, will arise when groups claim that state invocations of its police powers are not faithful to requirements of liberal toleration, but are inspired instead by its historical and sociological commitment to the values and beliefs of dominant groups. It would be unfeasible, however, to suppose that the criminal law in the United States should be sufficiently varied and nuanced to accommodate all the disparate groups alive and well in the polity. Law, moreover, is presumed to evince a generality guaranteeing that it will apply equally and evenly to all, and scrupulous attention to group variety would turn this commitment into a sham. But American law also recognizes group exemptions that unburden those groups that enjoy them from strict adherence to the letter of the criminal law, and this seems an appropriate and effective way to deal with the tolerance problems that arise under the collision of state responsibilities.

The use of exemptions in American law has been inspired largely by the liberal desire to accommodate certain group differences considered legitimate according to dominant liberal belief. The federal government, for example, has in the past exempted certain religious groups from its conscription laws, and several American states exempt Native-American religious groups from their controlled-substance laws if these groups use such a substance as part of their religious service.[24] But these exemptions are sprinkled around, in American law, like a kind of political grace, and although linked to the constitutionally supported free exercise of religion, they lack the status of a legal entitlement.[25] Liberal toleration, however, requires more than this; it justifies a group claim to an exemption when the requirements of the criminal law conflict with some practice or activity fundamental to a group's worldview or moral theory of the human good, including of course, but not limited to, a group's religious practices. This is because, liberal toleration requires the polity to allow group members to live their lives as they wish, free from the controlling paternalism of a government that thinks (inspired by its links to the beliefs and values of dominant groups) it knows best what is good for all members of the polity. It further frees groups from the need to participate in the broader activities of the polity that are inconsistent with group ways and worldviews, provided these activities do not involve the responsibilities of citizenship—responsibilities owed by every citizen to all members of the public that is the polity.

There are, however, reasonable objections to accommodating group autonomy by granting legal exemptions from otherwise valid state laws, and these deserve a hearing. For one thing, a policy of extending exemptions to groups allowing them to practice group ways is likely to put pressure on the notion of a group itself as individuals seek to claim group status in order to engage in activities otherwise prohibited by law. People in the United States have notoriously claimed a group status, for example, in order to avoid prostitution and controlled-substance laws, usually by insisting that these practices are integral features of their religion.[26] As these rather silly attempts demonstrate, the non-interference condition is grist for the mill of anyone who hopes to engage in activities prohibited by law either for reasons of profit or personal deviance. And they correspondingly invite us to tighten our understanding of a group in order to guard against this form of legal abuse.

But any attempt to explicate the notion of a group beyond the admittedly nebulous account offered above is dangerous because the notion of a group is itself caught within the ontological and normative orientation of disparate groups; thus any essentialist account of a group is likely to offend LP by excluding some individuals who see themselves as a group and even by identifying some individuals as a group even though they do not see themselves in this way. Liberals, for example, typically see groups as associations of individuals who voluntarily and deliberately have thrown themselves in together.[27] Groups thus become contingent features of individual life subject to modification and transformation according to the wishes of their members, and individuals, in turn, are presumed to enjoy the right to alter group affiliation as they see fit.[28] Catholics, on the other hand, see things differently and suppose that membership in the faith is not a matter of individual choice but of Church policy. Faced with this reality, theorizing about politics in a way that presumes a group-centered feature of individual life had best proceed by using the notion of a group as a place holder for the manifold forms of social relationships that endure within the polity—a point that merely repeats my earlier claim that groups are best recognized by looking to socio-political reality and avoiding contentious theoretical definitions. To recall the key aspects of group identification introduced above, it is perhaps best to concede that a group exists if (1) those individuals claiming to belong to it think of themselves and their association/identification with one another in this way, and (2) the group fixes or establishes at least some dimension of one's normative, ontological, and epistemological horizon according to the viewpoint of its members.

It seems reasonable to point out, however, that groups typically have a historical pedigree or cultural tradition that makes them easily recognizable, but these features of group identity are clearly inadequate as indicators of group status. The fact of flux works to transform groups and group membership, to cause groups to die out, and to generate new groups; consequently, a tolerant polity will need to allow for the natural evolution of group life, group generation, group transformation, and group mortality. To this we should add, as mentioned already, that groups are bound by a shared worldview and moral theory of the human good—an ontological and normative vision—that distinguishes them from the more transient and superficial affiliations that are also commonplace in the social life of modern states. But this too is a weak indicator of group status for we are left to wonder just how comprehensive a shared ontological and normative vision must be, how heartfelt it must be embraced, or how homogeneously it must be understood, in order to constitute a group.

Faced with the ambiguity that surrounds the notion of a group, the government's responsibilities under practical liberalism will come into apparent conflict with its group-centered responsibilities when individuals claim a group status for purposes of avoiding those laws that regulate dominant-group activities. In general, liberal toleration requires groups to forbear the practices and activities of the members of outgroups. But toleration is not license, and the members of dominant groups offend against the ways of their own groups if they claim an exemption to group-centered laws in order to engage in activities otherwise prohibited by the group. These are practical difficulties, however, and ones that belong to intragroup life and intragroup politics.[29] When faced with such issues, the government's responsibilities under LP take obvious precedence over its group-centered responsibilities. If it is to err, it should therefore err on the side of protecting group autonomy in the event of doubt about the status of some self-proclaimed group. In practice, however, it may not prove terribly difficult to discern those efforts to feint group identification for purposes of circumventing otherwise controlling morals laws; but even if this is difficult, the fact that some individuals may attempt to avoid group ways by claiming an exemption to which they are not really entitled is hardly reason to abandon the practice of giving exemptions to groups whose ways and beliefs are compromised by dominant views. Granting exemptions of this sort seems integral to realizing the ends of a politics of principle in the American context and reconciling the government's primary responsibilities under LP with the derivative responsibilities, to police dominant moral views, it has assumed in the United States, and to object to them on the grounds that some may abuse the practice looks like an effort to throw the baby out with the bathwater.[30]

If this is not reason to abandon the practice of granting exemptions, on the other hand, there is still some point in asking groups that request exemptions from otherwise valid state laws to demonstrate that the practice to be exempted really is integral to group ways and fundamental to group beliefs. If some group activities are actually inconsistent with recognized group beliefs and ideals, the group is hardly in a position to claim an exemption for them. Thus, mafia bosses could not claim that their hit men are exempt from state murder statutes since murder in the name of business still qualifies as murder even according to the moral viewpoint of the mafia.

A second and more compelling objection to the use of group exemptions has been pressed by Brian Barry in his provocative challenge to the special-rights claims advanced by numerous ethnic minorities.[31] Barry thinks that exemptions are only rarely justified if a law to which some group claims an exemption has an otherwise valid or compelling social purpose. His strong stand on equality inclines him to think that exemption claims virtually never outweigh laws that implement important social regulations. If a law protects or expresses an important social interest, then all elements of the polity should adhere to it. Exemption claims are compelling only if the law fails to implement an important social interest, but since such laws then have little reason to exist, he concludes they should be repealed. In the absence of some compelling social purpose, no one's liberty should be constrained by law. Barry is not oblivious to the concerns or interests of ethnic and cultural minorities, but while he appreciates the pull of cultural integrity, he appreciates more the social utility that is promoted by good law. Granting exemptions to cultural groups imperils this utility by allowing for the possibility of the very evil the law was intended to protect against.[32] Barry notes correctly that other groups or individuals may also have reasons, unrelated to ethnic practices, for wishing to disobey the law, and his strictly egalitarian stand inclines him to ask why ethnic practices should be granted exemptions while these non-ethnic reasons are not acknowledged as sufficient to justify similar exemptions.

This is a strong argument, but it does not hold against practical liberalism in the fashion Barry would apparently like it to. This becomes apparent if we keep in mind the dual responsibilities government has under practical liberalism. Governmental responsibilities under LP to respect the non-interference condition are non-negotiable; or rather, these responsibilities pre-empt governmental responsibilities to support and police the views and ways of dominant groups. Liberal toleration prohibits imposing upon outgroups governmental views about the good or the socially useful that are derived chiefly (and as they likely will be) from the norms and beliefs of dominant groups. To avoid this possibility, and thus accommodate outgroups as required by liberal toleration, it seems best to grant them exemptions to those laws that simply enforce the standards, beliefs, or ways of dominant groups.

To illustrate, consider the situation that the United States Supreme Court addressed in *State of Oregon Employment Division v. Smith*.[33] The State of Oregon denied unemployment benefits to two Native-Americans who were fired from their jobs as drug counselors because they used peyote in their religious practices. The state found that these individuals were fired for cause and were therefore not eligible for unemployment relief. Smith filed for legal relief from the state's decision on the grounds that the state was requiring him to choose between his job and the practice of his religion, and he believed this compromised his free exercise of religion rights under the First Amendment. The Court ultimately sided with the state for reasons we need not dwell upon, but the state's argument before the Court is worth considering. In a manner that Barry would likely find favorable (and interestingly one that squared with traditional free-exercise jurisprudence), the state argued that it had a compelling interest in prohibiting peyote use for all its citizens because peyote contains the debilitating hallucinogen mescaline, and this particular substance has deleterious physiological effects on those who ingest it. No one denied that peyote is a hallucinogenic substance or that it has a certain physiological effect on its users, and the state supposed that this was dispositive of the issue. The state argued that it has both the right and the responsibility, under the police power, to safeguard the well-being of the citizenry from the deleterious effects of such substances. But Smith responded by arguing that his religious beliefs and practices matter greatly to him and that being forced to choose between his faith and gainful employment worked a greater hardship upon him than did the use of peyote. The state, in arguably solid liberal fashion, supposed that the physiological harm caused by peyote was greater than the incidental intrusion upon Smith's religious convictions, but Smith calculated the harm involved differently. From where he stood, the state's imposition upon his religious practice was far more damaging to him than his use of peyote.

Although the Supreme Court refused to grant Smith the exemption from state law that he sought, such relief is surely justified under the noninterference condition. The State's claim that it has a responsibility to protect its citizens from the harm caused by the use of mescaline has some plausibility insofar as it reflects an understanding of harm that belongs to the attitudes of the members of dominant groups. While liberal sorts may wonder amongst themselves about the propriety of the paternalism on display here, it is at least plausible to suppose that the claim that mescaline causes deleterious physiological harm if ingested frequently will make sense to many liberals. But this is not the only way to construe the harm that is at issue, and to suppose that it is leaves us with a form of dominant-group imperialism. Disparate outgroups, with their own independent worldviews, may construe the harm question quite differently, as Smith in fact did.

By effectively forcing Smith to choose between the faithful practice of his religious beliefs and his ability to sustain himself, he was forced to bow to the coercive pressure of more dominant views about what constitutes harm. Such views hardly belong to the political morality introduced by LP; liberal toleration entitles groups to live by their own sense of what constitutes harm to them. During prohibition, Catholics were quietly allowed to use sacramental wine during mass, and we might suppose there were reasons for this beyond the simple fact that Catholics constitute a rather powerful group in American politics. No doubt these reasons involve acknowledging that the use of sacramental wine is fundamental to Catholic religious practices; and under practical liberalism, this understanding aptly captures the reasons why Catholics were entitled to such an exemption. The same holds for Smith and his fellow Native-Americans who use peyote as a part of their religious practices.

The alternative Barry allows to granting an exemption to Native-American peyote users, on the other hand, is to repeal all laws prohibiting the use of substances that happen to be used in the religious, ethnic, or ideological practices of any group in the polity. This too would guarantee that no group is imposed upon by the understanding of harm belonging to more dominant groups. But this suggestion has problems of its own. If those controlled substances used in religious practices are decriminalized, they might then be used recreationally by the members of dominant groups; and this is the sort of thing these groups hoped to prohibit by insisting upon their criminalization in the first place. This intrudes upon the ability of dominant groups to use governmental authority derivatively to police group ways and norms. (In the case at hand, it would prohibit the dominant culture from protecting its members from the harm caused by ingesting mescaline.) But this is a cost that does not arise under practical liberalism once we appreciate that LP mandates exemptions from otherwise valid state laws for groups whose ways and practices differ importantly from the ways and practices of dominant groups. Granting exemptions, then, is the least onerous way to honor the demands of a politics of principle and still enable the state to police the standards and ways of more dominant groups. It also assures that minority groups do not have a veto power over the ability of dominant groups to police their group ways and norms.

There will likely be situations, however, where exemptions are ineffective or inappropriate, and when they arise, non-interference will require the state to honor the demands of liberal toleration by not enforcing dominant beliefs if they intrude upon the ways or beliefs of minorities. The problem of required or compelled reference to the Christian Deity offers a case in point for the United States. Consider, for example, the 2002 decision by the Ninth Circuit Court of the United States holding that the words 'under God' should be struck from the Pledge of Allegiance because the phrase violates the establishment of religion clause of the First Amendment.[34] The Supreme Court has subsequently overruled the decision on jurisdictional grounds that did not address the merits of the case, namely, whether the words 'under

God' in the pledge violate the constitutional mandated separation of church and state.[35] Consequently, the issue raised by the case now hangs in legal limbo, and given the tenacity of the atheist litigants that pressed the issue in the first place, it seems reasonable to expect the matter to again find its way into the courts.

The Ninth Circuit's decision quickly galvanized public sentiment with Christian elites protesting the shabby treatment of religion in a country with a strong religious (read Christian) heritage, and atheists applauding the decision to keep religion out of politics. Following the decision, the politics of interests went into full swing, leading eventually to the Supreme Court's artful dodging of the issue. Justice William O. Douglas was certainly correct to note that Americans are a religious people and that the Christian faith has had, and continues to have, a prominent place in American cultural history.[36] But it is not the only religious tradition present in America, and there is also present in America a modest tradition of a secular humanism that deliberately avoids any reference to a Deity of any sort—not to mention the atheists in America who might prefer not to be subjected to theistic practices and rituals. If non-Christian groups wish to forego expressions of belief in or commitment to a Christian God because making such expressions or offering such commitments is inconsistent with their own beliefs and views, liberal toleration will support them. Under liberal toleration, groups are not permitted to force outgroups to engage in the rituals or practices that might matter to them, particularly if these rituals happen to be inconsistent with the beliefs and values of the groups that are imposed upon. (In addition to the intrusion upon the autonomy of groups not wanting to be forced to participate in the rituals of outgroups, there is something slightly assimilationist about all this.)

This is reason to grant non-Christian groups an exemption to, say, uttering the Pledge of Allegiance or praying in state-operated schools. But the use of exemptions in such cases may work a hardship on minority groups anyway. Consider, for example, the voluntary prayer programs introduced in many school districts once the US Supreme Court struck down compulsory prayer in the schools.[37] Where should the burden of tolerance go under these circumstances? Should dominant groups be allowed to engage in prayer in public schools on a voluntary basis, allowing outgroups to be released from the prayer or to stand by silently while those wanting to pray do so? Or should the burden of tolerance go the other way, requiring the Christian groups desiring to pray in the schools to put up with those outgroups (Christian or non-Christian) that do not want to engage in this sort of prayer?

The response I would recommend follows directly from the requirements associated with LP. Since LP defends the maximum equal freedom of all groups, the burden of tolerance in situations of this sort can be placed in either of two ways. First, liberal toleration might support the right of all groups to celebrate and practice their views in the public realm, including the public schools—restricted only by the control public officials need to maintain the effective operations of these public spaces. If any group is allowed to pray in public schools, then all groups should be allowed to practice their ways in these schools as well. If some Christians want to pray, they can do so while those not wanting to pray do something else. Second, liberal toleration could support the conclusion that no group should be permitted to use the public realm as a place to practice or display its own ways and beliefs. The choice between these two options may reasonably be left to independent school districts in order to resolve the school prayer problem. If school officials think the first option would be overly complicated and burdensome, they may elect the second option. Some schools, however, might prefer to implement generic release-time programs that would allow students a personal moment which may be used in silent prayer, meditation, or rest— depending only upon the wishes of the student. The US Supreme Court has frowned upon such programs, thinking that setting aside any school time for voluntary prayer offends the First Amendment's establishment clause.[38] If, however, the establishment clause is informed by the requirements of practical liberalism, such concerns would dissipate. Such programs appear to be a reasonably efficient way to accomplish the first option available under liberal toleration for resolving the school prayer controversy, and therefore, they are permissible under practical liberalism.

But the theoretical problem raised by the Pledge of Allegiance issue is not like this. The complaint raised against the words 'under God' was not based upon an objection to being forced to acknowledge a deity in which the complainant (or in this case the complainant's daughter) did not believe. If this was the objection, an exemption from being required to say the Pledge would have been in order. But the complainant's daughter was not compelled to say the Pledge; instead, the complaint objected to invoking a deity of some sort while pledging allegiance to one's country. Presumably, complainant Newbow has no problem with pledging allegiance to the United States, but he does have a problem with supposing that such a pledge must involve making reference to a deity in which he does not believe. This problem cannot be finessed by granting Newbow or his daughter an exemption from saying the Pledge of Allegiance, for the problem is with the Pledge itself, or rather, with the words 'under God' in the Pledge. Should a liberal polity allow a component of the worldview of its dominant culture to find its way into its political rituals or should it not?

To be sure, leaving the words 'under God' in the Pledge does not violate the non-interference condition. The government is not meddling in the internal affairs of any particular group or imposing outgroup ways upon some group, provided of course the Pledge is not made mandatory. But it still privileges some worldviews over others by linking the state with a specific religious conviction. This seems inconsistent with a spirit of toleration that requires the polity to put up with all worldviews in a manner that does not disadvantage or privilege any one in particular. If the liberal polity is dedicated, as it should be, to constructing and cultivating a social environment where all groups can coexist peacefully and profitably, its own commitment to toleration must guarantee that it puts up with all disparate viewpoints present in the polity in a balanced and egalitarian fashion; this follows automatically from the inclusiveness condition that receives formal expression in LP. If there is reason, as there would seem to be, to show respect for the polity to which one belongs by pledging allegiance to it, the ritual should permit all elements of the polity to do so in a manner consistent with their worldviews and moral theories of the good. If participating in such rituals is itself inconsistent with one's worldview, an exemption is in order at this point. But liberal toleration can hardly permit promoting or privileging some worldviews over others as a part of engaging in such rituals. So, here is a case where an exemption is inappropriate and where the liberal polity should make sure that dominant beliefs are not imposed upon the ways or beliefs of minorities.

## Group recruitment and retention

There is another situation where governmental intervention in what might be considered the internal affairs of a group is justified. The right of group autonomy supported by LP comprehends the derivative right of group self-preservation. This means that group retention and recruitment policies, which are crucial to a group's ability to sustain itself through time, are protected by LP against governmental intervention. In principle, then, groups have the right to control and determine their own recruitment and retention practices. Group outsiders, however, may think at times that these practices impact or compromise their own group retention or recruitment practices. Disparate groups may have conflicting views about group membership, for example, that raise troubling questions about who belongs to what group. Situations of this sort give rise to a tolerance problem that must be mediated by the liberal polity.

One of the most integral aspects of group life is socializing children in order to build in them an understanding and appreciation of group norms and group ways. The socialization process is crucial to group continuation, of course, but seen from the inside the socialization process involves educating children on the way the world is, what matters in life, and how one should behave in the company of others. To say, in other words, that groups want to pass along their worldview and moral theory of the human good is beside the point. The nature of a group's worldview is such that group members understand how to raise their children only in the terms it makes available to them. This, in turn, becomes an obvious point of intergroup conflict, for differences in worldview may incline outgroups to believe that the way a group raises its children, or conducts its recruitment and retention practices, is wrong, harmful, or morally objectionable. Under LP, however, group socialization of children, along with its recruitment and retention practices, must be tolerated; and given the moral concerns some outgroups may have for children, this might be reason to reject LP.

I shall have more to say about the group treatment of children in the following chapter. At present it is sufficient merely to emphasize that the socialization of children may be considered an inevitable and necessary feature of group life. Accordingly, government in the liberal polity should not interfere with these activities even if some (including some dominant) outgroups consider these practices objectionable. No doubt some traditional liberals will object to this on the grounds that group socialization tends to 'imprison' children within the group and deny them the ability to grow up independently and choose for themselves the type of life they will lead, what will matter to them, and how they think their lives should go. Liberal attitudes on this subject are rather obscure, however; while liberals encourage their children to develop the life that matters to them, they still cling to general parameters that guide and inform thinking about the good life. A life of mindless devotion to some perceived charismatic leader, for example, is inconsistent with liberal commitments to individual autonomy and is accordingly inconsistent with liberal ways. But others may see things differently holding that following and accepting the guidance of a wise prophet really is a good life. In short, liberal views about child development should be viewed as group specific, and liberal efforts to impose their views on group outsiders should be regarded as a form of intolerance under LP. Liberals may insist that they are right to see things as they do and that this justifies intrusion into the ways of outgroups. And they may in fact be right, but it does not follow that they are therefore justified in using the coercive might of the government to prohibit the socialization practices of outgroups. The claim of a right to interfere here would merely return us to a politics of interests with all the attendant costs.

In the event these costs are considered too great to override a commitment to LP, liberals, along with all other elements of the liberal polity, should concede to groups the right to socialize their young and take the steps necessary to retain their children within the group. Things are less straightforward and more problematic, on the other hand, when we consider the decision of an adult group member to disaffiliate and leave the group. Some groups claim jurisdiction over member decisions to disaffiliate as well as over group decisions about expulsion. If a right to group autonomy is to have much meaning, we should concede the right of all groups to set their own standards of group membership and to permit groups to enforce these standards against wayward individuals or factions within the group. Controversy over these standards may introduce serious problems that spark significant intragroup conflict. But as we saw in the case of the Pueblo, these are not matters that concern the polity, and so they are best left to the vicissitudes of intra-group politics.

Decisions to disaffiliate, however, are another matter. Faced with a defection of some sort, a group may claim that it will not allow or recognize disaffiliation, or it may attempt to make the cost of disaffiliation intolerably high for those wishing to leave the group. Sometimes individuals decide to leave groups because they have decided to take their lives in a different direction and no longer find fulfillment in their identification with the group, sometimes they leave because they have come to reject group ways and group practices, and sometimes they leave collectively because they disagree with group policies or viewpoints and intend to establish their own group around the beliefs and norms that have come to matter to them. In the event the parent group attempts to prohibit or block such disaffiliation, defectors can reasonably and justifiably expect support from the polity, and the polity, for its part, does not offend its responsibilities under the non-interference condition by providing the required support even though the group may think this an invasion of their internal affairs.

This is the proper stand for practical liberalism to take because, under such circumstances, the polity is called upon to decide whether the dispute in question is best understood as an internal group issue or an intergroup conflict. Here it seems appropriate for the polity to accept the claims of disaffiliates that they are no longer members of the group; if disaffiliates insist they are no longer group members, they have, in an important sense, actually left the group regardless of the contrary claims by the parent group. This is sufficient for the polity to suppose that we now really have either two distinct groups (in the event disaffiliation involves a splintering of the parent group) or an individual expatriate who no longer subscribes to group ways or beliefs (in the event disaffiliation involves a single individual). In the former case, the polity should now regard the conflict as an intergroup dispute requiring the parent group to tolerate the newly formed group. Policing forbearance will now require the polity to enforce the parent group's responsibility under LP to tolerate the new group. In the latter case, policing forbearance will now require the polity to make sure the parent group tolerates the new views of the expatriate and the new life he or she has set upon.

Groups claiming the right to control their own exit policies will consider this objectionable, and they may argue that an element of liberal individualism has crept into the argument here and biased the discussion in favor of liberal ways. It may be objected, for example, that my argument defends an individual right of disaffiliation, and it may be justifiably asked just where this right came from. Under the operating procedures for the defense of LP, it is impermissible to smuggle rights claims of this sort into the discussion. My argument, however, rests not upon any supposed claim about an individual's right of exit from the group(s) to which he or she belongs, but upon the rather obvious fact that people do leave groups from time to time. Once a person has made the decision to leave, once one *has* left the group in one's own mind, the person effectively—or for all practical purposes—has become a non-member. So, the polity has little choice but to side with non-members under these circumstances, not because of some need to recognize a right of individual choice, but because it no longer makes sense to conceive of someone who has consciously chosen in her or his own mind to disaffiliate from a group as a member of that group. This is but a practical, political implication of the fact of flux; the fact of group morphology needs to be built into practical liberalism in a fashion that respects the realities of group evolution and transformation. And while the polity cannot police all costs of member disaffiliation because some imposed costs fall within group juris-diction (if Catholics want to excommunicate apostates they are within their rights to do so), it can police those imposed costs that reach beyond the parameters of control that belong to the group.

Sometimes the costs of disaffiliation are high, to be sure. Consider, for example, the practice of shunning employed by some religious communities. Shunning is something of a punishment that accompanies excommunication from the religious group, and excommunication typic-ally follows upon a member's decision to leave the community. It prohibits community members from socializing, eating, or doing business with the excommunicated.[39] While the cost of shunning may matter little to some disaffiliates, it might matter a great deal to others and serve as a strong reason for unhappy members to want to stay within the community. In the curious case of *Bear v. Reformed Mennonite Church*, the Supreme Court of Maryland was asked to consider the legality of the practice of shunning.[40] The Maryland Court concluded that shunning may constitute an interfer-ence with areas of state concern, including marriage relationships and reas-onable business practices.[41] Kent Greenawalt, who takes exception to the decision, has argued that shunning should receive a religious exemption from state statutes protecting marriage and business relationships because shunning merely encourages individuals to behave in a way that is otherwise permissible.[42] Barry, on the other hand, thinks that this is reason to do away with state statutes designed to protect marriage and business relationships by allowing such interferences with them to be actionable in tort.[43] He would thus support shunning, at least in principle, but not by granting religious communities that practice shunning an exemption from state statutes.

Practical liberalism offers us an alternative reason to think the Maryland case was wrongly decided. Shunning looks like a powerful group strategy to maintain group loyalty and retain group membership. As such, it seems to be a legitimate exercise of group autonomy and reaches a sphere of influence clearly under group control. That individuals can shun independently if they so choose is simply beside the point; shunning, we can suppose, is a practice that makes sense within the context of the group's worldview and moral perspective. From the standpoint of the group, there is good reason to inter-fere with things like marriage and business relationships in order to sustain the integrity of the religious community, and deference to group autonomy would thus sustain the group's right to do so. On the other hand, there may be more dominant groups in the polity that believe others should not interfere with marriage relationships or fair business practices. This would justify governmental efforts to prohibit such things as reasonably tortious if we suppose that government here has assumed its auxiliary role of policing dominant-group ways and beliefs. But exemption claims by groups that practice shunning would then also be justified under liberal toleration and should be granted by the polity. From the standpoint of practical liberalism, then, Greenawalt reaches a right conclusion but for the wrong reason.

Still, shunning may seem objectionably coercive to some, and seen from outside the group this view would appear to be entirely legitimate. Seen from inside the group, however, things would appear to be different. If there was strong internal opposition to the practice, we would expect it to become a source of internal group conflict and disagreement; if, however, it is accepted as legitimate by group members, it fails to qualify as coercive within the parameters of understanding internal to the group.[44]

Barry, it turns out, is less unhappy with the practice of shunning than he is with the fact that Amish communities, which practice shunning, also require their members to opt out of social-security payments—a right granted them by the government for religious reasons.[45] Because shunning in conjunction with the inability of the Amish to develop a social-security safety net leaves Amish members financially dependent upon the community, Barry concludes that the Amish fail to qualify as a voluntary association, thinking instead that Amish members are, in effect, economically enslaved by their community. Nor does the fact that the Amish voluntarily submit to baptism alter his thinking, for he supposes, following Mill, that one is not at liberty to elect to live in a condition of slavery.[46] However, Barry understands slavery, and the Amish condition more generally, from the standard liberal viewpoint. Seen with Amish eyes, on the other hand, things would seem to be different, and the question that arises is whether liberal concerns for individual well-being should trump Amish views about how their lives should go. Under practical liberalism, these are matters entirely internal to the Amish community. Liberals may think it unwise or imprudent to commit to such a life, but this is not reason, under practical liberalism, to coercively interfere with Amish ways. Barry, along with everyone else, is justified in criticizing the Amish for undermining individual opportunities to leave the community; but if the Amish find all of this just a little silly, a politics of principle invites both sides to agree to disagree.

Let me turn now to group recruitment practices because they too can give rise to tolerance problems. Consider, for example, the activities of certain cult groups and non-traditional religions that have from time to time been accused of coercive recruitment practices in the United States.[47] Whether these groups are guilty as charged is a matter of some dispute, and not one that is easily adjudicated because the standards of coercion seem to be group specific.[48] What may be considered coercive to one group may seem like proper recruitment activity to another. Under LP, these disputes take on the character of intergroup conflicts, and accordingly they can be managed by appeal to the forbearance condition.

Given the fact that groups must forbear outgroups under LP, how might the polity fairly guarantee that group recruitment practices respect the demands of liberal toleration and do not fall into the category of impermissible assimilation? Since forbearance requires groups to permit outgroups to live their lives and pursue their moral theory of the human good as they wish, recruitment practices that objectionably intrude into group life and group practices run afoul of liberal toleration. Accordingly, the government may legitimately require all groups in the polity to employ only those recruitment practices that outgroups can recognize as consistent with the ability of their members to live their lives as they wish. It follows that the measure of the coerciveness of a group's recruitment is fixed by the sense of coerciveness associated with those groups to which the prospective recruit belongs and regardless of the viewpoint held by prospective or actual recruits who may already have suffered the effects of a coercive recruitment. Recruitment efforts that cut prospective recruits off from family and friends or that place prospective recruits under excessive pressure by denying them independent time and opportunity to reflect upon their choice will be objectionable to traditional moral liberals, for example, and the recruitment strategies of at least some alternative religious and cult groups are often criticized for operating this way. If so, then interference in group activities by the government to remove coercively recruited individuals is justified, though, by the same token, there is little the government can do in the event the recruits to such groups have been fairly recruited according to outgroup standards.

Some groups may object to this on the grounds that it makes them seem intolerant by virtue of their recruitment practices when in fact they are not so. The members of these groups might insist that they are merely attempting through recruitment to attract prospective group members and not to assimilate others they regard as damned, disgusting, repugnant, or misguided by virtue of who they are or what they believe. Nevertheless, efforts to recruit outgroup members in a manner that disregards what outgroups understand as the ability of their members to live their lives as they wish and practice their own group ways free from outside interference evidence a failure to forbear others in favor of a group's effort to expand its own ranks and promote its own ways and practices. While this is not strictly a form of intolerance, it does display a disregard for outgroups and a corresponding intrusion in the ways and beliefs of outgroups inconsistent with liberal toleration. While permitting the government to police such disputes may offend the recruitment commitments of some groups, it still protects group autonomy and group integrity against hostile outsiders, and this, in turn, is reason for groups, living under conditions of intergroup uncertainty, to find security and solace in LP. If it happens to make the recruitment of outgroup members more difficult, as it very likely will, it does not preclude recruitment practices altogether; and it should further assure groups that under practical liberalism, group life is protected against outside meddling to as great an extent as possible given the inevitable presence of normative and allocational rivals.

One final issue requires brief mention while we are on the subject of group recruitment and retention practices. If we keep in mind that the polity is itself to be conceived as a group that makes a home for a tremendous variety of normatively and ontologically disparate groups, what retention practices are appropriate for the polity itself? And do groups within the polity also have a (so-called) right of exit to be protected by the polity in the event they elect to disaffiliate as groups that emerge or evolve from an existing group do? Both these questions require more considered discussion than I can undertake here. At present it is possible only to anticipate the direction the discussion should take. Here it is necessary only to anticipate the direction the discussion will take. The polity, like all groups, has an interest in, and a need for, socializing prospective members into the group and orienting new groups that move into its jurisdiction. While we need not explore just what this means at the moment, it is important to emphasize that the efforts of the polity to socialize and integrate outsiders should be governed by an abiding concern for the integrity of group autonomy. Similarly, groups within the polity should also be understood to have a right of exit, including a right of secession in the event the territorial requirements of secession can be satisfied.[49] The case for practical liberalism, however, needs to include within its parameters some consideration of the reasons why secession is rarely, if ever, a good idea. In the event things are likely to get worse for a group if it secedes, or if it exits more generally, groups will have good reason to stay within, and remain faithful to, the liberal polity.

## Conclusion

According to the standards of liberal toleration associated with the acceptance of LP, groups are required to forbear one another, and the government, for its part, is required both to police the demands of forbearance and not interfere in the internal affairs of groups except under the circumstances introduced above. As a result, a maximum autonomy and independence for each group in the polity is guaranteed and promoted and is limited only by the requirement that groups permit outgroups the same autonomy and independence. The types of problems we have encountered under the notion of liberal toleration are almost certainly inevitable in a social environment where distinct and potentially hostile worldviews and moral theories of the human good coexist. If these groups are to manage to get along in a reasonably secure and amiable manner, concessions must be made, and this is reason to think that concessions should be made. Compared to the uncertainty and insecurity associated with a politics of interests, the concessions associated with liberal toleration discussed here should make practical liberalism, and the politics of principle it introduces, appear rather attractive. If the types of tolerance problems we have encountered are not resolved in a principled fashion, the normative rivalries from which they emerge are likely to explode beyond reasonable control or to continue to drive the pendulum of conflict and unrest typical of a politics of interests. So it would seem, so far, that the costs to groups of endorsing LP are not that great, and the autonomy guaranteed them should be most desirable. It follows that the defense of liberal toleration developed so far lends credible support to the basic argument and counsels in favor of accepting LP.

# 4
# Toleration and Group Autonomy

The theory of liberal toleration associated with practical liberalism safeguards a most capacious group autonomy. Fellow citizens are required under LP to forbear the ways and practices of the disparate groups present in the polity, and except for the situations discussed in the previous chapter, government is prohibited from interfering with or meddling in intragroup affairs. Accordingly, the jurisdictional parameters of political authority are defined primarily (though not exclusively) by governmental responsibilities to manage tolerance and coordination problems. Yet questions remain about how citizens are to understand their responsibilities under the forbearance condition, along with cognate questions about how government should resolve tolerance problems when they arise.

These questions may be formulated as follows: (1) What are the proper jurisdictional boundaries that establish the authoritative domains of groups within the polity and distinguish them from the authoritative domain of the group that is the polity? To answer this question it is necessary to explore the responsibilities of citizenship and distinguish them from whatever obligations and opportunities one has by virtue of her or his membership in specific primary groups. (2) How should the state place or identify the burden of tolerance when faced with a tolerance problem? Answering this question involves considering how the state should police forbearance in those tough situations where conflicting groups each make reasonable claims that the activities or practices of an outgroup violate LP by impermissibly encroaching upon their members' ability to live and do as they wish.

This chapter begins to develop a theory of liberal toleration by outlining some provisional answers to these questions. I offer here only a rough sketch of the demands of liberal toleration, for the full articulation of a theory of toleration ranges well beyond the limitations of a theoretical inquiry into the possibility of a politics of unity. The demands of toleration, on the other hand, constitute the primary cost of committing to a politics of principle and endorsing LP. So, it is important to examine these costs in order to see if they offset the advantages groups realize by accepting LP. If the costs do not outweigh the benefits to be gained under practical liberalism, the case for a politics of unity will be enhanced considerably.

## Liberal toleration and bad moral faith

In recent years, liberal political thinkers have shown an increased sensitivity for ethnic and cultural groups, largely because these groups have made a concerted political effort in many liberal societies to gain recognition and respect as independent autonomous units.[1] Perhaps predictably, liberal thinkers are divided on the question of the proper reach of ethnic or cultural autonomy non-liberal and even illiberal groups should be permitted within liberal states.[2] The question raises some tough issues for traditional moral liberals who regard liberalism as primarily a moral theory that yields certain moral principles that are to be put to service in society in order to promote social justice.[3] As we have seen, moral liberalism takes the individual as the primary moral unit and defends as basic to social justice a commitment to individual liberty and equality. This defense of liberty inclines moral liberals to support a right of free association that permits individuals to enjoy a high degree of group independence, and to prevent the scrutiny of group activities from the prying eyes of outsiders. At some point, however, all this makes moral liberals uncomfortable because groups can and on occasion do treat their fellow members in ways that violate the very commitment to individual liberty and equality that supports the liberal defense of group independence. This problem has generated a considerable amount of disagreement, in liberal circles, about when the state should intervene in the affairs of non-liberal or illiberal groups in order to enforce liberal norms within the group itself.[4]

This matter does not trouble practical liberalism, on the other hand, since all groups in the liberal polity are required to tolerate the internal ways and practices of all other groups living there. Yet this gives rise to a problem of a different sort. As noted in the previous chapter, liberal toleration asks groups to put up with the practices of others that their members may well consider deeply repugnant and morally objectionable. The nature of group diversity in the United States, for example, will require moral liberals to tolerate such unsavory things as polygamy; marital or gender inequalities; sacramental drug use; apparent child abuse, neglect, or homicide; intragroup discrimination; witchcraft; hate-group propaganda; snake handling; Santeria; and female genital mutilation—to mention only a few of the many practices that have at least a modest profile in American society and that are considered intolerable according to many moral liberals.

Moral liberals will surely want to ask how on earth anyone could seriously think of tolerating such things. And they will just as surely have little good to say about a theory of civil association that insists such things should be tolerated. Put in more general terms, the argument for rejecting LP that emerges from all this holds that if and when some group activities and practices are terribly immoral, as judged by dominant moral sentiment prevalent in the society, there should be little doubt that something should be done about them. And this something should be done by the government, according to traditional liberal thought, since a major part of its responsibility may be thought to involve safeguarding the moral integrity of society as a whole. While liberal toleration might be all to the good up to a point, it is simply pernicious to abandon heartfelt moral conviction for prudential reasons alone. To permit groups to engage in immoral practices that harm some of their members, or compromise their autonomy as independent human beings, is to turn one's back on an immorality that one should not ignore. If something *can* be done to prevent such immoral conduct, it *should* be done. To fail to do so is to act inconsistently with one's own moral convictions. It is, in effect, to practice a form of bad moral faith. If we suppose the liberal state was designed and intended to safeguard the freedom and well-being of all citizens, then the protections this affords all citizens cuts across group lines and requires the state to protect group members even against their own.

This is a powerful objection to LP; in fact, I suspect it conveys the spirit that powers all objections to LP. Our morality tells us what we must do to get along with one another, how we should conduct ourselves in the company of others, and when we should act to promote our moral ends in the face of dangers to them. This is because morality involves (perhaps among other things) a set of rules that control how we think human beings should associate; and from this point of view, morality (as conceptualized by the western liberal tradition) is deeply and unavoidably political. The public rules of civil association would seem to follow necessarily from the dictates of morality and not from anything else. If we are to live by our morality, we must insist upon a general adherence to its strictures; to do otherwise constitutes an abandonment of those principles and ideals of human association and interaction that we presumably hold dear and consider compelling and inviolate.

These reflections may incline one to wonder if it is either possible or desirable to continue supporting practical liberalism in the shadow of such a powerful moral rejoinder. One way (perhaps the only way) to counter this objection is simply to repeat the prudential argument already made to support LP, and in an important sense this is exactly what I intend to do. With the strength of the moral objection in plain view, however, it is necessary to reprise the prudential argument by situating the basic structure of the argument within a practical political context—to bring it to life within a specific political setting so to speak—and not simply to repeat the abstract form of the argument offered above. In doing so, two key points need to be established. First, it is important to notice that all elements of the polity are justified, in their own minds, in advancing and insisting upon the moral objection; it is not the personal property of any one group in the society.

So, where and when conflicting moral visions exist within a common social setting, the moral objection is bound to give rise to normative conflict powered by the deepest and most heartfelt sense that each group has justice on its side. Given the fact of pluralism, the moral objection would seem to encourage or underwrite ongoing civil conflict among competing normative rivals, and one should wonder, after a fashion, if this response to the problem of civil strife is really superior to the response mandated by LP. Second, it is also important to recognize that adherence to LP does not require the bad moral faith identified in the objection. In particular, it does not require groups to abandon efforts to have their own normative views recognized and endorsed by group outsiders. It does not prohibit discourse, argument, or proselytizing in support of one's moral beliefs and convictions; it prohibits only the pursuit of coercive strategies intended or designed to impose one's group ways on outsiders. This, I want to argue, does not constitute bad moral faith.

The power and pertinence of the moral objection to LP can be illustrated by an example that is perhaps as tragic as it is disturbing. The Followers of Christ is a relatively small religious sect that evolved from the Pentecostal movement. It has adherents living in Oregon, Idaho, and Oklahoma. Like certain larger religious communities, the Followers of Christ practice faith healing, believing that God's will should govern individual well-being. In 1998 following the deaths of three of the Followers' children, *The Oregonian*, a Portland, Oregon, newspaper, reported that at least 21 of the Followers' 78 children buried by the Oregon City community since 1955 would probably have survived if medical treatment had been available to them.[5] Predictably, the report sparked a small controversy that tended to galvanize the larger Portland metropolitan area against the small community. Fueled by the relentless coverage of the local newspaper, public sentiment quickly swung in favor of having the state prosecute the parents of children who die prematurely for negligent homicide in spite of the unusually 'liberal' religious exemptions associated with Oregon's homicide statutes.

The issue introduced by revelations about the child mortality rate among the Followers of Christ dramatizes what might be considered the worst-case scenario for a theory of toleration that recommends forbearing internal group practices. The case would probably not trouble to the extent that it does if adults were involved. If an adult opts to forego medical treatment for religious reasons and suffers an early death as a result, we could at least argue that he or she had a choice and made it according to his or her most cherished beliefs. If an adult decided that medical treatment was preferable to sticking to his or her religious beliefs and elected to leave his or her faith in order to receive such treatment, the government could support this decision and help enforce it against the group faithful who might try coercively to prevent him or her from leaving. At least some people could probably live with this, but things are different here because children are a part of the equation. Children under moral liberalism are generally considered both innocents and incipient adults. They require care and nurture until the age when they can make decisions for themselves, and their upbringing should equip them to be self-directing and self-determining individuals. To fail to provide the proper care and nurturing that will enable a child to become a responsible, self-determining adult is accordingly deeply offensive to liberal moral sentiments. The premature death of a child—and the death of a child is, from a liberal viewpoint, premature—is thus particularly horrible and should be prevented if at all possible.

Of course, a bit of imagination could make the example even more disturbing. Suppose, for example, some groups in the polity practice human sacrifice and select some child from their numbers to be sacrificed to their god. While this offense against the moral sensibilities of more dominant groups may inspire even greater moral outrage and even louder popular insistence that the state intervene in such practices, liberal toleration would still necessitate that even activities of this sort must be tolerated if they are perceived as legitimate group practices within the group. Liberal toleration, this is to say, seems troubling from a moral point of view because it does not permit outgroups a moral trump on internal group practices no matter how odious or repulsive group outsiders might consider them to be. But we need not stretch our imaginations to such extremes when there are more realistic and politically pressing examples, like the practice of faith healing, at hand.

Moral liberals may want to argue, with some plausibility, that it is wrong to permit some children to die unnecessarily simply because they happen to have been born into a particular religious community. This is a mere contingency of being (an accident of birth, quite literally), and such things should not hinder a child's ability or opportunity to live a fulfilling, independent, and worthwhile life, regardless of the group setting into which the child may happen to be born. Nevertheless, practical liberalism would prohibit the state from interfering with the practices of the Followers of Christ and denying them the opportunity to live according to their own beliefs. Yet when faced with the reality of the needless and pointless loss of the lives of children, moral liberals will most likely want to insist that such a practice is beyond the proper parameters of toleration, and with good reason. What sense does it make to suppose that moral norms matter (and arguably matter more than anything else) and yet admit that when it comes to civil association, these convictions must be set aside in favor of some alleged prudential need to tolerate others? If we suppose that moral liberals value toleration because it is necessary to allow the individual exercise of autonomy, any group practice that undermines the autonomy, or future autonomy, of group members ought not be tolerated.

It is occasionally supposed that anyone who defends a strong version of group autonomy, like the version supported by LP, must be something of a relativist, and the point is often made in a manner suggesting that the mere charge of relativism constitutes an argument against the position being challenged. This clearly is not so, but neither is it the case that relativism must be admitted before the strong sense of toleration at home in practical liberalism can be defended. The form of relativism at issue here, we can suppose, holds that the moral theory of the human good held and espoused by any group is as true as the moral theory of the human good held by any other group; moral truth, that is, is here regarded as relative to one's group and the moral beliefs of the group. Since the Followers of Christ believe that one's fate is in the hands of their god (or in God's hands from the viewpoint of the group), the practice of faith healing fits within the parameters of their faith. From their moral point of view, this is what they should do when confronted with an illness. And since this moral requirement is true for them, we lack solid moral grounds for an intervention.

A relativist might even press the point and insist that an intervention into the religious affairs of the Followers of Christ is arbitrary and unreasonable. Generally, liberal societies permit groups to raise their young as they see fit and worry only sporadically about child welfare. It could be argued, for example, that there is only modest social concern in the United States for protecting children against the ravages of poverty and redistributing wealth in order to guarantee that all children will have a basically equal opportunity in life. In fact, inequalities of opportunity are occasionally justified on the grounds that parents have a right to use the wealth they have amassed in order to make their children's lives go well.[6] Similarly, the major Christian faiths in America do not press government to intervene in the lives of parents who have fallen away from the church and fail to raise their children within the Christian tradition, even though this may be regarded as a dreadful disregard of the best interest of one's children. So it seems at best hypocritical to think that the state should intervene in the internal affairs of the Followers of Christ because their practices are regarded as immoral by the moral sentiments that happen to dominate American society.

The relativist might also note that the Followers of Christ care mightily about their children and firmly believe they are doing what is best for them. According to reports in *The Oregonian*, when a child becomes ill the entire community comes together and lays hands upon the child as a part of the healing process, and the immediate family will stay awake and in prayer night and day to affect healing. Such parents are hardly insensitive to the well-being of their children, and perhaps the state would do better to concern itself with parents who care little, if at all, about their children, abuse them, ignore them, or shunt them off upon unqualified baby sitters while they amuse themselves free from the burdens of parenthood.

The relativist may also make appeal to epistemic uncertainty. The Followers of Christ believe that faith healing works, and while the dominant liberal community in Oregon focused upon the disproportionate number of child deaths suffered in the Followers' community, neither the local newspaper nor the community at large wondered out loud about the success rate of faith healing. Nor did it ask whether the success rate of faith healing might actually surpass the success rate of healing brought about by current medical science. Yet instances abound where medical science has given up and yet recovery is still made, and perhaps as a result of the prayer asking for recovery. So then, what kind of liberal snobbery is it that supposes medical science is the only way, or even the best way, to deal with illness? This too might be considered a snobbery born of a sense of the infallibility of the liberal worldview and moral theory of the human good. But once we get outside this snobbery, once we appreciate the presence of other world-views and moral theories of the human good, we are properly chastened into allowing those who subscribe to these different beliefs and norms to live their lives as they wish.

This, I take it, is the relativist argument for the defense of group autonomy. It is not, however, an argument I want to use in defense of LP; nor is it an argument that has much to do with liberal toleration. In fact, relativists have no need for toleration. Perhaps relativism supports respect or appreciation for otherness and difference; but it can hardly support toleration because relativists do not ask us to put up with things we find repugnant, disgusting, or immoral. Instead, relativists chisel away at the certainty with which we can say that some group practice is disgusting or immoral. They would have us say, 'We think the As are morally wrong to practice X, but that's just us. Since the As think doing X is moral, that is good enough for us!' This is hardly toleration; toleration asks us to put up with things we consider (usually with great certainty) terribly and objectionably wrong and immoral.

To put the point the other way around, a theory of toleration presumes the presence of both moral and epistemological righteousness throughout the polity. It is intended to hold this righteousness in check, to render it politically docile, and not to eliminate it. In fact, liberal tolerance allows a great deal of intolerance to flourish in the polity. It does not require liberals, or anyone else, to sit idly by while others do things they consider immoral or unjustifiable. It allows liberals, and everyone else, to act upon their moral convictions by engaging the targets of their animus in open and reasoned discourse. It permits discussion and colloquy with others in order to persuade them, by means of reasoned argument, to see the wrong and injustice of their practices and to change their ways. What it prohibits, again for liberals and everyone else, is the coercive interference with the ways and beliefs of others in order to prevent them from practicing their ways and living as they see fit.

So, neither moral liberals nor anyone else should think they are not permitted to hold and practice their moral convictions under practical liberalism. This is protected under LP for moral liberals as a group just as it is protected for all other groups in the polity. Those who see a terrible injustice in the activities of the Followers of Christ are entitled to oppose their faith-healing activities by protesting their practice, engaging them in open discussion, exploring with them the foundations of their faith, and so forth. Liberal toleration, in short, does not require the bracketing off of one's moral beliefs in order to make allowance for the different ways and different beliefs of the groups extant in the polity. It qualifies only the kinds of strategies a group can employ in pursuing and promoting its moral ends by restricting the group to strategies and activities that do not compromise the ability of outgroups to live as they wish. Groups remain free under liberal toleration to protest the activities of outgroups, to discuss and debate group beliefs with outgroups, to encourage group defection through reasoned discourse, and so forth. But if reasoned argument and careful persuasion fail to get outgroups to change their ways and embrace a moral theory closer to one's own view, forbearance demands that citizens tolerate these ways even as they continue to advocate against them.

For some, including some moral liberals, this will seem inadequate; they will want to do more; they will think that their moral viewpoint both requires and justifies their doing more. They may attempt to leverage the government into interfering with group practices and, say, forcibly take the children of the Followers of Christ to a physician when they become ill. Or they may take matters into their own hands and, say, bomb abortion clinics in order to put what they consider an immoral practice out of business either directly or by means of intimidation.

From the standpoint of moral liberalism, illiberal practices of this sort raise a challenging problem—something we may think of as the problem of appropriate response. Kymlicka, for example, thinks that liberals ought to try and liberalize illiberal groups.[7] But he would restrict liberal efforts in this regard to reasoned discourse and insists that coercive efforts to prohibit these practices are not justified under liberal morality.[8] The liberal defense of liberal morality, according to Kymlicka, must respect the liberal commitment to honor individual autonomy, and thus Kymlicka's position is equivalent to the one recommended by practical liberalism. Yet it is not clear why this view should be thought to follow from the basic premises of liberal morality. If coercive interference might succeed in prohibiting some from compromising the autonomy of others, why should a liberal commitment to autonomy not permit, or even require, such an intervention? Since it does not appear that either response is necessarily or unambiguously entailed by liberal morality, it seems any response moral liberals might make here tends toward the arbitrary.

Dominant groups may resort to strategies of interference, coercive and/or violent as they are bound to be, with the moral confidence that they have right on their side. But having right on one's side is one thing, and behaving in a way that is best calculated to promote one's moral ends is quite another. The former belongs to the particularities of one's moral theory of the human good, whatever it may happen to be, while the latter belongs to the realm of strategic and prudential calculation. While some liberals may feel justified in invading the community of the Followers of Christ and carrying their sick children off to the doctor or holding parents criminally liable for the preventable death of their children, this strategy establishes a dangerous precedent. The Followers are likely to isolate themselves from the dominant culture even more than they have already, to hide the deaths of children from prying liberal eyes, and to become even more suspicious of and withdrawn from the larger community around them. Creating a sense of persecution in one's neighbors is not a particularly good way of getting along with them; nor is it a particularly good way of trying to help their children who might be in need of medical attention. It only makes enemies; it only estranges; it only encourages them to go about the job of living as they wish surreptitiously and clandestinely. It only exacerbates the politics of interests.

It is probably the case that the government could put an end to the Followers of Christ practice of faith healing if government officials really put their mind to it; the Followers, after all, are a particularly vulnerable group with few resources or immediate political allies. Government agents could follow the Followers of Christ into the hills; put them under constant surveillance; monitor their birth rates; and so forth. But other illiberal groups are sure to be watching and are sure to notice what they will consider to be a frightening intolerance toward illiberal practices. This will probably suggest something like a politics of dominance to these outgroups and encourage them to see these governmental actions as threatening and unjustified. In fact, the greater the success the government has in policing the practice of faith healing against groups like the Followers of Christ, the more its actions will tend to destabilize the status quo politics of interests and encourage illiberal and non-liberal groups to view government as little more than an extension of the moral inclinations of the dominant culture that threatens their way of life in ways that demand an appropriate defense. What looks like moral liberation to some will seem like oppression to others; and in the face of such oppression, otherwise vulnerable groups like the Followers of Christ will look for ways to improve their political circumstances and continue to survive—ways that may serve only to further expand and spread intergroup conflict.

Similarly, it does little good to bomb abortion clinics, even if one is thoroughly committed to fighting a terrible immorality and protecting the life of fetuses unable to protect themselves or insist upon their rights. This may only increase the resolve of those who want to make sure that the choice of an abortion remains available to women and inclines them to fight back, perhaps even by bombing fundamentalist churches. Historically, little has been gained by violence and coercive interference in the lives and ways of others, and it remains an enduring and embarrassing aspect of human stupidity that people should continue to think that their own righteous beliefs justify invading the lives of others in ways that will predictably increase animosity, distrust, hatred, and even violence. Few things have done more to set human beings at each other's throat; few features of human life have done as much to drive, direct, and inspire human predation. And consequently, few things have done as much to destabilize and endanger social life and turn man into a wolf to man. This, of course, is but a restatement of the argument for LP, but perhaps by giving the argument a more precise political context it will now seem more compelling because it has strength just where some (particularly moral liberals) had thought perhaps to find a weakness.

Still, it may be objected that practical liberalism does not offer much solace to anyone who worries about the dilemma of bad moral faith. While practical liberalism does permit groups to pursue non-invasive and non-coercive strategies in order to encourage outgroups to change their ways, this might seem too weak an effort to address the perceived injustice. If we take seriously the potential incommensurability of group worldviews and viewpoints presumed under the fact of pluralism, the likelihood that reasoned discourse will prove a successful way to get groups to change their ways would seem modest at best. If reasoned discourse is unlikely to mitigate the injustice that worries more dominant groups, might moral conviction not require more drastic measures?

Under practical liberalism, the realities of intergroup conflict suggest that more drastic measures may make things worse, particularly if all groups in a pluralist social environment feel morally justified in adopting them. But too, it seems pointless to speculate on the homogenizing power of reasoned discussion. It may be (and this is where I would put my money) that the ontological, epistemological, and moral differences that separate groups are so extraordinary that forging the kind of moral homogeneity necessary to eliminate normative intergroup conflicts is practically impossible short of the most tyrannical measures. But it may also be that this merely sells short the moderating powers of reasoned argument and discussion. Perhaps if we engage the Followers of Christ long enough and hard enough we can get them to change their beliefs and amend their ways. While this might seem unlikely, there is little reason why we cannot hope for this, or why we cannot act upon this hope. Practical liberalism is indifferent on such matters, as it should be. It requires only that groups pursue their moral ends in a fashion that respects the opportunity and ability of all others to do so similarly. This allows for plenty of room for intergroup engagement and discussion, qualified only by the fact that groups must be willing to participate in the process of exchange and not have it imposed upon them. This, I think, is an effective response to the charge of bad moral faith. Groups are still permitted to work toward bringing their social world into what they consider proper moral alignment. They can still do something to realize their moral ends, but they cannot do just anything. Seen from inside a group's worldview, we might say that practical liberalism limits the things people can do to make their world better, but it also goes some distance toward assuring that their world will still be a safe and secure place for them.

It may be objected, however, that this strong stand on group autonomy does not follow as readily from LP as I have supposed. The objection I have in mind trades on what might appear to be an ambiguity in the meaning of the liberal principle. Recall that LP protects a most capacious group freedom/independence compatible with a similar freedom for all groups. Suppose, then, we interpret this to mean that all groups have a right to coercively interfere in the internal affairs of all other groups in the event outgroups find the internal practices of some group(s) intolerable according to their own moral theories of the human good. Since this interpretation of LP satisfies the formal conditions of the principle—all groups enjoy the same amount of equal freedom—there appears to be no reason, internal to the principle itself, why LP should not be understood in this manner. So, any attempt to insist that LP protects group autonomy by prohibiting coercive interference in the internal affairs of outgroups must be either purely arbitrary or motivated by subterranean moral concerns.

By way of response, it is important to keep in mind that LP is intended as a focal point for a politics of principle that solidifies and coheres a common polity. The principle can realize this end, that is, it can establish a viable politics of unity, only if it constructs a workable framework for managing normative rivalries and resolving distribution problems. An interpretation of the principle that does not facilitate this end is thus clearly inconsistent with the intent and spirit of the principle. But this is exactly what an interpretation of the principle that licenses intergroup predation happens to do. To interpret the principle in a manner that permits outgroup interference in the internal affairs of a group hardly puts an end to the politics of interests and hardly checks the slide toward a politics of dominance. Instead, it pushes in this very direction, and thus it cannot overcome the conflict that inspires the need and desire for a politics of principle in the first place. Since it makes no sense to interpret LP in a manner that frustrates the end it is designed to realize, it is necessary to reject this reading of LP in favor of a construction of the principle that protects and safeguards group autonomy. This, after all, is the good that groups have prudential reason to pursue when evaluated against the fact of pluralism as supplemented by the fact of flux, and so this is also the background spirit against which to measure competing interpretations of the principle.

## Hatred, prejudice, and bigotry

This brings me to another, albeit related, objection to liberal tolerance that now needs to be considered. Under practical liberalism, toleration is the keystone of a politics of unity. Yet this unity coexists under the fact of pluralism with tremendous diversity and group difference. This may seem to be a terribly odd type of unity since it allows, even accommodates, an extraordinary amount of hatred, prejudice, and bigotry within the polity that is the stuff of serious and troubling normative rivalries. A viable politics of unity, it might be supposed, should properly be characterized by friendship and mutual respect regardless of the differences that separate us. These differences, it could be argued, should be considered mere contingencies that separate by accidents of birth or circumstance. Such things should not be allowed to fester within the polity and possibly erode the unity required for the polity to endure. Insofar as we share a common social setting, we are all thrown together in the struggle to live worthwhile lives and realizing this should encourage us to understand that we must sink or swim together.[9]

I do not wish to denigrate this vision of a communal polity. It is certainly right to insist that the ties that bind us to our polity matter, and if a polity is to endure, they must matter more than the internal forces that pressure the polity to fly apart. It is the basic and minimalist understanding of practical liberalism that these ties can matter more, at least at the initial stage of forging a politics of unity, only if they are recognized to have a strong prudential claim on our attention, regardless of our worldview or moral theory of the human good. Beyond this, one can argue that the identification of citizenship should come to matter in its own right and to have a significance throughout the polity that will incline groups to attach a moral and not just prudential importance to their association with the group that is the polity.

I will have considerably more to say about this in the chapters to follow; at present, however, I want to consider how we should approach the tolerance problems that will invariably arise in a polity that endeavors to build political unity amidst the intergroup hatred and animosity associated with entrenched normative rivalries. Because we cannot suppose that these will disappear given the realities of the fact of pluralism and the depth of intergroup hatreds that bedevil social life in pluralist settings, bearing the burden of tolerance is a cost of endorsing LP that needs to be carefully evaluated. If groups cannot be expected to put aside their intergroup animosities, the price of a politics of unity involves the need to tolerate those outgroups considered damned, disgusting, repugnant, or misguided by virtue of who they are or what they believe. So then, is this cost too great for groups to endure?

In American political culture, concepts like prejudice, bigotry, and their cognates are deeply ingrained in the politics of interests. It is presumed, in dominant liberal circles at least, that there is something wrong with prejudiced or bigoted behavior, and if others can hang one of these concepts on the members of some group, they can make considerable political gains under a politics of interests. Nonetheless, these terms are as judgmental— I am tempted to say as prejudicial—as one can hope to find. The views that some will want to condemn as prejudiced and bigoted will seem like reasoned insight to others. Name-calling is an integral feature of a politics of interests because it is an obvious way to capture and control politically salient rhetoric. A politics of principle, on the other hand, does not transcend name-calling; in the presence of normative rivalries, it is still likely to be a commonplace activity. But in the liberal polity, name-calling lacks specific political purpose. It may exacerbate intergroup animosity, but it serves no practical end other than to emphasize and illustrate certain forms of intergroup hatred and contempt. This does not mean, however, that groups whose members are subjected to vicious and demeaning verbal attacks will not be concerned about name-calling. They cannot be expected to like it, but should they be required to tolerate it?

Problems emerge for the liberal polity when the efforts of some group to be heard, efforts frequently intended to demonstrate the depth and sincerity of group beliefs, bump up against the ability of the members of target groups to go about their business and live as they wish. Racist and religious or ideologically inspired groups cannot within the limits of liberal toleration kidnap, torture, kill, rape, beat, rob, or otherwise harm outgroup members. These are obvious intrusions upon the ability of the members of such groups to live as they wish, and as such they are just as obviously inconsistent with the requirements of liberal toleration. They illustrate the most extreme instances of the failure to forbear the members of outgroups. While such behavior is uniformly prohibited in American jurisprudence, it is an additional wrong under liberal toleration to commit such acts when motivated by intergroup hatred, animosity, or disregard. In most American legal jurisdictions, this additional wrong—a wrong that can be characterized under LP as an act of intolerance—is expressed in terms of state hate-crime statutes. If it is presumed that LP is a governing principle of the polity, such displays of intolerance reach a level of political injustice beyond the wrong displayed by the more garden variety motives that often inspire such brutal and unacceptable behavior. From the standpoint of practical liberalism, then, there is reason to applaud state efforts to enhance sentences, or even better, to redefine the nature of the crime involved when intolerance motivates such criminal conduct.[10] But these too are easy judgments to make when compared with group activities that express hatred and animosity but that are less invasive with regard to their impact upon outgroup members. Here is an area where troubling tolerance problems arise. While LP requires groups to forbear one another, it also protects the freedom of group members to express their views and beliefs, including their views and beliefs about others, as they see fit. And as noted above, it also entitles all groups to advocate for their preferred way of social life by means of open discussion and reasoned argument. How, then, are we to draw the line between legitimate expression, on the one hand, and the failure to forbear on the other?

To situate the discussion, consider again the much-discussed Supreme Court decision in *R.A.V. v. St. Paul, Minnesota*.[11] The case involved the prosecution of Robert Viktora and other juveniles who had burned a cross on the lawn of an African-American family in the early morning hours. They were convicted in local court of violating Minnesota's Bias-Motivated Crime Statute, making it a criminal act to burn a cross on public or private grounds among other things.[12] By way of defense, Viktora claimed he was merely exercising his First Amendment right of free expression, and this defense took him all the way to the US Supreme Court where it eventually held good. There is no reason to be overly concerned with the specifics of the case, just as there is little point in second-guessing the Court on whether its decision squares with the general flow of free-speech jurisprudence. But the particulars of Viktora's behavior are of interest if we are to assess accurately where the burden of tolerance should go under these circumstances. Did burning the cross violate the forbearance condition, or should we view his actions as legitimate speech that necessitates placing the burden of tolerance in the other direction and asks the black family to tolerate Viktora?

Suppose we approach this question by first asking whether speech should be protected under practical liberalism. It certainly looks like it should be because people may well wish to express those views, beliefs, and convictions they hold dear. This is a derivative feature of the control to which group members are entitled if they are to be able to live their lives as they wish. It would make little sense to allow group members to hold and practice their beliefs without also permitting them to articulate these beliefs from time to time. Moreover, and as I mentioned above, groups whose members dislike the practices of certain other groups may engage the members of these groups in conversation and express their objections in the hope that these people may sense the need to change their ways. So the right of open discourse and discussion is robustly protected under practical liberalism, and this is consonant with defending a right of free speech.

But *R.A.V.* introduces circumstances that suggest things might not be so simple. Speech can at times become invasive, even to the point where it might obstruct the ability of some of those within earshot to live their lives as they wish. Sometimes speech is invasive because of the method or manner of expression, but sometimes it may seem invasive simply because of its content and regardless of the manner of expression involved. If we suppose that speech is an integral element of the freedom protected by LP, but acknowledge at the same time that speech can be invasive as well, we encounter the tolerance problem raised by *R.A.V.* There may be circumstances where the invasive dimension of speech puts the burden of tolerance upon the speaker, but at times the burden may go the other way, even when the speech in question is reasonably held to be invasive. This allows the hardly remarkable conclusion that the right of free speech under practical liberalism is not absolute. How then should we place the burden of tolerance when generally protected speech is at issue?

To begin, we should perhaps admit that Viktora's conduct qualifies as speech; his actions had a communicative purpose. Cross burning is a particularly intimidating way to convey certain racist viewpoints. Its message and its meaning are embedded in the history of America's racist past. But it is still speech, and if there is reason to defend free speech under practical liberalism, there is reason to think that the burden of tolerance here is on Viktora's side. The existence of the St Paul anti-bias crime ordinance is evidence that city elites did not particularly want to hear speech that displays certain types of intergroup biases, and it is perhaps fair to say that the black family that awoke to Viktora's bonfire did not want to hear this sort of thing either. But this is hardly sufficient to place the burden of tolerance on their side. In a pluralist polity full of normative rivalries, it is all but certain that some groups will not want to hear the convictions or viewpoints that others wish to express. So, we must decide whether everybody should enjoy some right of self-expression or whether everyone should hold their tongue. Since the opportunity to express one's beliefs and viewpoints is central to having and holding such things, and since open dialogue and discussion about proper and improper lifestyles between groups depends upon a right of free speech, some right of free expression would seem preferable to a social condition where everyone had to keep quiet for fear of offending the members of disparate outgroups. It follows that we should think LP protects the right of group members to speak their mind on things that matter to them and that this is a dimension of the protected group autonomy supported by the liberal principle.

This, in turn, is reason to object to the St Paul ordinance. By making some expressive acts subject to criminal liability, it effectively censors some groups on the grounds that others do not want to hear their views or see them expressed; or rather, it allows some groups a right of censure over their normative rivals. And few groups would want to accept a political arrangement that allows their normative rivals to silence them in this manner. If the expression of one's viewpoints deserves government protection under liberal toleration, as I am suggesting that it does, the St Paul ordinance evidently violates the non-interference condition, and the statute should go. But this does not necessarily throw the burden of tolerance onto the side of the black family or the city elites in St Paul. Viktora and friends could have been prosecuted by St Paul for any number of possible legal transgressions, including trespass, disturbing the peace, and starting a fire without a burning permit.[13] Although city ordinances that protect property, public tranquility, and public safety are not ordinarily designed or intended to curtail speech, they can do so if they affect a speaker's method of expression. But these ordinances also have a valid social purpose; they protect individuals and safeguard their ability to live their lives as they wish. Insofar as this is their chief end, they are altogether legitimate under LP as social regulations that anticipate and diffuse coordination problems and control intergroup conflict.

At its most practical level, the freedom protected by LP involves the ability and opportunity of groups collectively and their members individually to go about their daily business without obstruction from outsiders; it guarantees a maximum control of one's life, one's actions, and those things or properties that are recognized to be one's own. With this in mind, two aspects of Viktora's conduct trouble, and together they introduce the tolerance problem he created. First, Viktora did his communicating at night when he had good reason to believe that the family members were asleep in the comfort and security of their home. One can surmise that the family would have wished to remain asleep and unbothered by Viktora's efforts to communicate with them. His speech act thus counts as an intrusion and a disruption of the personal control the family enjoys in their own home at a time when efforts to speak to others is typically found objectionable. Second, his communicating involved an act that may well cause property damage. Even if Viktora and friends were careful to make sure the burning cross did not cause a larger fire, it was likely to burn the grass, leave ashes, and generally make a mess that invades the family's property and leaves them with a mess to clean up.

In either case, Viktora's actions intrude into the life of the family in a way that suggests an imposition upon their ability to do as they wish. If we suppose the family did not wish to be awakened in the early morning hours—hardly an unreasonable supposition—then Viktora's actions, which we can correspondingly presume were designed to awaken and intimidate the family, constitute an interference with their ability to do as they wish. Similarly, if Viktora left a mess behind or singed the lawn, the family would have some unwanted repair work to do, and this too constitutes an intrusion into the freedom protected by LP—for the freedom to do as one wishes involves the right to control one's own private space.

This seems sufficient to indicate that Viktora's conduct violated his responsibility to forbear those he finds damned, disgusting, repugnant, or misguided by virtue of who they are or what they believe. Liberal tolerance requires him to express his racist views, if he must express them, to the black families in his neighborhood in a manner that does not obstruct their ability to live their lives as they wish. This is the burden that toleration imposes upon him; his right under LP to speak his mind does not override his responsibility to forbear others. Consequently, his right of free expression in the liberal polity does not protect the expressive methods he used, and St Paul would have been entirely justified to prosecute him for violating any or all of the city ordinances he transgressed (except the anti-bias statute which, as we have seen, violates LP). And because he transgressed these laws in the process of failing to forbear his normative rivals, because, that is, he acted upon an intolerance inconsistent with his responsibilities as a citizen of the liberal polity, St Paul could have legitimately prosecuted him under a properly worded hate-crime statute.

To connect the requirements of liberal toleration with American free-speech jurisprudence, we can say that practical liberalism supports standard time, place, and manner restrictions upon speech, but it condemns, *in principle*, all content-based restrictions.[14] In the liberal polity citizens must tolerate whatever others have to say, but they must also forbear others in the process of speaking. Seen in this light, the problem posed by *R.A.V.* might no longer seem terribly problematic. The invasive aspects of Viktora's behavior are evident enough, and it is not difficult to see that his conduct disrupted the targeted family's ability to go about their business and control their personal affairs as they wished. But the line between protected speech and intrusive conduct is not always easy to see.

Consider, for example, a case from Oregon State University that occurred several years ago. An engineering student at the University, an African-American freshman as it happens, left his dormitory and headed toward the library.[15] As he crossed the campus, he was 'joined' by several white students who began to shout abusive racial epithets at him. He kept walking, but the white students raised the level of harassment, attempting finally to urinate on him. At some point along the way, the confrontation instigated by the white students went from protected speech to intolerant conduct; but where? Had the white students not attempted to urinate on the black student, would their speech have remained protected? Here, it seems, the details are everything. While the white students have a right to discourse on things that matter to them in a public arena like a college campus, this right ends when their efforts obstruct the ability of others to go about their business. If, however, the white students did nothing but speak to the black student as he walked, if, that is, they made no overt effort to obstruct his path or physically intimidate him, have they obstructed his ability to go about his business?

While their presence and their speech invariably made the black student uncomfortable, this is but the viewpoint of a hostile normative rival. If the black student feared for his safety, he might turn around and go back to his dormitory, and if this happened, there is a sense in which the actions of the white students caused him to alter his activities. But the imposition here is indirect nevertheless; the change of plans results from the fear or concern that arises because of the behavior of the white students but not directly from any physical intrusion. If the black student felt no fear, if he supposed that the white students were both racists and good liberal citizens and therefore willing to forbear him in spite of their hatred, he would have continued along his way to the library. Moreover, this enables us to place the burden of tolerance in a well-developed liberal polity. I will suppose that citizens in such a polity not only understand their responsibility to forbear normative rivals and make every effort to do so, but that they also practice their moral theory of the human good by speaking to and with others about their views. With this in mind, racist speech, even racist speech specifically directed to a particular individual and presented in a particularly disgusting or obnoxious way, should be tolerated provided the speaker does not physically intrude upon the customary sphere of personal control enjoyed by his audience. Both speaker and audience should understand the limitations upon the methods of speech that liberal toleration requires, and this should do something to mollify any fears or concerns the audience may have that otherwise legitimate speech could lead to something else.

This strong stand on the burden of tolerance in free-speech cases may not be altogether appropriate in the American context given America's long history of racism and racial violence, however. The black student may have had reason to think that something other than speech was coming (as in fact it did) and think it prudent to abandon his plans for the library and seek safe harbor at the nearest opportunity. If practical liberalism was to inform American free-speech jurisprudence, then, some appreciation for this should be built into the process by which the burden of tolerance is placed under these unique circumstances, and this invites the need to qualify, in the American context, the claim that liberal toleration will not permit *any* content restrictions upon speech. If we were to put ourselves in the shoes of the black student and if we think under these circumstances the student had legitimate reason to fear that something beside speech was coming, there is a failure to forbear in evidence. Speakers have a responsibility under practical liberalism to calculate the type of impact their speech will have on their audience. Where circumstances are such that speech, by virtue of the manner of its presentation, can be ordinarily understood to elicit fear, intimidation, or concern for one's safety from the audience, the boundary that separates forbearance from intolerance is crossed. While mere speech is unlikely to elicit such concerns in an audience within a fully developed liberal polity, adjustments of this sort may be necessary in the United States by virtue of its past history of racial conflict and the intergroup hatreds that still linger.[16]

This gives us some inkling of the costs of endorsing LP with regard to free-speech matters. In many respects, the costs are not great because the demands of liberal toleration here correspond to a large degree, though by no means completely, with much of American free-speech jurisprudence. But racists, in particular, may think the costs too great and now be disinclined to endorse LP. If they accept LP, they are prohibited from working positively toward bringing about a social condition where their normative rivals are either segregated or eliminated. So, if they are really devoted to their racist beliefs, the acceptance of LP would seem to require the effective abandonment of their moral theory of the human good. This is strong reason not to accept LP. Racists will likely find small solace in the fact that they are still entitled under practical liberalism to preach racist views, articulate their racist agenda, and convey their racist beliefs even though they cannot do anything beyond this in order to bring about their desired racist end state.[17] This too looks like a kind of bad moral faith; racists may stump for their views on the one hand but must not engage in coercive measures calculated to actually bring about their desired goal.

Just as liberals are unlikely to warm up to groups like the Followers of Christ, racist groups are unlikely to warm up to those outgroups they think inferior or disgusting. But these others are present in the polity and efforts to segregate or eliminate them may prove terribly costly or even suicidal. Racists are entitled to their worldview and moral theory of the human good under practical liberalism, but accepting LP requires a rethinking of their political agenda. It requires, in effect, a decision to try and live with those one dislikes because of who they are rather than to go to war with them. Such a war is unlikely to be won, but it is very likely to be costly. When measured against their chances of victory in such a war along with the costs of fighting it, the costs associated with LP should not seem all that great. Those we dislike because of who they are or what they believe will not go away; so, live with them we must. And if we must live with them, then we (racists and non-racists alike) are better off to forsake a politics of interests in favor of a politics of principle. Under a politics of principle, racists can speak their mind at least without fear that dominant groups will attempt to shut them up by introducing regulations of the sort on display in the St Paul Anti-Bias Motivated Crime Ordinance.

Needless to say, the targets of racial, ethnic, religious, and ideological hatreds are not likely to be overly happy with practical liberalism either. They must put up with all manner of racial, ethnic, religious, and other such insults and continue to hear from those who happen to consider them damned or disgusting. But if the spirit of practical liberalism takes hold alongside these hateful views, the targets of hate groups can at least appreciate that under LP they will be free from unwanted, although only direct, intrusions into their ability to live and do as they wish. No doubt they would prefer things if the haters would go away and their intergroup associations were more amicable, but faced with the presence of normative rivalries and the fact of pluralism, this seems an unrealistic possibility. Knowing this and facing the realities of intergroup hatred and animus should again make the acceptance of LP look like a good bet. A politics of unity requires compromise from all groups in the polity, and practical liberalism proceeds against the background conviction that a suitable compromise is preferable, for all concerned, to the uncertain and destabilizing consequences of unregulated intergroup conflict.

This is also reason for anti-racists to like LP just a little—for LP strikes a balance between hostile groups that maximizes protection for group autonomy while also insisting upon the need to practice toleration. This domesticates hateful and prejudiced views, though it falls short of eliminating them. Still, domesticating groups holding such views assures a public environment where groups are allowed to hold and promote (within the confines of liberal tolerance) those views and ways that matter to them and where political unity is still manageable. This is reason for liberals to endorse LP. But the cost of this endorsement also requires liberals to practice toleration themselves, especially when they confront groups like the Followers of Christ. So, liberals must decide whether toleration is a good thing for all groups or whether they would prefer to live in a society where toleration is not cultivated and where the politics of interests is allowed to run its course—whatever this turns out to be. Once again, it seems like opting for toleration is the best bet, though not the preferred political arrangement. Ironically, practical liberalism is not going to be anyone's preferred political arrangement, and its attractiveness as a doctrine of political compromise amongst normative rivalries lies in this very fact.

## Toleration and the practice of private discrimination

The liberal polity, like all civil associations, will need to develop institutions and offices in order to meet its manifold responsibilities. Here too liberal tolerance should guide the process by which decisions are made regarding how offices and institutions are to be staffed, managed, and allocated. Participation in the political process (involvement in the activity of government, holding political office, and accruing political authority) is something that might matter to the members of all groups in the polity. This need not be true in practice, of course, and certainly it is not true in the United States. Groups may opt out of political involvement if this sort of thing is no part of, or is anathema to, their moral theory of the human good. But under practical liberalism, groups cannot block the ability of outgroup members to seek office or involvement in the public that is the polity by virtue of who they are or what they believe. State offices, this is to say, should be open and available to all.

It will be worthwhile, however, to see exactly how this conclusion follows from LP. As we have seen, LP safeguards a maximum amount of freedom for group members to live their lives as they wish compatible with a like amount of freedom for the members of outgroups to do so as well. Consequently, no group can claim a privileged access to the offices and institutions of the public that is the polity; nor can any group wanting access to the offices and institutions of the public that is the polity insist that their normative rivals should not have similar access. Such claims involve the assumption that groups are entitled to a greater range of freedom than their normative rivals, and these are the sorts of claims that are explicitly excluded under LP because they violate the inclusiveness condition.

Suppose, however, a group elects to forego certain freedoms in order to insist that other groups not have these freedoms. Not all possible activities potentially available to all elements of the polity will matter to all groups; some groups may have little use for or interest in, say, the opportunity to participate in governmental service. Or, some groups may be relatively neutral on the freedom to participate in governmental service but may not want their normative rivals to have the freedom to do so, and these groups

may insist that they do not want this freedom and do not want their normative rivals to have it either. Consequently, the amount of equal freedom
they would be willing to accept under LP would not include the freedom of
all group members to participate in the civic enterprise.

I doubt, however, that such a construction of LP can be sustained.
A construction of LP that would frustrate the ability of the polity to function
is obviously inconsistent with the initial commitment to a politics of unity,
and allowing group A to have veto power over the ability of the members of
group B to participate in civil service would potentially frustrate the polity in
just this way. Moreover, groups would hardly find much reason to support
LP if it safeguarded only the freedom that mattered to their normative rivals
(thus violating the supportiveness condition). There may be some lifestyles
that the Crazy Betas find repugnant but that matter greatly to the Innocent
Alphas. This might incline the Crazy Betas to think that the freedom that
matters to them under LP should not include the freedom to practice these
particular lifestyles; but to understand LP in this way would be to give the
Crazy Betas a veto over the acceptable lifestyle practices of the Innocent
Alphas, and vice versa. This is just the sort of thing groups would not want
to accept, and so it must be understood to be the sort of thing that is actually
prohibited by LP. It follows that LP safeguards the maximum freedom for
groups to live as they wish; and while all groups enjoy a similar maximum
freedom, there may be many things that group members are free to do
under LP that they do not want to do because they are inconsistent with
the group's moral theory of the human good. Consequently, the freedom
group members enjoy under LP to live as they wish includes the opportunity
to involve themselves in the affairs of the public that is the polity if they
so desire. Such a freedom may not, and certainly need not, be exercised,
however, if group beliefs or the policy statements of group elites prohibit
such activity for some, or all, group members.

By extension (and consistently with the inclusiveness condition), the same
point permits us to say that participation in all aspects of the public life of
the polity should be open and available to all. Group efforts to deny such
access to outgroups simply because they find them disgusting, misguided,
repugnant, or damned by virtue of who they are or what they believe appear
on their face to be segregationist (if they are intended to marginalize these
groups or limit their presence in the life of the public that is the polity)
or assimilationist (if they place outgroup members in the tough position
of having to choose between their group ways and involvement in the
governance of the polity). This point, however, raises some problems of its
own that introduce additional questions about the boundary between group
jurisdiction and the jurisdiction of the polity. These issues, in turn, may
create further tolerance problems.

As we have seen, under practical liberalism groups control their own
membership criteria, and this may well be a source of intragroup political

conflict. They also control their own expulsion criteria, although membership exit or withdrawal is enforceable by the government against group efforts to retain or reclaim expatriots. Often, however, groups offer or provide services or opportunities to outgroups and individuals beyond the boundaries of their own group practices and ways. In some cases, this involves selling services for a fee either as a part of the ways of one's group or because the members of a group are involved in some private enterprise unrelated to group ways for the purpose making money either for the group or for themselves. In other cases, it involves employing individuals from outside the group in a group-operated business or institution serving the group or society at large, or in a business or institution operated by group members (but not officially affiliated with the group) that again serves the group itself, society at large, or both.

Catholics in the United States operate many colleges and universities, for example, and they may elect to open their doors only to fellow Catholic students or to both Catholic and non-Catholic students. Similarly, they may elect to hire only Catholic instructors or both Catholic and non-Catholic instructors. No problems arise under practical liberalism if, say, the Catholic Church elects to serve and employ only its own faithful. Catholics, along with all other religions, are free to see to the educational development of their own, just as they are free to service their own needs without interference from outsiders. Suppose, however, some group opts to operate its own college system and to open it to all elements of the polity except, say, Catholics; or suppose a hotel, owned and operated by the members of some group, serves all elements of the polity except, say, Irish-Americans. Do such private discrimination practices demonstrate a failure to forbear group outsiders? Let us suppose that in each case these discriminatory practices are motivated by intergroup hatred and animosity. Imagine, for example, that the Ku Klux Klan (KKK) has decided to operate its own college system and declares that everyone except Catholics and African-Americans are eligible for admission, or that a group of Italian-American entrepreneurs in San Francisco's little Italy have opened an upscale hotel that will host anyone able to meet its room rate except Irish nationals or people of Irish descent as evidenced, perhaps, by the fact that they have an Irish surname, red hair, or refuse to take an oath stipulating they do not believe leprechauns exist.

If we suppose that a Catholic really wants to attend a KKK-operated college, or that an Irish-American really wants to stay in the hotel operated by Italian-Americans, and that their exclusion is due to others' failure to forbear them, we have the makings of a tolerance problem. Catholics and Irish-Americans can claim that they are excluded from a service available to everyone else because of who they are or what they believe, and this violates LP. But the KKK and Italian-Americans can counter that they are practicing group ways and operating group-affiliated institutions as they wish. Thus they can insist that their exclusion of certain others from group businesses is both consistent with and justified by LP. Here, then, is a first-class tolerance problem.

This problem is driven by a familiar ambiguity that is built into LP. Should we understand the maximum equal freedom required by LP as the freedom to prohibit a group from acting upon convictions that deny certain opportunities to their normative rivals (A is unfree to restrict B's freedom to do X), or should we understand it as the freedom to exclude normative rivals from their group practices, even if these practices are extended to some other group outsiders (A is free to restrict B's freedom to do X)? It seems on its face that LP could be interpreted either way. It could be supposed that the freedom to discriminate against normative rivals is a part of the freedom all groups would want to protect; and since all groups might be willing to concede that all groups should retain the right to discriminate against normative rivals under LP, the maximum equal freedom condition would be satisfied under this interpretation of the principle. Nor is it necessarily implausible to suppose that the right to discriminate against normative rivals might matter more to groups than the alternative right not be discriminated against by a group's normative rivals.

Nonetheless, this does not seem to be the most compelling interpretation of LP, even if it happens to be the interpretation favored by all, or a great many, groups in the polity. The freedom to discriminate again provides group A with the opportunity to veto some of the activities and opportunities (and an indeterminate number at that) open to the members of group B. Even though groups may value the right to discriminate against their normative rivals, the right they value involves the right to affect or influence the way their normative rivals elect to live their lives and the opportunities that happen to be available to them. That is, this reading of LP permits the As to place limitations upon the options and opportunities available to the Bs even though these options and opportunities are available to the Cs (where the Cs are not a normative rival of the As). The As are thus claiming the right to diminish the freedom of the Bs and to create an inequality of opportunity between the Bs and the Cs. This is manifestly inconsistent with the maximum *equal* freedom requirement of LP, and thus this reading of LP should be rejected, even though it is in principle possible (though unlikely in practice) that all groups would prefer this reading to the alternative defended here.

As we have seen, the basic right of group autonomy supported by LP guarantees that groups are entitled to control their own internal affairs free from outside interference. But when group activities move beyond the group parameters, groups must tolerate all outgroups that their activities may happen to touch, even if they find them disgusting, damned, repugnant, or misguided by virtue of who they are or what they believe. If a group undertakes some productive endeavor, it need not employ outsiders provided production remains entirely an internal group matter. Nor need the group offer its product to outsiders, but if it does, liberal toleration requires it to offer the product to all outsiders and not just those outsiders it happens to look favorably upon. Suppose, for example, the Old Order Amish (a religious community famous for its tight communal control of group ways and a favorite target for discussions of the problems posed by multicultural considerations) produce lovely quilts that they sell on occasion to interested outsiders. The Amish are at liberty under practical liberalism to control the production of the quilts; they need not hire a pushy outsider who wants to find employment in the Amish community as a quilt maker unless of course they want to. If, however, they decide to hire outsiders to help with the production of quilts, they offer opportunities to outsiders that previously did not exist. This shifts their enterprise from a group-specific matter to an activity open to all elements of the polity under the maximum equal-freedom condition of LP. Once they elect to hire, say, a helpful Mennonite, they may no longer discriminate in their hiring practices; helpful atheists too must be considered for employment when outsider openings arise. Similarly, if the Amish elect to sell their product to the community at large, they may not discriminate between buyers; if they are willing to sell to interested Mennonites, they must also sell to interested atheists.

Once again, however, groups might insist that this misconstrues their right of group autonomy. They may wish to argue that as long as the production of some good is fundamentally a group affair, the right of group autonomy entitles the group to decide who will be employed in the productive process as well as to whom the product will be marketed. Now, a group that pushes this argument is supposing that the polity should not interfere with its productive activities provided they are operated or sponsored by the group, pursued in the name of the group, or perhaps undertaken for the good of the group. Correspondingly, groups that assert a right of non-interference here are also supposing that they have no responsibility to forbear certain group outsiders just because they employ tolerable outsiders or market their product to tolerable outsiders. But the burden of tolerance, I have argued, falls the other way; once groups take their economic activities into the realm of the public that is the polity, they must play by the rules that govern participation and involvement in this group. That is, they must practice the toleration expected of them as citizens according to LP; they must respect the freedom of all group members equally and not claim a veto power over the ability of normative rivals to live their lives as they wish. Employment and marketing practices that discriminate against certain outsiders by virtue of who they are or what they believe expand the opportunities of members of friendly groups without similarly expanding the opportunities of a group's normative rivals. A group that favors certain tolerable outgroups in its hiring and marketing practices creates an imbalance between the economic opportunities and rewards available to those outgroups it can abide and those it cannot. This effectively denies these rewards and opportunities to some citizens even though they may wish to compete for them, and consequently, it displays an intolerance that is impermissible under practical liberalism.

Once a group moves its activities into the realm of the public that is the polity, liberal tolerance requires it to make those offices, opportunities, and products it makes available to some elements of this public available to all its elements.[18] Whether this counts as a cost of accepting LP or a benefit from doing so is, of course, impossible to ascertain in the abstract. While I have emphasized that all groups may value the freedom to discriminate against normative rivals, they may also think it prudent, particularly in the face of the fact of flux, to endorse a principle that guarantees they are not themselves the victims of discrimination by their normative rivals.

Things are rarely so simple in practice, however, and sometimes group practices fall into a gray area between internal group practices and participation in the public that is the polity. Consider in this regard the stand the Boy Scouts of America (BSA) has taken regarding the use of gay scoutmasters. The BSA administration has decided that the use of gay scoutmasters is inconsistent with the moral values and ideals of their organization and in 1990 revoked the membership of a gay scoutmaster in New Jersey. The US Supreme Court eventually upheld the scoutmaster's dismissal on First Amendment expressive association grounds.[19] There is no need to worry here about the particular legal spin put on this situation by virtue of its First Amendment construction, but the case does introduce a serious tolerance problem. On the one hand, the BSA is a private, non-profit association dedicated to instilling 'values in young people and, in other ways, to prepare them to make ethical choices over their lifetime in achieving their full potential.'[20] Among other things, the values in question, as reflected in the Scout oath, involve being 'morally straight' and 'clean.' The BSA administration apparently understands the values of moral straightness and cleanliness to be inconsistent with a gay lifestyle. Therefore, gays practice a way of life inconsistent with the moral theory of the human good the BSA wishes to promote (according to BSA administrators), and this is reason (again according to BSA administrators) to exclude them from their association.

On the other hand, the BSA's commitment to instill the values it cherishes in 'young people' suggests that the organization is (or should be) open to all young people, or to the youth of the public that is the polity. Not only does past practice bear this out, it also seems that many young people are attracted to the Scouts because of the experiences it offers in outdoor activities and the like, and not simply because they wish a certain type of moral training. Nor has BSA done much historically to exclude people wanting outdoor experiences from those wanting moral training. This too suggests that the Scouts serve the public that is the polity. Is this general openness, in conjunction with the apparent appeal to openness, sufficient to conclude that the BSA serves the public that is the polity in a way that should override its decision to exclude gays from membership? Should the BSA be expected to forbear gays because it services the public that is the polity, or should gays be asked to forbear the BSA because it is a private association with a specific moral theory of the human good it wishes to promote?

The Supreme Court, along with other commentators, focused heavily on the question of whether the BSA's exclusion of gays really is consistent with its moral agenda.[21] The BSA's commitment to moral straightness and cleanliness is exceptionally vague and does not clearly or unequivocally imply opposition to gay lifestyles. But this is not a matter that can legitimately be second-guessed under practical liberalism. Whether or not gay lifestyles are inconsistent with the values of the BSA is up to the membership itself to decide. This is a matter of internal associational politics. So, we must take it as given that the BSA considers gay lifestyles inconsistent with the values it seeks to espouse and cultivate in young people. While there might be disagreement on this point internal to the Scouts, the official position adopted by Scout leadership seems apparent. We need not take as given, however, the conclusion that the BSA can exclude gays from its membership if it serves in some way the public that is the polity. The United States Tennis Association (USTA) is also a private, non-profit organization. It welcomes as members individuals interested in promoting and participating in the sport of tennis, and in this regard it is open to the public that is the polity. I doubt, however, anyone would be willing to concede that the USTA could justifiably reject gays from membership consistent with the demands of liberal toleration because the USTA opposed gay lifestyles. And I think this conclusion would be sound even if the USTA leadership decided that the aim of their organization was to promote participation in the sport of tennis for heterosexual Americans only.

The tolerance problem in evidence here is perhaps best resolved by searching for a nexus between the moral, religious, or ideological vision held and promoted by the association claiming protection for group autonomy and the nature of the activities the association makes available to its membership. The BSA, for example, seeks to instill the values it promotes in young people by 'instructing and engaging them in activities like camping, archery, and fishing.'[22] Imagine now that the USTA adopted a policy toward gays like the BSA's policy and further insisted that it seeks to instill certain moral views in its membership through instructing and engaging them in the sport of tennis. We should ask here whether the purpose of the association is (1) the claimed moral agenda, or (2) promoting the sport of tennis throughout the society at large. Is (2) merely the means by which the USTA wants to realize (1) or is (2) the actual end of the association, and by claiming (1) it is just discriminating against a group it finds repugnant or disgusting by virtue of who its members are (in violation of LP).

One way to answer this is to ask if (2) is a viable, plausible, and effective way to realize (1). In the case of the sport of tennis, I should think it clearly is not. Teaching and nurturing the sport of tennis certainly can instill certain moral values in the participants of the game—the ideals of fair play, honesty, and civility come readily to mind here. But it would be a reach to suppose that something about gay lifestyles is inconsistent with any of this. What then about the BSA? Learning about things like camping, archery, and fishing may well be of interest to the members of many disparate groups in the public that is the polity. But are these effective and viable ways for the BSA to cultivate the values in its members that it seeks to cultivate? Does camping and fishing cultivate moral straightness and cleanliness as these notions are understood by the BSA? Learning to camp and fish in the company of others might again facilitate a sense of fair play, honesty, courage, patience, and the like, but again it seems a reach to conclude that there is something about gay lifestyles that is inconsistent with any of this. So, the required nexus between the activities promoted by the association and the values it seeks to instill is not met here—or at least I do not see that it is met, although this is an issue for further democratic discussion. If this is right, the burden of tolerance falls, in this case, to the Boy Scouts of America. Here is a case, then, where the public involvement of a private association trumps their claim of group autonomy because the activities they make available to prospective members is too unrelated to the moral theory of the human good that they presumably wish to promote.

I could be wrong about this, of course; it could be that the BSA can establish the required nexus. But there is little reason to worry about this here. What matters from the standpoint of practical liberalism is getting clear on how the burden of tolerance should be assigned under such circumstances. The BSA is certainly entitled to argue for the requisite nexus, but it falls to the courts, in this case, to decide whether the nexus is satisfactorily established, just as it falls to the public as a whole to critically examine the judicial reasoning in such cases and deliberate on what toleration requires here. This is an integral feature of resolving tolerance problems of this sort, and the government hardly offends against the non-interference condition by adjudicating this type of tolerance problem.

We are now in a position to draw with some precision an important boundary between groups and the public that is the polity. While groups may operate their own internal markets, the marketplace that serves the polity belongs to the polity as a group and is governed by the requirements of liberal toleration. Groups that may find others disgusting, damned, repugnant, or misguided by virtue of who they are or what they believe must then tolerate these others in the public places of the polity. And to this extent, private discrimination in hiring or serving practices is impermissible under practical liberalism. Is this reason for groups that loathe others by virtue of who they are or what they believe to reject LP in favor of a politics of interests? It might seem so since under a politics of interests, groups wishing to discriminate against certain outgroups may eventually achieve sufficient political control to realize their desires, whereas this is not possible under a politics of principle.

It seems unreasonable to think, however, that a group's desire to discriminate against its normative rivals in the realm of the public that is the polity could be so great as to incline its members to assume the risks associated with a politics of interests. Any success discriminatory groups might have in this regard may well prove to be transient and fleeting. Given the fact of flux, there is always the real possibility that these groups will lose more under a politics of interests than they can hope to win. If they lose control of political conceptualizations, for example, their normative rivals may find themselves in a strategic position to invade their group autonomy and undermine their independence and status as a group. As the historical ebb and flow of racial politics in America demonstrates, the gains and losses for hostile normative rivals under a politics of interests are difficult if not impossible to control, and the future is inevitably uncertain. Given the unpredictability and seriousness of such normative conflict, endorsing LP should seem attractive to all concerned even if it means abandoning practices of private discrimination in the public space.

A similar reasoning applies to private discriminatory activities with regard to group control of its physical environment. While groups cannot under practical liberalism pursue policies or strategies that impose segregation upon others, they may if they wish, and in accordance with their right to group autonomy, segregate themselves from outsiders. In many instances, territorial control is an integral feature of group life and may be required in order for the group to practice those ways tied to the land or to a given region.[23] If and when groups can demonstrate that physical segregation from the polity is a fundamental aspect of group ways, groups can claim under LP a legitimate right to control the territory they occupy and exclude outgroups from intruding upon their space. Others seeking to move into the region, to develop the land, or otherwise intrude into the physical life of the group should thus be prohibited from doing because this demonstrates a failure to forebear on their part. Isolationist groups may, in effect, run their own system of restrictive covenants, but only isolationist groups may do so. Accordingly, members of the KKK who happen to share a neighborhood in common cannot operate a restrictive covenant to block the purchase of one of their properties by an African-American family, for the Klan has no ethnic, religious, or cultural tie to a specific place that is the center or source of group life. And while Klan members may claim, in solid nativist fashion, that America itself is *their* place, both American history and the mere presence of other groups puts the lie to this. The Klan is free to segregate itself in the fashion of, say, the followers of the Bhagwan Shree Rajneesh, but under LP it should be obvious that no group can claim the polity as its own.[24] Such claims just set off a struggle characterized by the politics of dominance (and Klan members should be sufficiently prudent to want to avoid this).

The geographical or territorial control permitted to some groups under practical liberalism introduces another source of possible problems that requires at least a passing comment. Sometimes, group ways will involve engaging in certain practices that may have deleterious consequences for the environment or neighboring communities. Amish farming practices, for example, are not altogether environmentally friendly and they may raise riparian problems for the larger community affected by them.[25] Such things raise coordination problems that are appropriate for the polity to address and mediate. While I cannot explore here the various approaches for dealing with coordination problems available under practical liberalism, it is worth mentioning generally that such things should be handled by looking (1) to efficient and fair compromises and (2) to the general welfare of the polity itself. The appropriate outcome to a coordination problem involves placing the burden of deference in a way that not only is least intrusive upon group autonomy, but also guarantees group ways will not indirectly or unintentionally intrude upon the ability of outgroups to live and do as they wish. This, in turn, may necessitate some corresponding limitation upon the practice of group ways. But this too is the price groups must pay because they happen to live in the presence of others.

Coordination problems, like tolerance problems, need careful and thoughtful mediation, and we can presume that affected groups will be involved in the discussions that serve to propose possible deference strategies. But it falls to government in the liberal polity both to referee these problems (thus working toward a fair compromise when the welfare of the polity as a whole is not at issue), and to manage them appropriately when it perceives that the welfare of the group that is the polity is at issue. The alternative to governmental control of these issues under a politics of principle is to submit to the mercy of the politics of interests and allow groups to take their chances in the hope of capturing government sufficiently to realize their own ends against their allocational rivals. But we already know the potential costs associated with this strategy, and it seems fair to suppose that few group practices that generate coordination problems are so integral to group life that a group would be willing to defend the practice by jeopardizing the continued well-being of the group itself rather than reach some form of political compromise.

## Toleration, social stability, and civic education

There is another potential source of tolerance problems that requires brief comment. The education of their young is sure to be of considerable importance to groups because their members invariably want their children to live a good life. Since thoughts about what counts as a good life are internal to the worldview and the moral theory of the human good held by the group, group concerns amount to the desire to make sure that their children are properly introduced to group ways, beliefs, and norms. This also includes the public that is the polity which also has both an important stake and a clear interest in seeing that its children become good citizens. The basic idea of a good citizen under practical liberalism involves practicing toleration and deference to other groups when group interests or group ways come into conflict with outgroups. It will involve other things as well, of course, including meeting the maintenance responsibilities (e.g., paying taxes, serving in the military, etc.) that assure the polity is able to function and endure. But the practice of toleration is perhaps the most urgent and pressing responsibility citizens have, given the ugly realities of intergroup hatred and animosity that I have supposed is unavoidable under pluralism.

It follows that both primary groups and the polity (as an ancillary group) have an interest in child education, and both, therefore, have a legitimate right to have some input into the educational curriculum a child encounters. Given the strong defense of group autonomy associated with practical liberalism, we might suppose that groups are entitled to provide for the educational needs of their children, and this supposition is generally reasonable. But because the polity also has an interest in this education, it may involve itself in group educational practices in order to assure that one's responsibilities as a citizen are made clear to children and the importance of meeting them are discussed and emphasized.

This is the potential source of another tolerance problem. Influenced by America's liberal legacy and in keeping with their *parens patriae* responsibilities, all American states require some education for all children; and since education is presumed to be both a public good and a necessary condition of living a good life (understood in liberal terms), states also operate public schools that take children from all elements of society. In principle, there is nothing wrong with this. Since the liberal polity should insist on citizenship training for its incipient citizens, it is appropriate for it to provide for this education. But the dual role of government is also on display here. While the primary educational responsibility of the polity is citizen development, government may also serve the interests of dominant groups by providing educational opportunities for the children of these groups.

Groups need not send their children to these public schools, of course; parents may elect to send their children to private or group-sponsored educational institutions if they wish or even to practice home schooling. The US Supreme Court has not only upheld these alternatives to public schooling, but it has also wisely insisted that 'certain studies plainly essential to good citizenship . . . be taught . . . and that nothing be taught which is manifestly inimical to the public welfare.'[26] Under practical liberalism, this is an altogether appropriate policy, but it does not necessarily introduce an option all groups may be willing or able to use. These options come with a considerable cost to groups in terms of time, training, and finances, and groups may prefer to take advantage of available state-operated schools rather than assume these burdens themselves. If they do so, they can justifiably assume that state schools operate in the liberal polity within the constraints imposed upon the public that is the polity by the non-interference condition. Curricular decisions are sure to be burdened by the need to observe the non-interference condition, however, and what some groups consider proper educational policy for members of the polity might seem to others to violate the non-interference condition. The resultant disputes will take the form of a tolerance problem.[27]

Let me elaborate by taking brief notice of another Supreme Court decision that has become a favorite target of ridicule with many moral liberals. The case of *Wisconsin v. Yoder* involved an action brought by the Old Order Amish claiming that Wisconsin's requirement that children stay in school through age 16 violated their right to the exercise of their religion under the First Amendment.[28] The Amish argued that they should be exempt from this requirement since education beyond the eighth grade was unnecessary for an Amish way of life and because additional education may incline Amish children to forsake their faith, thus endangering the welfare of the group itself. For reasons that are unnecessary to discuss, the Court upheld the Amish claim, but not without first hearing an impassioned liberal dissent from William O. Douglas:

> It is the future of the student, not the future of the parents, that is imperiled in today's decision. If a parent keeps his child out of school beyond the grade school, then the child will be forever barred from entry into the new and amazing world of diversity that we have today. The child may decide that is the preferred course, or he may rebel. It is the student's judgment, not his parent's, that is essential if we are to give full meaning to what we have said about the Bill of Rights and the right of students to be masters of their own destiny. If he is harnessed to the Amish way of life by those in authority over him, and if his education is truncated, his entire life may be stunted and deformed.[29]

Douglas's concern has been repeated by more than one moral liberal, perhaps rarely with such eloquence but always with equal conviction.[30] Nonetheless, Douglas's comments illustrate an intolerance that is impermissible under practical liberalism. Douglas expressed, with his characteristic efficiency, an inclination to see children as potential persons requiring a full (liberal) education in order to be sufficiently prepared to chart their own course through life. As a practical matter, it is unclear whether any of us ever manage to receive such a comprehensive education, even if we are subjected to a curriculum that moral liberals would endorse. All education directs, limits, selects, and focuses upon what the groups in control of determining curricular matters consider appropriate or necessary. (That this is frequently a matter of intragroup politics in liberal circles hardly needs mention.) Students attending most traditional schools are not introduced to alchemy, creationism, astrology, witchcraft, phrenology, or any number of other 'schools of thought' that are simply dismissed by the dominant culture as misguided, false, or foolish. Should we complain because students are not permitted to consider these matters for themselves and make their own judgments about their value?

To quibble just a bit more with Douglas, it is, to say the least, presumptuous for him to suppose either that staying in school through age 16 will equip students 'to be the masters of their own destiny,' or that receiving the kind of education Wisconsin planned for them will make them masters of their own destiny. It makes more sense to suppose that if they stay in school as long as Wisconsin would like, they would be more inclined to elect a destiny more in line with liberal presumptions about how a life should go. That is, by staying in school the student becomes pulled by a greater range of influences, but why anyone should think this makes the student master of her or his destiny is beyond me. From Douglas's liberal perspective, the introduction to a greater range of (liberal) influences was a good, but to the Amish parents it was not a good. And while Douglas wanted to hear from the children to see what they thought, it seems most unlikely that either side would really care a great deal about this. How could these children hope to know, at this point, what was in their best interest; in fact, if they were already sufficiently astute to be cogently aware of this, they would hardly need much additional education, though perhaps they might require and desire additional training of some sort.

But let me put these quibbles aside and ask how the burden of tolerance should be placed under the circumstances raised by *Yoder*. The question invites us to ask a second: Who should control the type of socialization process Amish children receive? This asks, in a sense, who has the primary responsibility to raise these children, look after their safety and security, and determine how their lives should go in the future? It is something of a commonplace in American society today to suppose that parents have the primary responsibility to raise their offspring, but if they do not do so in a fashion considered appropriate by the state, the government is justified in taking over the process itself. Of course, we have already encountered problems with this view of the matter in the circumstances surrounding the Followers of Christ. I argued there that the right of group autonomy protected by LP allows parents to raise their children and care for them in the manner they consider appropriate according to their worldview and moral theory of the human good. If this holds in the case of the Followers of Christ, it should also hold with equal vigor for the Amish.

When it comes to the matter of education, the Wisconsin Amish evidently see things differently than liberals like Justice Douglas. While liberals may regard children as non-affiliated neophytes, the Amish no doubt regard their own children as future Amish. This is a difference lodged in the basic worldviews of two competing groups, both insisting that they know what is best for the Amish children. But the control the liberal polity can claim over the well-being of children is governed by its primary responsibility to bring to life the ideal of maximum equal group autonomy for all groups living there. It is manifestly inconsistent with group autonomy to suppose that the views associated with equipping children for dealing with the rigors of life that belong to dominant groups should be imposed upon outgroups. This is the logic that requires us to side with the Followers of Christ, and it also requires us to side with the Amish in *Yoder*, at least provisionally.

I say 'at least provisionally' because the concerns introduced both by the litigants and by Justice Douglas misrepresent the actual nature of the tolerance problem raised by the case. While we should concede that groups have a primary interest in the education and development of their young, these children should also be recognized as future members of the public that is the polity; and just like primary groups, the polity also has a legitimate interest in the education and development of its young. Practical liberalism, like its Rawlsian counterpart, holds that the polity's interest in the education of children spins upon its concern for children as future citizens and not upon any deeper moral concern about them as individuals in need of receiving the appropriate equipment to live a good life.[31] If the Court's decision in *Yoder* to grant the Amish an exemption from Wisconsin's educational requirement troubles from the standpoint of practical liberalism, it does so because there is room to wonder whether an educational experience through the eighth grade is sufficient to guarantee that children, Amish or otherwise, are sufficiently introduced to the nature and demands of citizenship to operate viably in the polity as citizens and not just to operate in the Amish community as members of the faithful. Acceptance of LP means that the Wisconsin Amish, along with all other groups that elect to join the polity, must meet the demands of citizenship, and these rights preempt those group concerns that might come into conflict with it. This is but another way to state the costs associated with the acceptance of LP.

If it turns out that proper citizenship training requires an educational experience beyond the eighth grade, the Amish would have reason to reject LP, and they would arguably be justified in doing so if this additional educational requirement doomed the Amish community to eventual death from the loss of membership.[32] It would be foolish to join a political unit in order to best preserve a group's well-being if joining the unit met committing to responsibilities that would eventually destroy the group. If this is right, groups like the Amish must face a ticklish situation from the standpoint of practical liberalism. If they opt for a politics of interests over a politics of principle, the Justice Douglases may win the next round and the Amish community will be in trouble. But they might also endorse LP and work to find ways to provide proper citizenship training for their young that does not also require them to send their children to government-operated schools whose curricula are controlled by dominant groups. When faced with the uncertainties of a politics of interests, this looks like the more prudent decision.

This conclusion invites some further comment on just how citizenship training—or better, education on citizen responsibilities within the polity and on being a good citizen—should be undertaken. Here too we find the possibility of tolerance problems arising. To illustrate, let me consider the interesting difficulties raised by the case of *Mozert v. Hawkins County, Tennessee*.[33] While *Mozert* never made it to the Supreme Court, it has nonetheless been the subject of extensive Monday-morning quarterbacking by theorists concerned with exploring the extent to which the state's interest in educating children can trump parental concerns about the curriculum to which their children are exposed. The Mozerts, plaintiffs of record in the case and members of a fundamentalist religious community, raised objections to a reading text adopted by the County school system for teaching critical reading.[34] The plaintiffs did not object to the teaching of critical reading, but they objected on religious grounds to the text's presentation of certain lifestyles they considered morally objectionable according to their religious beliefs. They felt the text presented these lifestyles in a favorable light, and thus constituted teaching about the good life in a manner inconsistent with their beliefs about how life should go. The County, for its part, seemed to be out to kill two birds with one stone. It not only wanted to teach critical reading (whatever this means) but also to develop a sense of respect and appreciation for diverse lifestyles in the children of the County. It had in mind, in short, a social message in addition to its effort to cultivate literacy in its population.[35] If the message squared with the County's responsibility to develop good citizens, this would have been all to the good. But did it do so?

The Mozerts initially hoped to have their children exempted from using the text, and when this attempt was rebuffed, they insisted that the use of the texts should be accompanied by a statement from the schools indicating that the Mozerts's religious beliefs are true and correct while the views expressed in the text are false.[36] Needless to say, the school district was unwilling to accept this position, and neither were the federal courts. But the Mozerts's request that the school system stipulate the truth of their beliefs merely turns the tables on what they supposed the school district was doing. The point of contention reduces to the fact that Hawkins County was doing more than teaching literacy; it was also advocating a particular substantive view about how people should regard difference and diversity. The text portrayed, for example, a standard role reversal—a husband cooking dinner with a wife returning home from a hard day's work—in a favorable rather than hostile fashion. The quiet message of the text, a message the County well understood and even endorsed, was that such new-age lifestyles are all to the good. Yet according to the religious convictions of the Mozerts, such lifestyles are all to the bad, and they did not wish to have their children subjected to the falsehoods and stupidities of a world (in their judgment) gone wrong. At best, such perversity might confuse and confound their children, an impressionable and vulnerable constituency to be sure, and at worst it might generate the very moral corruption the Mozerts were committed to protecting their children against.

The Mozerts's request that the County declare their beliefs true and correct and the views expressed in the text false seems facially objectionable. Why should the Mozerts be allowed to dictate to the rest of the County what beliefs are true and which are false? Making such proclamations in a public school—institutions belonging to and operated by the public that is the polity—would seem to violate the non-interference condition. They intrude upon the ability of outgroups to live as they wish by imposing a viewpoint on their children with which they disagree, and consequently, they invade an area where group members have a right under LP to primary, though not exclusive, jurisdiction. The education of group young, after all, is crucial to the transmission of group ways and beliefs, something protected by the defense of group autonomy as an important element of the freedom groups hope to secure by endorsing LP in the first place. But we might suppose that the Mozerts knew exactly what they were doing in making this request; they were asking judicial permission to do to other groups in the County exactly what they believed the County was doing to them. The same principle that should protect the County from suffering the imposition of views the Mozerts liked but others disliked should protect the Mozerts from suffering the imposition of views they disliked just because the County supposed them to be true or socially valuable. The politics of interests is evidently at work here, and if practical liberalism is to introduce a more politically desirable arrangement, we need to find a principled resolution to this problem.

County apologists, on the other hand, might object to this on the grounds that the County's heart was in the right place, as even the most hard-headed practical liberal should admit. The case for the County's politically correct reader turns on the question of whether it is appropriate for teaching the responsibilities of citizenship under practical liberalism. It might be supposed that the reader was appropriate to this end since its aim was to encourage toleration of the sort integral to a politics of principle. But this confuses a commitment to toleration with the advocacy of a worldview and moral theory of the human good held specifically by dominant groups in the County. In the absence of a clear understanding of the demands of liberal toleration under practical liberalism, this confusion is understandable. Under a politics of interests, groups will have a natural inclination to suppose that their vision of the good corresponds with the political ends of the polity, and this seems to be what happened in Hawkins County.

The claim that the County's preferred reader should be accepted by all elements of the polity because it is appropriate for teaching liberal toleration is flawed for two crucial reasons. First, it assumes that a sympathetic presentation of difference will lessen contempt, or at least mitigate this contempt in children and thereby lessen their contempt when they become adults.[37] But given the realities of intergroup animus, it is difficult to believe that familiarity will do much to lessen contempt; in fact, the old saw from which this way of putting the matter is derived seems equally if not more persuasive. The backlash against the text driven by the fundamentalist opposition to it is testimony to this possibility. No doubt the Mozerts and the other fundamentalist parents involved did much to offset whatever 'domesticating impact' the text might have had on their children. Indeed, the whole incident seems to have raised the level of intergroup contempt by politicizing the issue, setting the politics of interests in motion, and further alienating the fundamentalist community from the larger society around them. The whole affair looks like it did more to exacerbate intergroup contempt than it did to mollify matters.[38]

There is, moreover, a lesson of some importance in all this. It is simply foolish to suppose that liberal toleration can be fostered by increasing group exposure to diversity. Diversity and diversity alone is hardly the problem; rather, the problem is produced by the real conflicts generated from normative rivals. It is merely naïve to suppose that these rivalries can be overcome, and the hatred and animosity at their heart eliminated, by exposing children or anyone else to the diverse ways and beliefs practiced by various groups. It seems ridiculous to suppose that members of the Ku Klux Klan will begin to embrace Catholics as brothers if, through exposure to Catholics, they suddenly discover that Catholics no longer torture heretics or march in lockstep to edicts issued by the Bishop of Rome. Members of the KKK may already know this, but they still have reasons—compelling reasons in their judgment—to loathe Catholics, and these are hardly likely to change in the event members of the KKK are exposed more immediately to Catholics.

If this holds in the case of adults who cling to their group ways and beliefs in spite of the proximity of those they happen to despise, it should hold for children as well. Children are most likely to adopt those ways and beliefs pressed upon them by the dominant and significant influences in their life. These are surely to be parents and group elites and not the teachers and schools that the parents view with suspicion or disdain. For their part, these parents and group elites are likely to work harder to inculcate 'right belief' in their children if they sense that outgroup influences are working to impose 'wrong belief' upon them. So it seems unlikely that putting 'positive images' of alternative viewpoints and practices in front of the young and impressionable will do much to foster toleration, respect for diversity, or much of anything else championed by liberal sensitivities. Instead, it is more likely to further complicate the challenge of promoting toleration by making intergroup animosity all that much more extreme.

The second flaw with supposing the County's reader might teach liberal tolerance is that the claim is simply a *non sequitur*. One cannot teach liberal tolerance by working to cultivate respect for diversity; this goes beyond toleration presumably in the hope of eliminating intergroup animosity altogether. Toleration, once again, involves putting up with those one happens to find damned, disgusting, repugnant, or misguided by virtue of who they are or what they happen to believe. Cultivating respect for others would eliminate the need for toleration by making us at least indifferent to one another if not positively gleeful because of the socially enriching aspects of ethnic, cultural, and perhaps even religious diversity. If the elimination of intergroup animosity is the goal, then ironically it is a goal inconsistent with the requirements of practical liberalism, for it involves an effort to alter group beliefs and norms and to bring group thinking into line with a specific vision of the good. This is, to say the least, an assimilationist policy, and as such it displays the very intolerance that practical liberalism hopes both to expose and to prohibit.

There is considerable irony in all this. It is hard to imagine how anyone could think it sensible to generate respect for diversity by doing away with it; yet this is precisely what this line of argument hopes to achieve. It reduces, in the end, to the claim that some sorts of diversity are okay because they square with the way those groups advocating 'respect for diversity' want the world to be, but other sorts of diversity are not okay, and have to go, because they generate disrespect for diversity, that is, for the way those groups advocating 'respect for diversity' want the world to be. From the standpoint of practical liberalism, this view is as naïve as it is convoluted, and consequently, it is likely to exacerbate the very intergroup conflict it hopes to transcend. In fact, this is the dynamics of a politics of interests and merely returns us to the troubles associated with this manner of civil warfare. Groups that feel threatened by what they perceive as a form of group imperialism will likely retrench, fight back, and resist the assimilation being imposed upon them. Thus the dynamics of intergroup rivalry suggest that such assimilationist strategies (strategies associated with a politics of interests) are likely to have the opposite of the intended effect. The legal meanderings that bubbled out of Hawkins County offer compelling testimony in favor of this conclusion.

This is hardly a reasonable way to achieve a stable and secure political order. If such stability is to be achieved, the cultivation of toleration is required, and toleration is about the only thing that it is sensible to hope for here. Robert Fullinwider's quip that 'Politics requires that I respect that others are different, not that I respect them for their differences,' gets to the heart of the matter.[39] If, on the other hand, it makes little sense to insist that groups whose members regard certain outgroups as damned, disgusting, repugnant, or misguided by virtue of who they are or what they believe should learn to respect the targets of their animus, it does seem plausible to insist that they concede the desirability of tolerating them. Practical liberalism recommends a politics of principle as the most effective and enduring way for a polity to confront intergroup hatred and animosity. To succeed in such a politics, it is necessary to surrender the idea that we can or should try to transform diversity into unity and to focus instead on the effort to forge unity in the presence of diversity, where the diversity in question takes the society as it is and supposes the fact of intergroup hostility and animus.

Ironically, the conflict on display in *Mozert* suggests an apt approach to the teaching of toleration and citizen responsibility more generally. The lesson begins by admitting the disingenuous nature of the County's protestation that the text was used not just to teach critical reading but also to cultivate a sense of respect for diversity. In actual fact, the text presented a vision of social life endorsed by traditional moral liberals coupled with the Orwellian attempt to seize the moral high ground by contending that this vision displayed the morally necessary requirement to respect diversity. But there are some things good moral liberals should respect and other things they should not put up with. It seems unlikely, for example, that the moral liberals in Hawkins County would want to adopt a critical-reading text that gave a sympathetic presentation of members of the National Socialist Party of America stoning a Hasidic Rabbi or members of the Aryan Nation beating a black child. Liberals will see such things as an instance of the hatred that they love to hate. They are instances of disrespect, prejudice, and bigotry of the sort a civil society should work to eliminate. But this can be seen, when viewed through the prism of a different worldview, as a form of hatred and bigotry in its own right; and from a practical standpoint, it also demonstrates the politics of interests at work. Consequently, those worldviews and moral visions labeled disrespectful, hateful, or bigoted are dismissed as unworthy of respect or appreciation. What looks like an effort to teach respect for diversity thus reduces to another page in the saga of intergroup conflict; instead of teaching respect, the County's reader was a part of a larger political process that exacerbated intergroup animosity and inspired further conflict.

The resolution of the *Mozert* problem appropriate to practical liberalism is now reasonably clear. As a lesson in toleration, the County's reader was a crashing failure, and this itself is a lesson in toleration. The Mozerts would have been happy with a compromise that exempted their children from use of the reader, and this possibility makes some sense. Given the moral message of the text, it would seem that the educational elites in Hawkins County wanted to impose the worldview and moral theory of the human good to the liking of dominant groups in the community upon all groups in the community. Since the school district was operated by the County, this constitutes a violation of the non-interference condition. But of course even here the dual responsibilities of the government should be considered. Public schools are important elements of the socialization process of dominant groups, and the government can and should serve these interests also. It can do so, of course, provided it does not violate the non-interference condition in the process; and since this is precisely what it did in *Mozert*, an exemption for the children of fundamentalist families of the sort proposed would seem to be in order.

Yet, while this might seem like a sensible resolution to the tolerance problem posed by *Mozert*, things are not quite as simple as this. As centers of education about the responsibilities of citizenship, public schools should be required to explore the requirements of toleration and deference and to discuss how these things can be brought to life within the liberal polity. As the educational wing of the polity, this is a primary responsibility of publicly operated schools as well as a primary responsibility of all group-sponsored alternative modes of education. The education system is hardly the only social institution that carries this responsibility, however, though it certainly carries it more immediately than others. But if toleration is to come to life in the liberal polity, it must be promoted and discussed by groups in their intra-group institutions and arrangements and by other official institutions of the polity. Political education does not begin and end at the schoolhouse door; nor does it begin in kindergarten and end with high-school graduation.

In this regard, there is something to be said for allowing Amish children to leave public schools after the eighth grade. If we worry that this is not sufficient schooling to achieve a satisfactory appreciation for the responsibilities of citizenship, we can find solace in the fact that political education is an ongoing process to which the Amish, along with all other elements of the polity, will need to dedicate themselves. By leaving school, Amish children do not necessarily leave the educational process. The Amish in America, along with everyone else, continue to live in a fluid and shifting political climate. New intergroup conflicts arise; old political fissures reemerge; but the challenge of finding ways for disparate groups to live together remains essentially the same. Insofar as this challenge is continuously in front of us, the demands of a politics of principle also remain in front of us, and this can and should be a source of inspiration for ongoing education on the requirements of citizenship within the liberal polity.

If, however, the primary public responsibility of the educational system is instruction in citizen responsibility, can or should schools (public or private) teach things seemingly inconsistent with the demands of toleration and deference? This arguably is what the Hawkins County reader was doing. It presumably carried the message that we should not tolerate any manner of disrespect for others—or at least let us suppose that it carried this message. If so, then the text implies that we should not tolerate some of the groups that liberal toleration indicates that we should. This is reason to think that an exemption, which would free the Mozert children from the requirement to use the reader, does not go far enough. By advocating a moral viewpoint inconsistent with the responsibilities of citizenship, the text works against the ends of civic education, and this is reason to exclude its use altogether.

This suggests a possible cost for endorsing LP that may be too great for any group to bear. If groups are unable to teach group values and norms to their children because these things are inconsistent with the political morality inspired by practical liberalism, these groups are in trouble and their autonomy would seem to be severely compromised. Since it would be foolish for any group to endorse a political system that threatens group autonomy and integrity, groups might be better off taking their chances under a politics of interests. This is particularly troubling in the case of comprehensive groups that seek to control to the greatest possible extent the worldview and moral theory of the human good held by their members. The logic of practical liberalism, however, still seems consistent with the ends of even the most comprehensive groups. Acceptance of LP does not require any alteration or abandonment of basic group ways and beliefs; it requires only that one make necessary political accommodations that take into account the presence of others.[40]

In any event, in the particular circumstances that surround *Mozert*, things need not go this far. What matters is the ability of educators to distinguish their dual roles as facilitators for understanding civic responsibility and as spokespersons for the ways and understandings of the groups they represent. Moral liberals can still teach their children the importance of respecting certain forms of lifestyle diversity, and they can still teach them to suppose that those who fail to respect diversity display an unacceptable prejudice and bigotry. But as members of the public that is the polity, teachers must also make it clear that even moral liberals still need to learn to live with these people, and without making social conflict any worse than it already is. Ironically, these educational messages—the message of the group and the message of the polity—go hand in hand. Learning about a worldview or moral theory of the human good that inclines or encourages one to sense difference and disagreement with others may be essential if groups are to sustain themselves, but it is also the sort of thing that generates normative rivalries and inspires further intergroup hostility. So, learning at the same time about the challenges of living together in the presence of this hostility may be the best way to cultivate political unity amidst tremendous social, moral, ideological, religious, and cultural difference and hostility.

## Conclusion: The price of toleration

While some groups may think the price of endorsing LP high, there is reason to think it is not too high given the alternatives of a politics of interests or a politics of dominance. In at least one sense, understanding toleration in terms of putting up with others one finds loathsome and disgusting is misleading. Toleration does not mean that we cannot oppose these people, object to their way of life, and work to get them to change their ways or alter their beliefs. We are completely free under practical liberalism to attempt this sort of thing; liberal toleration limits only the means and strategies we can use to achieve our desired ends. As I have emphasized, here we must rest content with reasoned discourse and peaceful colloquy. We must try to reason with these people into changing their ways, but in doing so we cannot confront them in a manner that invades their ability to live as they wish, something social convention generally makes readily apparent. Given the depth of difference and incommensurability of group views associated with the fact of pluralism, recourse to reasoned discussion alone may not hold out much likelihood that groups will manage to get outgroups to see things their way and change their practices. Nevertheless, liberal tolerance does not lead to bad moral faith; it merely circumscribes the ways one can operate in the name of one's moral ends. There will be those who think this is too liberal, too equivocal, too tolerant. When confronted with grievous moral wrong, drastic measures are sometimes required to end it. But it is important to measure the social costs of such measures. The ebb and flow of intergroup conflict is generated all too frequently by moral righteousness on all sides, and all too often this exacerbates the very conflict practical liberalism hopes to pacify. While such conflict will hardly come to an end under LP, the divisive character of this conflict can at least be mollified in a manner that supports the maximum possible amount of group autonomy consistent with the same autonomy to be enjoyed by other groups, and this is an important reason why groups should endorse LP.

We have seen that liberal tolerance has other costs, but it does not seem like any of these costs are so great that groups would be better off under a politics of interests rather than under a politics of principle. Nevertheless, some worries should linger in this regard. Supporting political unity at the same time that one is defending normative and ontological diversity should now seem rather perilous. Practical liberalism gives rise to a political morality of toleration and deference to which government should resort when it comes to resolving tolerance and coordination problems. But this morality will also infuse itself in the hearts and minds of the polity, requiring good citizenship of people who also belong to groups with differing worldviews and normative schemes. Is it possible to be confident that with time the political morality of practical liberalism will not erode or transform the normative convictions of primary groups and thereby alter the nature of these groups themselves? If this is a real possibility, it might also be a reason for groups to reject LP and live with (at best) a politics of interests. These remain lively concerns to which we must now turn.

# 5
# Stability, Legitimacy, and the Liberal Polity

So far we have seen that groups living under the conditions identified by the fact of pluralism have strong prudential reasons to endorse and accept the politics of unity associated with practical liberalism. The failure to commit to such a politics leaves groups to fend for themselves amongst the uncertainty and instability invariably associated with a politics of interests and thus to risk falling victim to a politics of dominance. In the face of the uncertainty associated with the fact of flux, the stability that a politics of principle has to offer should seem terribly attractive, particularly since groups maintain, under LP, a maximum amount of group freedom limited only by the demands of liberal toleration and the requirements of deference. But doubts on this score are sure to linger, driven, perhaps, by either skepticism or cynicism about the likelihood that prudential reasoning can deliver on the promise of political stability. The purpose of this chapter is to explore and address these doubts.

The doubts I have in mind raise questions about the general stability of the liberal polity imagined by practical liberalism. These doubts might be expressed by imagining two problems that practical liberalism must address. First, one might wonder whether enough has been said to persuade reasonable skeptics that anyone would accept a politics of principle in the first place. Is the prudential argument sufficiently strong to guarantee that all groups in the polity would endorse LP? Second, and presuming a satisfactory response to this question, reasonable skeptics might also question whether the prudential argument is sufficient to demonstrate that the liberal polity will remain stable through time. If some group or coalition of groups thinks it has amassed sufficient political capital to successfully dominate its normative rivals, what is to prevent it from abandoning the *modus vivendi* established by the acceptance of LP and proceeding to pursue a politics of dominance? These are not really separate problems, however, but separate faces of the same problem. These concerns, presumably endemic to a *modus vivendi* arrangement, introduce the dilemma of political stability, and to address this dilemma it is necessary to develop further the prudential argument introduced above.[1]

## The theory and practice of political stability

There is a quick, ready, and incontrovertible response to the problem of stability that needs to be offered at the outset. Practical liberalism cannot *guarantee* that a polity that commits to LP will remain stable and not decay back into a politics of interests or toward a politics of dominance. Nor, for that matter, can any manner of theorizing about politics offer such a guarantee; all theorizing about civil association must make some presumptions about how people think and reason, and these might prove false on some occasions or under certain conditions. So, if it is a guarantee of political stability that is expected from practical liberalism, readers are sure to be disappointed, but not just in practical liberalism. But it does seem possible to say some things about how and why the problem of stability ought not be considered theoretically problematic, and this is what I want to do here.

The problem of political stability, as it has emerged in recent times, can be traced to the efforts of John Rawls to demonstrate the practical viability of his majestic theory of justice. Rawls endeavors to establish the stability of what he takes to be just institutions or a just civil arrangement by expounding on the conditions he thinks must obtain if people *qua* citizens are to remain loyal and committed to these institutions and this arrangement more generally.[2] Stability is a problem for a freestanding political system, he rightly contends, because the realities of pluralism indicate that there is no underlying comprehensive moral system that legitimates and justifies even just political institutions for all imaginable elements of the polity. Political institutions, this is to say, cannot be supposed to follow from and give political expression to some fundamental and presumably objective moral claim considered binding upon all elements of the polity.

This, as we have seen, is a viewpoint shared by practical liberalism. It is worth emphasizing, however, that practical liberalism is simply agnostic about the existence of some fundamental and objectively true moral viewpoint. The fact of pluralism as it is understood within the context of practical liberalism does not presume the truth of something like Berlin's theory of value pluralism, for example.[3] Practical liberalism avoids moral theory in general and for practical reasons; it presumes (under the fact of pluralism) that pluralist societies are composed of groups whose members share differing, mutually exclusive, and potentially hostile moral theories of the human good. Consequently, no univocal moral theory, even if it happens to be true, will be able to command the attention and acceptance of all elements of the polity. For reasons internal to the group beliefs of those groups whose moral theory of the human good happens to diverge from moral theory others think true, the latter theory (even if it really is true) will be unable to convince these groups of the justness or legitimacy of the political principles it articulates and the political institutions and arrangements it inspires. This, again, is why practical liberalism proceeds by initially severing political theorizing from moral thought and moral argument.

But this severance is the source of the problem of political stability. As Rawls poses the problem, 'How is it possible that there may exist over time a stable and just society of free and equal citizens profoundly divided by reasonable religious, philosophical and moral doctrines?'[4] Put this way, however, the question is apparently loaded, for Rawls is presuming in the question itself that the disparate doctrines that characterize pluralism, as he understands it, are *reasonable*. In general, Rawls seems to understand reasonableness as a characteristic of persons, although we may read him in a manner that suggests the reasonableness of persons is itself a consequence of the reasonableness of the moral theory of the human good to which they subscribe. Rawls characterizes the reasonableness and unreasonableness of persons as follows:

> Persons are reasonable in one basic aspect when, among equals say, they are ready to propose principles and standards as fair terms of cooperation and to abide by them willingly, given the assurance that others will likewise do so.[5]

\* \* \*

> Reasonable persons, we say, are not moved by the general good as such but desire for its own sake a social world in which they, as free and equal, can cooperate with others on terms all can accept. They insist that reciprocity should hold within that world so that each benefits along with others.

> By contrast, people are unreasonable in the same basic aspect when they plan to engage in cooperative schemes but are unwilling to honor, or even propose, except as a necessary public pretense, any general principles or standards for specifying fair terms of cooperation. They are ready to violate such terms as suits their interests when circumstances allow.[6]

Rawls does not think that a *modus vivendi* arrangement of the sort employed by practical liberalism can establish or guarantee the stability of the liberal polity because we cannot be sure of the reasonableness of the parties to the 'treaty arrangement.' Rawls imagines a *modus vivendi* as a treaty arrangement that works merely because it serves the current interests of the parties to the treaty. But he thinks these parties will be ready and willing to defect from the agreement if and when it is in their interests to do so.

'This background highlights the way in which such a treaty is a mere *modus vivendi.*' And by extension,

A similar background is present when we think of social consensus founded on self- or group interests, or on the outcome of political bargaining: social unity is only apparent, as its stability is contingent on circumstances remaining such as not to upset the fortunate convergence of interests.[7]

As is well known, Rawls's solution to the problem of political stability is to lobby for the presence of an overlapping consensus where the disparate moral theories of the human good present in the polity all recommend and advocate, each in their own way, acceptance of Rawls's political conception of justice for moral reasons, albeit reasons internal to these moral theories themselves. Thus Rawls supposes stability is achieved if his political conception is regarded as also a moral conception from the internal perspective provided by (what turns out to be) reasonable moral doctrines. Rawls answers his question about the conditions under which reasonable religious, philosophical, and moral doctrines will accept a political conception of justice (and thus assure its stability) by saying, in effect, that they will do so *because* they are reasonable. Put differently, this means that political stability is possible if (and only if) the moral demographics are right.

It is no doubt true that if the moral demographics are right (or to put the point differently, if a type of moral homogeneity exists in the polity), the problem of political stability will dissipate. And Rawls implies at times that states like the United States have achieved the stature of reasonableness. Put more cynically, we might take this to mean that liberal states, or states with historical liberal influences have become evermore liberal, that is, groups in the state have infused basic liberal views into their moral theories of the human good. It is far from certain, however, that all groups in liberal states, and particularly the United States, qualify as reasonable in Rawls's sense; and from their point of view, the cultivation of 'reasonableness' in Rawls's sense takes on the appearance of a politics of interests or a politics of dominance. They become the unseen or discounted minority that remain a source of potential instability and ongoing social conflict. And the politics of interests, from this perspective, continues apace. It may continue to marginalize and quiet these 'unreasonable' groups, or these groups may at some point manage to turn the politics of interests to their favor and possibly destabilize the state or transform the uncertain meaning of social justice in the state to favor their views.

So then, while an overlapping consensus argument might address the problem of political stability adequately when and where all groups in the state qualify as reasonable in Rawls's sense, this condition does not appear to exist in states like the United States where it is not difficult to find 'unreasonable' groups. When and where this is the case, the demographics are simply not right, and appeal to an overlapping consensus cannot resolve the problem of political stability—it can only shroud from view the ongoing dynamics of a politics of interests that tends toward a politics of dominance. This is the difficulty that practical liberalism seeks to address. Perhaps ironically, this is a problem of political stability, and contra Rawls and his followers, practical liberalism proceeds by insisting that this problem can only be resolved by appeal to prudential argument.

It is worth dwelling on the problem of stability a bit longer, for the implications of my concerns about the failings of Rawls's response to the problem of political stability complicate the problem somewhat. Hobbes, it will be recalled, insisted that the end of civil association was to establish a condition of peace, which could only be managed by escaping a condition of war. Hobbes, of course, understood this to involve surrendering oneself to a secular authority with sufficient power to forcibly (if necessary) maintain domestic tranquility.[8] A sovereign capable of maintaining social peace by means of force of arms may achieve political stability by coercive means, even if all elements of the polity refuse to acknowledge his authority, but this was hardly sufficient, in Hobbes's view, to guarantee political stability. Individuals and groups that refused to consent to his social contract remained in a state of war, both with the sovereign and presumably with all other elements of the state. A similar situation may arise under Rawls's overlapping consensus. The moral viewpoints of a considerable majority of powerful groups in the state may endorse Rawls's just political institutions; that is, a powerful majority of groups may qualify as reasonable in Rawls's sense. Backed by the support of these groups, government may be able, again by means of force of arms, to sustain a type of political stability. This will prove to be the case, for example, if unreasonable groups are too weak or diffuse to oppose effectively the power of the government supported by the dominant influences of 'reasonable' groups.

But this remains a potentially unstable condition. As times change, as the fact of flux works its magic, the balance of power may shift, and the stability of the state will be jeopardized accordingly. In Hobbes's terminology, what may look like a stable political system really is not all that stable because it remains a subtle condition of war and falls rather short of establishing the condition of peace Hobbes believed essential to political stability. As Hobbes recognized, genuine political stability is possible only if all elements of the polity commit to civil association. To put the point in the terminology of practical liberalism, real political stability is possible only by the establishment of a politics of unity. Correspondingly, political unity, I have argued, is possible only by means of the establishment of a politics of principle. But given the fact of pluralism (as this is understood under practical liberalism), it is not possible to make either a moral or an epistemological argument to support such a principle.

The account of liberal toleration above indicates that it is likely that no group in the polity will find complete favor with the politics of principle established by LP. It seems likely, that is, that all groups will think that desirable action plans are restricted by adherence to the demands of liberal toleration. It is possible that some (and perhaps a great many) groups in the polity will have moral reasons to think that the civil condition established by LP is acceptable from their moral point of view. In spite of the constraints it imposes upon their action plans, these groups may still conclude that this civil condition is morally desirable on balance, resulting in a political stability generated by a type of overlapping consensus. Such a possibility is necessarily considered a happy coincidence under practical liberalism, however, and not one that can be considered terribly realistic given the fact of pluralism. It follows, in a fashion Hobbes seems to have understood, that the only way to defend a genuine politics of unity is to rely upon prudential argument and to establish that it is in the short- and long-term interest of groups to accept a politics of principle both at present and into the future.

### The theory and practice of prudential argument

Rawls, following Brian Barry, supposes that *modi vivendi* are necessarily unstable because demographic changes may make it reasonable for some groups to defect from the 'treaty' in order to realize their interests.[9] The political unity achieved by endorsing LP must be considered to be at best the second-best social arrangement for all groups in the polity. (This may not be the case, of course, and will not be the case if some group's moral theory of the human good actually inclines them to endorse LP. But this is not a possibility that can be factored into the argument and for reasons just discussed.) Groups can thus be presumed to favor a civil arrangement premised upon their own moral theories of the human good and be willing to press in this direction if circumstances seem to be right. If and when they consider circumstances right, it is to be supposed that they would defect from the *modus vivendi* and endeavor to bring about their more desired social arrangement. So it would seem that any form of civil association premised upon a *modus vivendi* is bound to be unstable. Even if the prudential argument could work to establish an initial politics of unity, things would remain precarious. Groups would constantly be looking for an opening in which they could transform the civil arrangement into something more to their liking.

Given our operating assumption about the prudential rationality of the group members constituting the state, it can be supposed that prudential argument does speak importantly to everyone. Because group members are prudentially rational, they will accept the conclusions of arguments demonstrating where their best overall interests lie. As noted above, however, such arguments must be presented in hypothetical terms; prudential argument does not speak categorically to prudentially rational agents. When I introduced the prudence and profit arguments (Chapter 2), I mentioned three conditions that need to be satisfied in order to establish the prudential value of LP, and it would be good to review them here:

1. The cost LP imposes upon groups is slight.
2. The dangers to group life and group well-being under alternative forms of association are greater than the costs of accepting LP.
3. The risk of confronting these dangers is either great or indeterminate in the event groups elect to reject LP, while the costs of LP are certain and determinate.

The basic argument for LP attempts to show that under the dramatized social situation presented in Chapter 2 these conditions can be met, and therefore, prudent group members (or group elites) should endorse LP—and would do so if they behaved prudently.

We have also noticed three possible objections to the basic argument that correspond to the three conditions that its acceptance hangs upon:

1. The cost of endorsing LP is too great, perhaps because of the bad moral faith it requires.
2. The dangers to group life are not great, or not perceived to be great, because groups are confident about their dominant position in society and in their relative strength (as measured in terms of recognizable political resources) compared to other groups in the polity.
3. Group members are not as risk averse as the *prima facie* case of LP presumes. In the face of indeterminate risk situations, they may be inclined to take chances particularly if they think the moral stakes involved are high.

By way of response, it has been argued that LP does not lead to bad moral faith; it only imposes limitations upon the type of strategy that groups can use to promote their own moral ends in their dealings with outgroups. And it has been argued that the fact of flux undermines the confidence dominant groups can have in their ability to control their social environment and realize their own moral interests. Social change is perhaps the only constant of social life, and the forces that drive social change seem well beyond the control of groups short of the thorough-going domination imagined by George Orwell, a domination which is hard to imagine becoming a practical reality. And as I shall argue momentarily, the fact of flux confronts groups with such uncertainty that it is impossible to calculate the nature of the risk groups run if they contemplate defecting from the polity and working to promote a social arrangement more to their liking. If this is right, groups cannot effectively calculate the likely chances of success in such a move, and this is likely to make risk aversion an altogether prudent strategy.

We might take all this to mean that groups at some initial point of inquiry have reason to endorse LP and move to a politics of unity. But introducing the problem of political stability at this point jeopardizes this conclusion by suggesting that groups also have reason to defect from this arrangement if they suppose it is in their interest to do so. The basic argument for LP appeals to the fact of flux to trump or at least moderate the inclination of dominant groups to take advantage of whatever momentary advantages in strength or political resources they might have and therefore opt to pursue more imperialist strategies. According to the objection raised by the problem of stability, however, the fact of flux may just work in the opposite direction.[10] If social flux brings about a condition where a given group (or coalition of groups) is clearly dominant, why would it not be reasonable for that group to seize the opportunity to impose its will on others, perhaps confident that it now enjoys the strength to control the fact of flux. Since the fact of flux may work for, as well as against, them groups thinking they have come into a dominant position may (and not unreasonably) think it worth their while to defect from their commitment to LP and work to dominate the state. Since LP must be presumed always to introduce (at least) only the second-best civil arrangement for the social setting, groups whose members come to believe that they *can* dominate the polity and realize their most desired form of civil association at some point will surely be inclined to do so. Since this is always a possibility, the politics of unity imagined here is invariably going to be unstable and insecure, and so, at the very least, some reasons need to be presented in order to indicate that dominant groups should elect to be more risk averse than might initially seem plausible.

The problem being introduced is exacerbated by the fact that groups (or group elites) may not see or understand their social environment in the generalized (and perhaps rather antiseptic) terms employed by the prudential argument. They may be unaware of the group diversity actually present in the polity, or they may discount some groups as 'mere merchants of unwanted ideas' who are so far on the social fringe that they cannot be considered viable forces in society.[11] They may, in short, see their social environment more immediately, if less clearly, than is supposed by the prudential argument. Instead of seeing and being sensitive to intergroup conflict in general, they may see only certain conflicts; and with their own historical view of their social setting before them, they may see social consistency and the historic dominance of certain groups as an enduring feature of their social world. There is, for example, a commonplace view of American political culture that sees the United States as a predominantly (if not dominantly) liberal culture that is growing more liberal by the day.[12] From this vantage point, illiberal groups hovering at the social fringe need not be taken all that seriously, and the social conflict I have associated with the politics of interests in the United States might be dismissed, by dominant groups and students of American political culture alike, as a false and fraudulent problem. If groups do not see the problem of intergroup conflict and the politics of interests it inspires, if they do not recognize the social demographics in the manner critiqued by practical liberalism, they will not be inclined to endorse the politics of principle practical liberalism advocates. It is hardly necessary to embrace a remedy to a problem groups do not recognize.

This returns us, of course, to the problem of audience and the corresponding need to establish the legitimacy and pertinence of the social pathology that serves as the inspiration for political theorizing. If groups laboring or existing under a politics of interests do not see the social dynamics in the manner advocated by the theorist, theoretical inquiry is bound to fall on deaf ears. Prudential argument depends, in the final analysis, not simply on the presumed prudential rationality of all elements of the polity, but also upon the ability of theoretical inquiry to establish and defend the salience of the social pathology it has identified. This includes establishing the legitimacy of the account of the social environment that situates the theoretical project. If groups do not see the social dynamics and political conflict in the manner imagined by practical liberalism, group members will not calculate their best short- and long-term interests in the fashion anticipated by the basic argument.

To illustrate the importance of this problem, it will be helpful to look carefully at the prudential argument pressed by Hobbes, and to explore what I will call Hobbes's mistake. Hobbes is properly renowned for presenting a somewhat bleak picture of human nature. People in Hobbes's judgment are driven by fear and pride, and their behavior (to put it mildly) tends toward the asocial. Unless human beings manage to regulate themselves by suitable political institutions, they will live in a condition of war where 'there is no place for industry; because the fruit thereof is uncertain: and consequently no culture of the earth; no navigation, nor use of the commodities that may be imported by sea; no commodious building; no instruments of moving, and removing such things as require much force; no knowledge of the face of the earth; no account of time; no arts; no letters; no society; and which is worst of all, continual fear, and danger of violent death; and the life of man, solitary, poore, nasty, brutish, and short.'[13]

This is, to be sure, an ugly situation, and human beings would be idiots to settle for it if it is possible for things to be otherwise. Hobbes had no need for the heavy guns of moral argument to defend the legitimacy of civil association under the circumstances; the guns of simple prudence were heavy enough. If we do not put aside the problems that set us to preying upon one another and bickering with one another, we have little to look forward to. But if we do put them aside at least to the extent necessary to embrace civil authority, we have lots to look forward to. Faced with the stark and inhospitable circumstances imagined by Hobbes in his famous state of nature, anyone who was willing to risk the decay of civil association in the name of some religion, ideology, or moral conviction must be dismissed as a great fool. The case for prudence under these conditions seems unassailable. If it is almost certain that the life of man will be little more than a constant war of all against all in the absence of civil association, and if it is almost certain that humankind will live comfortably and prosperously under civil association, who would not opt for civil association regardless of the normative attachments they might happen to have?

But like any prudential argument, Hobbes's conclusion will be acceptable only if his audience is convinced that this accurately describes the choice situation that they actually face. But some of Hobbes's immediate critics, particularly Cumberland and Pufendorf, rushed to the apparent defense of humankind by insisting that Hobbes's characterization of human nature was well off the mark. Human beings, Pufendorf replied, were hardly the asocial creatures imagined by Hobbes; they are instead sociable beings who necessarily live in one another's company.[14] Pufendorf's account of human sociality is both more appealing and more reasonable that Hobbes's stark vision, but the corrective to Hobbes pressed by Pufendorf and Cumberland largely vitiated the force of Hobbes's prudential argument. The costs and benefits associated with endorsing some form of civil association were no longer as evident as Hobbes had imagined them. Or rather, the rational-choice context Hobbes imagined failed to move Pufendorf and Cumberland because neither believed his empirical generalizations that set the choice context were valid. If we reject Hobbes's bleak view of human beings, we simply refuse to embrace the empirical conditions that background Hobbes's rational-choice problem, and this is just what Cumberland and Pufendorf did.

In effect, Hobbes was hoist by his own petard. In order to make the choice of opting for civil association obvious and evident, he dramatized a choice situation in which presumably rational actors have everything to lose if they failed to opt for civil association and a great deal to gain if they did. But the dramatization proved largely unbelievable, and this was Hobbes's mistake. If the theorist's audience refuses to accept the choice context that situates prudential argument, prudential argument will be stillborn.

How, then, should practical liberalism proceed to address the problem of political stability in light of the reemergence, or reworking, of the problem of audience? Perhaps enough has already been said to convince my audience that the politics of interests, as on display in the United States, is a source of political instability and that a politics of principle is a preferable political scenario—but I doubt it. There is, then, reason to dwell further on the politics of interests as it operates in the United States in order to make it a more believable, a more realistic, account of the American political condition; but unhappily, doing so would take us well beyond the limitations of the present discussion. A second (and no doubt less satisfying) way to proceed is to beg this question and continue to examine the force of prudential argument by presuming or hypothesizing that the account of the politics of interests in the United States developed at the outset is accurate and compelling. *If* we concede the existence of the social pathology introduced by the politics of interests, can prudential argument establish a compelling case for a politics of principle capable of meeting the challenge posed by the problem of political stability? This is the theoretical difficulty (but not the practical dilemma) that the problem of political stability poses for the *theoretical* articulation and defense of practical liberalism.

The presumption being made supposes that the dramatization of the social conditions extant in the United States sketched at the outset is reasonably accurate, and that with sufficient study and reflection all elements of the polity can see that this is the case. It is important to emphasize, however, that this presumption does not violate the necessary commitment of practical liberalism to defend a theory of civil association that does not rest upon any normative or ontological claims that may be (and no doubt will be) considered controversial or objectionable to any group given the group's worldview and moral theory of the human good. It must be supposed that groups can grasp these demographics and understand the group dynamics present in the social environment independently of whatever worldview or moral theory of the human good they happen to hold. A simple description of the nature and dynamic of group life in a given social setting, this is to say, can (and from the standpoint of prudential argument must) be regarded as normatively and epistemologically naïve. I take this to be a reasonably innocent and unobjectionable component of the presumption being made. If, however, I happen to be wrong about this, prudential argument cannot serve the needs of theoretical inquiry, and the case for a politics of unity would appear to be hopeless.

Suppose, then, we rehearse again the sociology of liberal politics introduced above. The first key component of this sociology is the fact of pluralism. The fact of pluralism, once again, tells us that the social environment is composed of an extraordinary diversity of differing and potentially (and very likely) hostile worldviews and moral theories of the human good that are reflected in the belief systems and normative convictions of the groups they bring into being. The fact of pluralism is at the heart of the normative conflict that haunts the social setting, and this form of political conflict is a particularly unsettling and divisive presence in the social environment. Groups, in turn, have differing and shifting political resources that create political imbalances in the social setting.

If this accurately mimics the social environment in which groups find themselves, it might be instructive to imagine how they might be expected to behave under such circumstances and in the absence of organizing and coordinating agreements among them. There is in this regard a parallel with the interstate system that might be worth exploring. In international-relations theory, a group of thinkers inspired by the work of Hans Morganthau and associated with the school of political realism suppose that the international environment is characterized best by thinking of states as entities driven by the need/desire to increase their power vis-à-vis their fellow states.[15] In an uncertain and potentially (if not actually) hostile international environment, power seeking is the best way for states to sustain their security and promote their interests. Given the presence of normative and allocational rivalries in a given social setting and the corresponding absence of any generally accepted organizational structure, it would seem that groups would be inclined to behave this way as well.

Perhaps, however, this is beside the point since the group politics that concerns us here is already embedded in the organizational matrix supplied by the state. After all, the state's government exists (both in liberal theory and practice) to moderate and manage conflict, including the conflict generated by normative rivalries. But there are deeper problems here, for the state is not necessarily a neutral arbiter of intergroup conflict; it may, instead, be a mechanism that conflicting groups use and manipulate to their own advantage. If it is captured and controlled by dominant groups, or if it is up for grabs and able to be enlisted by currently dominant groups to their advantage, the government becomes a weapon that groups can use to their own advantage rather than an impartial referee of intergroup conflict. Realist logic still applies under this scenario, then, because groups now have reason to marshal what political resources they can in order to put the government to use to their advantage or defend against rival groups that use government in this way. Further, this is the scenario characterized by a politics of dominance and a politics of interests. Under such political arrangements, groups can be supposed to look for ways to strengthen their power and position vis-à-vis other groups. Under the politics of interests American style, this means groups will attempt, as best they can, to control the terms of political legitimacy and perhaps to expand political conflict in the event this fails. The result is intergroup struggle with groups exercising the resources at their disposal to maintain and expand whatever political advantage they may happen to have. Thus a politics of interests invariably tends toward a politics of dominance. And just as groups will seek to maximize their own power, they will also struggle against the similar efforts of outgroups to do so as well, for the struggle for dominance is also a struggle to make sure one is not dominated. So, a politics of interests is invariably unstable, and it will remain so until either some group or coalition of groups manages the thorough political domination that Orwell has so frighteningly imagined or a politics of unity is established.

A politics of interests is sure to make for strange political bedfellows (the enemy of my enemy is my friend), and will likely cause otherwise politically quiet groups to become politically active and mobilized as the ebb and flow of intergroup struggle brings about shifts in the political landscape. Presently more dominant groups cannot remain confident that they can marshal sufficient political resources to maintain their current political advantages, a point groups can readily understand if they recognize two basic features of realist politics. First, even the strongest states that have occupied a place of prominence in human history have collapsed with time. In the international environment, political dominance seems a fleeting thing, and the same seems true within state borders as well. The religious elites of Massachusetts Bay no longer control life in Massachusetts, and the Catholic control of Connecticut politics proved to be a fleeting thing. Mexican culture lost its control in Texas and California, though it now seems to be making something of a comeback.[16] Second, the nature of intergroup conflict is likely to shape and influence the nature of intragroup politics within all groups, including dominant groups. As new normative issues arise under the politics of interests, groups will need to evaluate them from their own normative standpoint, and this can generate change within the worldview and moral theory of the human good of the group itself, perhaps even splitting the group at least on specific issues.

Both these points illustrate aspects of the fact of flux. And it is worth entertaining the possibility that the greater the group diversity in a given social setting—the larger the realm of pluralist beliefs and normative convictions—the more uncertain and unstable group life becomes. Groups, and particularly larger groups, are bound to have strong and weak identifiers, and while some group members may walk in lockstep to the orders/instructions of group elites, it is probable that not all of them will do so. Weak identifiers, or individuals who belong to different and disparate groups, may split from the official position defined and articulated by group elites, or they may defect from group viewpoints and policies at some point in time. Consequently, group elites and group leaders cannot remain confident of the loyalty or commitment of their rank and file.

The fact of flux, then, is premised upon a simple history of the nature of inter- and intragroup life. Intragroup politics is an inescapable dimension of group life, and it is hard to imagine that anyone could hope to manage or control the drift and flow of intragroup dynamics, particularly when we appreciate the fact that group members are likely, in pluralist cultures, to identify variously with more than one group. But our understanding of the fact of flux should be further developed and embellished by noticing the way uncontrollable external factors affect and influence intragroup practices and intergroup conflict. The history of American politics can be told, for example, either by fixating upon the ability of the 'dominant culture' to assimilate immigrants, or by the struggles caused by the clash of immigrant groups as they bring new ways and new beliefs into the social setting.[17] There is a certain point and pertinence either way one tells the story, to be sure, but one fact remains regardless of how one elects to tell it: Immigration has changed the American socio-political landscape by introducing an ever-shifting power

172 The Liberal Polity

balance between groups and generating new and unpredictable sources of intergroup conflict. States can, of course, attempt to control their borders and thereby to control the nature of social change generated by the influx of new social influences. But in pluralist states, this too is likely to become politically controversial and the potential source of additional intergroup conflict.[18]

This description of the social environment and the workings of the fact of flux might not generate the concern and anxiety that follows from Hobbes's state of nature; but it should suffice to signal that even under a politics of interests American style, there is still reason for groups to worry about the insecurity and instability inherent in such a political condition. Under such a scenario, groups must face the tough challenge of managing to defend their own interests and ways of life. It should thus make sense for them to ask how they might construct a stable political arrangement that also maximally protects the ability of their members to live their lives as they wish. It looks as if groups can pursue either of two possible strategies to secure this desired end. They can endeavor to manage or control social change in order to sustain their ways of life against outside intrusion or aggression—a choice that leads ultimately to a politics of dominance. That is, they can attempt to amass sufficient political power to dominate their social environment and thus manage it to their liking. Or they can hit upon and support a workable *modus vivendi* and reach an agreement with the other groups in the social setting that permits all groups a maximum amount of autonomy compatible with a like autonomy for each group—a choice that heads in the direction of a politics of unity. The first choice, of course, is hardly viable; it is merely a continuation of the realist logic that generates problems of insecurity and instability in the first place. So, if groups see their political condition in the manner described above and if they respect the problem of instability that they consequently face, the choice of moving toward a politics of unity looks like the only acceptable move to make.

The basic argument for LP has already placed great weight on the fact of flux. Introducing the fact of flux into the social environment shifts the nature of the rational-choice problem groups (and group elites) face when considering the propriety of a politics of unity. Hobbes, it will be recalled, cast his prudential argument against the background of claims to scientific certainty. He sought to offer a compelling account of human nature, and if this account is right, only a great fool would not endorse Hobbes's conclusions. But few people believed his account, and so it became relatively easy to dismiss his argument. The basic argument for LP, on the other hand, rejects appeals to scientific certainty. It must do this, of course, because of the problem of audience. But there is little reason to attempt certainty of some sort here if recourse to uncertainty can do the same job, and perhaps even do it better. In the face of uncertainty, what sense does it make to risk the reward of a politics of dominance if it is hardly possible to calculate the likely chances of success and if there is historical reason to think that one cannot begin to calculate the multitude of variables likely to influence or control the likelihood of success? Of course, the risk factor associated with attempting or committing to a politics of dominance (or resting content with a politics of interests), indeterminate though it is, must also be balanced against the gains and losses associated with opting for a politics of principle. The discussion of liberal toleration provides at least some reason to think that the costs associated with accepting LP are not all that great, regardless of the group facing the choice situation, and the benefits are quite high. This is because with the acceptance of LP, groups are at least guaranteed by liberal toleration a reasonably extensive amount of group autonomy.

With this in mind, we can now make an effective response to the problem of political stability. The Barry/Rawls critique of prudential argument suggests that groups will opt for LP if (and only if) there is a basic balance of power between the groups that are party to the choice situation, and these groups would accept LP because *under these circumstances* it is in their best interest to do so. If these circumstances change, however, and it appears to groups that they can realize their interests more effectively (or realize more of their interests without the need for compromise) by defecting from the *modus vivendi*, they would surely do so. The same concerns that incline groups to accept LP at time $t$ should incline them to defect from LP at time $t + 1$, namely, the strategic pursuit of their basic interests. But the uncertainty introduced by the fact of flux alters the nature of the choice predicament, and this is why the prudential argument does not (and does not need to) hypothesize a basic balance of power in the initial choice situation. As we have seen, groups cannot calculate accurately or effectively the costs associated with staying with the status quo politics of interests, even if at time $t + 1$ they have (or believe they have) an advantage of political resources that might make them short-term winners in the politics of interests. For all they know, they will turn out to be long-term losers, and they cannot, with confidence, think otherwise. This uncertain and undesirable possibility must be balanced against the modest costs associated with committing to a politics of principle and the certain benefits that follow from making this move. The basic argument depends upon the conclusion that opting for LP under the circumstances is the prudentially rational thing to do, regardless of any group's evaluation of its political dominance at any particular point in time.

The choice situation groups face, it is important to add, is complicated by the fact that there is an indeterminate but apparently large number of groups involved in the equation. The As may dislike the Bs and thus be disinclined to enter a treaty arrangement with them, but the As might also worry about the fact that the C's hatred of the Ds might destabilize the social environment, that the E's hatred of the Fs might do so as well, and so forth. While the As might be willing to take their chances in open warfare with the

Bs, they must also reckon with the problems caused them by open warfare between the Cs and the Ds, and so on. This complicates any one group's ability to control the social environment and suggests that political unity may be preferable to dominance as a strategy for sustaining a stable and peaceful social environment.

So, the problem of stability seems to dissolve once it is recognized that the fact of flux is a constant in the equation. If it makes sense at time $t$ to opt for LP because of the indeterminacy of the risk associated with not doing so, coupled with the significance of the costs associated with running this risk and the benefits associated with not doing so, it makes sense at time $t+1$ to make the same choice. While the relative dominance of groups will change from time to time, this constant of political life should be understood as reason to sustain a prudential commitment to LP, rather than as reason to abandon this choice. The choice situation groups face, this is to say, does not change from time to time even though the relative political strength of groups will change—and no doubt change again. The ebb and flow of social forces—the workings of the fact of flux—is simply too indeterminate to make defection from the *modus vivendi* a viable option. It would invariably set off a chain reaction that groups contemplating defection cannot fathom and thus cannot begin to hope to control. The appreciation of this cost of defection through time is the source of the enduring stability of a political *modus vivendi* based upon prudential rationality.

It may be objected, however, (and rightly so) that this argument depends ultimately and unhappily upon the belief that groups will see and understand socio-political history in the manner recommended by practical liberalism, and this is hardly reasonable. The objection, I think, must be conceded, and in fact I have already conceded it. While it does not seem that the appeal to the fact of flux rests on any controversial or group-specific epistemological claims about historical forces or the like, and instead depends only upon a naïve review of the enduring ebb and flow of conflict in human history, some groups may have their own epistemologically, ideologically, or religiously driven view of history that fixes their understanding of things. Some groups, for example, may think that they are God's chosen people and that their god guarantees their final triumph in their ongoing struggle with outgroups. So, rather than live with these outgroups, they feel compelled by their faith to continue to war with them, confident in the end that their god will see to their final victory.

These groups will thus have reasons internal to their own worldview to continue their struggle with outgroups in the manner they think demanded by their god; and if this is understood to involve the use of violent and coercive strategies, there is little more anyone can say to them. By way of responding, albeit modestly, to this objection, however, it is worth emphasizing that there is little that any theoretical argument can say to such groups. No form of liberal theory, or republican theory for that matter, will have much practical impact on them. They elect, as they think they should, to live in what Hobbes would call a condition of war with the social world around them, and they qualify as unreasonable not only in Rawls's moralized sense of this notion but in the more prudential sense at home in practical liberalism as well. They have placed themselves beyond the reach of political theorizing, and consequently, they are problematic and unsettling not just for practical liberalism but for anyone who holds out hope that theorizing about civil association can contribute in some, perhaps small, way to furthering the stability and domesticity of the human condition.

But practical liberals might also point out to such groups that a commitment to a politics of principle of the sort associated with the acceptance of LP does not prevent them from dedicating themselves to their imperialist ways. Once again, it only places limits upon the strategies that can be used to further their group agenda. They are still at liberty to promote and advocate the universal acceptance of their group ways, but by means of reasoned discourse and open discussion only. If this is not sufficient, and if they prefer placing themselves in a state of war with the social world around them, the rest of us have no recourse but to deal with them accordingly. In the presence of such an ongoing and seemingly endless struggle with their adversaries, one wonders how long such groups will be inclined to suppose that their god demands such a strategy. One wonders if perhaps the counsel of prudence might not eventually make itself evident even to such dogmatic groups, and one can hope that with time and the costs of intergroup warfare, prudential insight will eventually prevail. It is difficult for the liberal spirit to believe that even the most dogmatic groups will continue to pursue destructive and catastrophic political strategies in the face of increased evidence that they are invariably counter-productive. Perhaps this is simply a failing of the liberal spirit, but it can still serve as an inspiration for keeping channels of communication open even with groups of this sort in the hope that at some point they will recognize the wisdom of listening to the counsel of prudence.

## The pursuit of political legitimacy

The embellishments to the basic argument for LP offered above present what I take to be an effective response to the problem of political stability. *If* groups are persuaded by the argument that endorsing LP is the right thing to do and a politics of principle is the best prudential choice open to them at any point in time, this conclusion will remain compelling regardless of any future changes in their political resources or political position in the polity. The fact of flux, in short, works to support rather than defeat the basic argument for LP. While we can still follow Rawls in likening the *modus vivendi* arrangement imagined under practical liberalism to a type of treaty, it is also a treaty condition that will continue to serve the prudential interests of groups through time and regardless of changes in the political strengths of the groups constitutive of the polity. The recognition and acceptance of this point provides groups with reason to develop socio-political mechanisms in the polity that will further promote and safeguard political stability. The primary move in this direction involves cultivating a sense of political legitimacy in the polity.

Political legitimacy is the keystone of a stable polity. No matter how just, decent, or fair a system of government happens to be, it will be in trouble if it fails to be recognized as legitimate. Correspondingly, no matter how unjust, indecent, or unfair a system of government might be, it will likely endure if it is generally accepted as legitimate. Discussions of political legitimacy typically begin with the introduction of a key distinction between the type of authority enjoyed by government. The notion of *de facto* authority focuses attention on the question of whether a political system has the acceptance and allegiance of the people subject to its authority. Although outsiders may think there is precious little to be said for a particular state, it still qualifies as *de facto* legitimate if its government is accepted as authoritative by a sufficient number of those citizens subject to its authority. *De facto* authority, in other words, is fundamentally a sociological matter. *De jure* authority, on the other hand, is concerned with the justness of the political system in question. A state is considered authoritative or legitimate in this sense only if it meets certain basic and compelling standards of justice, regardless of whether it is actually accepted as legitimate by those subject to its authority. Political systems that are legitimate in the *de jure* sense are authoritative as a matter of right and not because they are considered legitimate as a matter of fact.[19]

With this distinction in mind, it could be argued that there is no room for the notion of *de jure* political authority within practical liberalism. Before it is possible to talk intelligently about such legitimate authority there must be some independent moral standard against which to measure the justness (and hence the rightful authoritativeness) of a political system. But because practical liberalism proceeds from prudential argument alone and deliberately rejects the relevance of any antecedent moral concerns for political argument, it cannot avail itself of any moral grounds upon which to evaluate the legitimacy of the state. This, in turn, might seem to jeopardize the ability of practical liberalism to defend a theory of political legitimacy capable of promoting political stability in the polity. If practical liberalism cannot establish independently the *de jure* authority of the liberal polity, it lacks the necessary antecedent normative foundation necessary to show that the polity ought to be considered legitimate by its own citizenry. And if this is the case, it is bereft of the necessary normative base required to develop and promote a form of actual legitimacy in the polity. If it cannot promote this legitimacy by means of reasoned argument that proceeds from unassailable moral premises, it can hardly hope to achieve the political stability that comes with the general recognition of the legitimacy of the polity.

But it would be a mistake to suppose that practical liberalism is void of the normative grounds upon which a sense of *de jure* authority in the polity can be based. It is important to distinguish here between the reasons one has to commit to some form of civil association and the nature of the commitment one makes for either moral or prudential reasons. While we cannot suppose that groups have moral reasons to commit to LP (though they might have such reasons) and while we must suppose, in turn, that prudential reasons are compelling in this regard, the commitment to LP is itself a commitment to a normative posture—a form of political morality—that controls and determines (for the most part) the role and responsibilities of government in the liberal polity. Thus the demands of liberal toleration and deference that follow from LP, or that are accepted under LP after public discourse and deliberation on the subject, generate the normative base that powers a sense of legitimacy within the liberal polity. I shall have more to say about the nature and significance of this political morality in the following chapter; at present it is sufficient to recognize its presence in the liberal polity and grasp the important contribution it can and should make to the legitimacy, and hence the stability, of the polity.

By committing to LP, the groups constitutive of the polity commit to a particular and distinctive political morality. They commit, that is, to organizing themselves according to the requirements of a principle that promotes and safeguards the maximum amount of equal freedom for all groups in the polity. By committing themselves to this principle, and by recognizing that doing so is in their best interest on balance, they must also be understood to dedicate themselves to this principle and to the political morality that it brings into existence. They dedicate themselves, in other words, to a common commitment in spite of the significant normative and ontological differences they may have. And they expect other groups in the polity, as well as political officials, to dedicate themselves to the ends associated with this political morality as well. Under practical liberalism, all groups in the polity must be understood to be linked to one another by a common commitment and dedicated to a common enterprise, namely, making sure that the liberal polity measures up to the motivating ideal articulated, albeit obliquely, by LP. This is the pivotal spirit of a politics of unity, a spirit driven by the conviction inherent in practical liberalism that political unity is possible in spite of the normative and ontological diversity that might separate groups sharing a common social setting.

Legitimacy of the sort required to sustain political stability must be cultivated in the polity, of course; and this returns us to our earlier reflections about the importance of educating the children (*qua* future citizens) of the polity on the value and necessity of civil association. Given the implications of the fact of flux, groups must be understood to commit to a politics of unity through time, and thus to promote political stability by passing along the tradition of civil association that characterizes the polity to their

children. This begins with the cultivation of an appreciation for the importance of civil association as the best means for enabling groups existing
under conditions of pluralism to coexist under the peaceful conditions that
permit their members to maximally live their lives as they wish. While this
is itself a prudential and not a moral commitment, it involves committing
to the distinctive political morality introduced by LP. So, while civic education begins with the development of an appreciation for the practical need
for civil association, it must quickly continue by fostering some sense of
the requirements of liberal toleration and deference as well as some understanding of why these things matter.

The cultivation of a civic consciousness and civic identity will require
group members to develop a fairly complex sense of themselves as members
of disparate groups, namely the primary group(s) to which they happen to
belong as well as the group that is the polity. And just as group members
will largely define themselves in terms of the normative and ontological
convictions of the primary group(s) to which they happen to belong, they
will also define themselves, as least partly, as members of the public that is
the polity by internalizing the group norms (liberal toleration and deference)
that help define and orient this particular group.

This latter requirement may seem like tough duty, particularly for those
imperialistic groups with clearly defined normative rivals they consider
damned, disgusting, repugnant, or misguided by virtue of who they are
or what they believe. According to internal primary group norms, these
outgroups are not to be tolerated; instead, they must be eliminated, segregated, or assimilated in the name of the internal norms and ideals that these
groups hold dear. Yet according to the internal norms of the group that is the
polity, these groups are to be tolerated in spite of the basic conviction that
they should, according to primary group norms, be eliminated, segregated,
or assimilated. *If* we see and regard this as a contradiction, the legitimacy
of the liberal polity is again cast into doubt—and the stability of the liberal
polity cast into doubt, once again, at the same time. Why would primary
groups become unfaithful to their basic group norms and convictions and
adopt a set of norms and convictions inconsistent with their moral theory
of the human good?

This concern, however, is simply a restatement of the problem of bad
moral faith already discussed. To respond further to this problem, it should
be recognized that there really is no contradiction here. Groups are not asked
under practical liberalism to surrender, amend, or abandon their basic beliefs
or moral theory of the human good; instead, they are asked/required only
to alter/amend the kinds of strategies they can properly employ for the realization of desired ends. As we have seen, they remain fully able and entitled
to argue and lobby for the elimination, segregation, or assimilation of their
normative rivals, but they are not permitted to act upon coercive strategies
designed and intended to bring about their desired ends. If toleration, as a

political virtue, is to make any sense at all, it must be considered possible for groups to balance these separate concerns and put up with outgroups, in the minimalist sense required by LP, while still holding their convictions about the need to do something about them. Practical liberalism holds that it is in a group's best interest to find ways to live with its normative rivals rather than remain in a volatile and hostile social environment where political stability is a mere chimera; and it also holds that if groups recognize this point, they will be willing to cultivate a sense of the political morality that accompanies practical liberalism even though this requires them to amend or alter the types of strategies they might prefer to use in dealing with their normative rivals.

Themis, the Greek goddess of justice, is notorious for the blindfold she wears. The blindfold is supposed to symbolize the fact that justice does not see those subject to her authority and works her will by focusing only upon the salient standards of desert that guide her decisions. Under practical liberalism this means that groups must commit to the idea that the same standards of justice that work to safeguard their group autonomy also work to safeguard the autonomy of their normative rivals. The requirements of liberal toleration and deference hold for all groups or they cannot work their magic for any group. This is not only reason for groups to take seriously a commitment to the ideals associated with LP, it is also reason for groups to discuss, explore, and develop the demands of social justice under practical liberalism. This too is an element of the cultivation of a political morality necessary to sustain the legitimacy of the polity. As we shall see, groups not only need to know what social justice requires, that is, what liberal toleration and deference demand of them, but they also need to be willing to reason through these demands in order to formulate viewpoints on how the operative standards of social justice should be implemented in order to best resolve future tolerance and coordination problems. It follows necessarily that the cultivation of a sense of political legitimacy in the polity involves open debate and discourse between *and within* groups on the meaning and implications of those normative standards of legitimacy that animate the polity.

It may be supposed, however, that this would be objectionable to some particularly authoritarian groups because it necessitates taking political discussion to the rank and file and removing it from the (perhaps paternalistic) control of group elites. Practical liberalism has no objection to leaving the civic relations of groups in the hands of group elites if this is characteristic of group ways. But two important qualifications must be noted in this regard. First, groups may have no ready way of determining who their future elites will be or which of their children will emerge as group leaders in the future. When this is the case, the education of all children in the group should include the cultivation of the standards of political legitimacy. Second, because the commitment of the group to LP is presumed to endure through time, the importance and logic of civil association should be made apparent to the children of all groups. Groups whose children fail to understand or appreciate the necessity and logic of civil association, but who learn to recognize certain outgroups as normative rivals because of who they are or what they believe, may find that their children are inclined to defect from the *modus vivendi* because they are motivated by the normative ideals of the group and are not sufficiently aware of the political costs and dangers of doing so. It follows, then, that even the most authoritarian groups should be expected, under practical liberalism, to see to the citizenship training of their children, even if these children play no crucial or significant role in the political involvement of the group in the polity once they reach adulthood. To assure political stability based upon a general appreciation of the legitimacy of the polity, all citizens of the polity should be expected to have some familiarity with the standards of legitimacy that underwrite the polity and regulate intergroup relations.

## Uncertainty, risk aversion, and choice

So far, I have presented the problem of political stability, as it arises under practical liberalism, as something of a rational-choice problem. In fact, it might seem like the choice predicament that groups must face according to the basic argument for LP is really just a version of the famous Prisoner's Dilemma and is best characterized in these terms. If we understand the argument in this fashion, it may also be argued that the parties to the choice problem must be terribly, perhaps even unnaturally, risk averse to set aside working toward their most preferred social arrangement in favor of the compromise advocated by practical liberalism. This way of understanding the case for LP has important implications for the problem of political stability because defection is a classic problem for rational-choice argument. To conclude my defense of the stability of the polity under practical liberalism, then, I want to explore this view of the prudential argument.

The problem of defection that accompanies rational-choice argument is simple enough. Suppose a group of neighbors are accustomed to burning the leaves that litter their yards in the fall and have found that if everyone burns their leaves the air around the neighborhood is foul and hazardous to the neighbors' health. They agree among themselves to stop burning leaves and independently assume the cost of carrying their leaves to the city dump for disposal. Suppose, however, that one of the neighbors, Jones let's say, discovers that he can burn his leaves and not have any appreciable effect on the air. If he defects from the agreement, he can benefit from the clean air produced by the agreement and avoid the cost of taking his leaves to the dump. This, it seems, is the rational thing for him to do, and so Jones has reason to take a free ride under the circumstances. So, of course, does everyone else in the neighborhood; yet if everyone in the neighborhood elects to take a free ride, the *modus vivendi* arrangement collapses, and the neighbors are back at square one. Is this the sort of problem that will plague the prudential argument for LP?

We should keep in mind here that the good jeopardized by defection from the *modus vivendi* is both a collective and non-excludable good, that is, a good that will benefit all parties concerned and that cannot be denied individual defectors if enough participants in the agreement do not defect, thus assuring that the good is realized. If Jones, and only Jones, defects from the agreement not to burn leaves, Jones, along with all the neighbors, will still realize the good of clean air, for there is no way the neighbors can deny him this good. So, if Jones is confident that the other neighbors will keep their word, it is rational for him to defect and take a free ride, that is, realize the desired good without assuming the accompanying cost. So, the agreement is inherently unstable; if it is rational for Jones to defect if he assumes others will keep to the agreement, it is rational for everyone to defect under the same circumstances.

In the case of practical liberalism, the good to be realized by keeping to the *modus vivendi* is the social peace and political stability generated by the acceptance of LP, a peace that guarantees participants the independence necessary to live their lives as they wish. It should be evident, however, that this is hardly a collective good. The polity as understood under practical liberalism is typical of political life more generally because we can suppose that the parties to the *modus vivendi* anticipate the possibility of defection and attach a cost to it in the form of criminal punishment. The enforcement powers granted the government constitute an external incentive not to defect by attaching a cost to defection presumably greater than any benefit gained from defection. In effect, the imposed cost of defection is (at least) a partial loss of group autonomy because outgroup sanctions are bound to interfere with internal group governance, and of course freedom from such interference is the major benefit of group participation in the *modus vivendi*. Consequently, the good of peaceful coexistence with one's neighbors cannot be properly conceived as a collective good. Defectors can be understood to reject LP and thus to place themselves in a state of war (to borrow from Hobbes) with the polity around them. Since nothing is owed to defectors of this sort, they are no longer guaranteed the group autonomy they would enjoy under LP, and they are subject to the coercive might of the government without the benefit of the rights and liberties that are enjoyed by members of the polity.

Further, it seems reasonable to suppose that defection will be readily apparent under practical liberalism, for it involves committing to strategies designed and intended to eliminate, segregate, or assimilate outgroups by coercive means. Outgroups are sure to notice such strategies and appeal to government for aid and relief. If defecting groups defend their behavior by insisting that the burden of tolerance is on their side (claiming, in effect, that they are not defecting at all), it falls to government to adjudicate the question. If a group loses this dispute, it must either live with this decision or, by failing to do so, establish itself as a defector. Since the costs of defection would seem to be high—the value of group autonomy is presumed to matter greatly to groups and not worth risking—and would also seem to be reasonably certain, the likelihood that a group will manage to take a free ride seems quite remote. Accordingly, the likelihood of defection should be considered quite remote.

But of course, this argument does not take into account the relative political strengths of the disparate groups that make up the polity. More powerful or dominant groups may feel confident that they can defect with impunity and avoid political sanction by controlling or capturing the power of government. Only rather weak and politically vulnerable groups would be disinclined to defect, fearful of the coercive might of government as sustained by the more dominant groups in the polity. But the defection of dominant groups is almost certain to rip the *modus vivendi* apart. If weaker groups see that dominant groups have defected from the treaty, the *modus vivendi* will collapse because they can no longer look to government for defense against the coercive strategies of outgroups. This will send the social environment back into a politics of interests or toward a politics of dominance and set off a political dynamic that (as we have seen) dominant groups cannot be certain they can control—and almost certainly cannot control through time. So even dominant groups cannot manage to take a free ride either. If they defect, the desired good of social peace and stability is automatically placed in doubt, for their defection puts an end to the treaty and thus to the good the treaty assures.

Still, this argument will fail to satisfy anyone who remains puzzled over what might look like a paradox within practical liberalism. Groups are supposed under practical liberalism to opt for a form of civil association that is (at best) their second most desirable socio-political arrangement. Given their moral theory of the human good, groups can be supposed to prefer to have everyone live according to their moral vision and to eliminate from the social environment (one way or another) groups that refuse to do so or that are considered anathema by virtue of who they are or what they believe. In spite of the social demographics of the polity and/or the relative political strength of various groups, practical liberalism holds that the polity will be stable because this arrangement is the best bet (most prudential choice) for groups, all things considered, *provided certain sociological conditions associated with the fact of flux obtain*. I have already discussed an objection to this possibility based upon a group concern of bad moral faith. But a similar objection can be pressed from the standpoint of rational-choice argument that further exposes the apparent paradox lurking within practical liberalism. From a rational point of view, groups can be supposed to remain wedded to their most preferred socio-political arrangement and choose to pursue it if and when they think they can get away with it. It would be irrational for a group to adhere to a politics of unity if they supposed their most preferred socio-political arrangement can be realized with a bit of work and effort. Dominant groups must therefore be supposed to be extraordinarily risk averse to elect not to pursue their most preferred arrangement if and when the time seems right.

The paradox is this: Why should dominant groups remain faithful to the *modus vivendi* if they calculate that their chances of realizing their most preferred socio-political arrangement are sufficiently good to be worth the risk? If groups do happen to calculate the odds to be in their favor and if they are seriously committed to their own moral theory of the human good, defection is the rational choice, and so much the worse for practical liberalism. It is simply paradoxical to suppose, as practical liberalism seems to do, that groups would be risk averse to the point of irrationality.

Suppose we consider this a rational-choice problem. According to practical liberalism, groups are presumed to make choices premised upon their understanding of their best interests; this as we have seen is the point of prudential argument. Groups are presumed not to be so irrational or suicidal that they will jeopardize their best long-term interests in order to achieve some desired but seemingly unattainable good. But gambling or risk-taking is not necessarily itself irrational. If a group calculates that it has a ninety-eight percent chance of realizing its most desired socio-political arrangement and a one hundred percent chance of not doing so if it opts for a politics of unity, it might seem altogether reasonable for the group to take the gamble. And where this possibility exists—as it does under practical liberalism—the stability of the *modus vivendi* hangs daily upon the way various groups calculate their chances of success if they elect to defect.

This means, in effect, that the question of political stability under practical liberalism hangs upon the types of calculations groups are likely to make regarding their chances of success if they defect from the *modus vivendi*. So it is worth exploring how such calculations might be made. Jon Elster has suggested, cogently in my view, that there is something inherently irrational about making rational choices.[20] Rational action differs from impulsive, irrational, erratic, or emotionally driven action on the grounds that a rational chooser is presumed to act upon beliefs which he or she has reason to think are true and accurate. Rational choice, this is to say, depends upon the presence of certain data that the chooser accepts as valid and determinative. But how does one know one has sufficient data to make a reasoned choice? It is always possible that the data one has is not sufficient, and therefore a rational chooser should always be searching for more data before making a choice. To suppose that, at any point in time, a chooser has sufficient data to make an informed choice is to presume infallibility, and no group can have sufficient data, or sufficient faith in the data it has, to make such a presumption. So it would seem that either one must choose arbitrarily or not choose at all because one is still collecting the data required to guarantee one will make the right choice.

In actual practice, of course, conventional wisdom supplies us with the data we need to make rational choices, and we make such choices because we are confident both in the data we have and in the belief that we have sufficient data. Risk aversion, in turn, is best measured by weighing the likelihood of desirable outcomes against the likelihood of undesirable outcomes in conjunction with an estimation of the desirability and undesirability of the projected outcomes. Imagine that Smith is contemplating the possibility of surgery. Suppose, according to current wisdom, there is a one hundred percent chance that she will die of dreaded disease X in two days if she does not have surgery and a ninety-eight percent chance that she will not survive the surgery if she has it. Provided Smith has reason to believe the percentages, she will opt for surgery. This, to be sure, seems a relatively easy case. But suppose instead that there is a one hundred percent chance that Smith will live in minor pain for the rest of her life (however long that happens to be) if she does not have the surgery and a two percent chance that she will not survive the corrective surgery that would relieve the pain for the rest of her life if she survives. Would it still be rational for Smith to opt for the surgery?

The latter situation introduces, I think, a much harder call. Yet the call again hangs upon our confidence in the attached percentages. Gambles make sense, at least from a rational point of view, only by calculating the odds; or perhaps this is not really gambling at all, for by calculating the odds one hopes to take (something of) the gamble out of the decision process. Risk taking, to be sensible, involves being clear on the nature of the risk undertaken. I have heard people who enjoy bungee jumping say that they engage in this activity because they enjoy taking risks. Bungee jumping, of course, involves jumping off a high bridge with an elastic cord tied to one's ankles; and while the cord seems rather long, it is guaranteed to be shorter than the distance to the ground. I fail to see the risk in this; while one is jumping off a high bridge and hurtling toward the ground, the jumper is presumably confident that the cord will prevent him from falling to his death. Perhaps there is a small chance that something will go wrong—the cord will break perhaps or not be fastened properly to the bridge—but this possibility does not seem to be a part of the jumper's calculation. One wonders, on the other hand, how many bungee jumpers there would be if it was understood as a part of the activity that the cord would not be fastened to anything for one jumper in ten, leaving one jumper in ten to fall to his death.

Guaranteeing that one bungee jumper in ten would fall to his death would no doubt not only put risk into bungee jumping, but it would likely also diminish the number of people who go in for this sort of thing. Perhaps more people would get involved (and we would get a better sense of the psychology of risk aversion) if we changed the odds somewhat. Would more people pursue the 'thrill' of bungee jumping if the odds of certain death were one in one hundred (or one thousand) rather than one in ten? Presumably, the less the likelihood of death (ostensibly an undesirable outcome) the more less-risk-averse individuals would be inclined to experience the thrill of bungee jumping and the risk of death. Again, however, the logic of risk aversion depends upon a calculation of the odds of a positive outcome coupled with a clear sense of the good to be gained by running the risk balanced against the severity of the undesirable outcome that is risked.[21]

If this aptly characterizes the psychology of risk aversion, we can appreciate the problem rational choosers face when it comes to remaining faithful to LP. Here, uncertainty is present on two fronts. First, there is no way to calculate the likelihood of an undesirable outcome; the fact of flux guarantees that groups will be unable to calculate the likely consequences of their defection from the *modus vivendi*. They can have no way of knowing how other groups will respond to their actions or deal with the threat to the civil peace generated by their actions. Second, and largely because of the first uncertainty, groups are unable to calculate the severity of the possible evil their actions generate. Not only do groups have no way of determining the odds of realizing an undesirable outcome if they defect; they also have no way of calculating the extent or magnitude of the undesirable outcome they risk by opening this Pandora's box by defecting. Groups can know, of course, that the consequences of defection may be potentially great and will be great if it thrusts the polity back into a politics of interests they are unable to control, but of course they will also know that things might not actually turn out this way. However, they cannot assign odds to either possibility—the variables involved are just too great to allow for such calculations.[22]

In the face of such uncertainty, there is simply no basis upon which to calculate the reasonableness of the gamble associated with defection. Imagine someone who values his life deciding whether to take up bungee jumping and being told that if he elects to jump there is just no telling what the outcome will be. He could fall to his death or the cord could break his fall; there is just no way to know. Consequently, there is no way to calculate the odds of achieving either a desirable or an undesirable outcome.

Uncertainty, however, troubles only half the choice equation associated with accepting and adhering to LP. The certainty of political stability and the accompanying social peace and tranquility should also be factored into the choice situation. This stability guarantees all groups a maximum amount of group autonomy and prohibits groups only from interfering coercively in the ability of outgroups to live as they wish. If we assume groups are not suicidal, if, that is, we assume groups are prudentially rational in the sense discussed above, this does not seem like such a terrible cost. If this is still a second-best political condition for all groups in the polity, it cannot fall very far below any group's most desirable political condition on a preference scale, no matter how intensely a group may detest its normative rivals. If the Crazy Betas would rather die en masse than live peaceably with the Innocent Alphas, there is nothing practical liberals (or any other theory) can say to them to prevent ongoing and probably violent conflict between these two groups. The presumption of the prudential rationality of groups, as we have seen, is a necessary precondition of the theoretical project. But it is also the most minimal presumption necessary to attempt to make a theoretical case for a politics of unity amidst tremendous normative and ontological diversity. With the presumption in place, however, we can conclude that the social peace possible under a politics of unity will have considerable attraction to groups that otherwise face uncertain and unknowable outcomes from a politics of interests, leading perhaps to the most undesirable outcome of a politics of dominance where they happen to be the dominated.

## Social dynamics in theory and practice

It seems, then, that concerns about the instability of the *modus vivendi* associated with practical liberalism are misplaced. Treaty arrangements that depend upon a balance of power are indeed unstable if we suppose the distribution of power is alterable in knowable and predictable ways and if the arrangement is less desirable than some other arrangement that each party lacks the power to realize. If A enhances his power vis-à-vis B, then B will be in trouble. Since there is no reason to suppose that A will not try to enhance his power, it is in B's best interest to do so as well. This explains Morganthau's contention, aimed at the international arena, that states not only do, but should, seek power.[23] If states continue independently to seek power, the power balance that initially made the treaty seem like a good idea may be distorted, but it is difficult for states to be certain of this—for they need to continually assess and reassess the power of their adversaries. By continuing to seek power, states continue to build stability into the treaty arrangement.

In the case of the social dynamics associated with accepting and adhering to LP, an accurate reading of the power balance is made problematic by the fact that groups cannot know what their defection will do to the existing power distribution. Given the fact of pluralism, there are just too many groups in play to calculate accurately the consequences of defection, and it is hard to imagine, given the fact of flux, that any group will become powerful enough to control through time the response all other groups will have to its defection.

So then, the strength and stability of a *modus vivendi* depends upon the type of uncertainty I have been exploring. Where this uncertainty is present, and where the good realized by some treaty ranks high on the preference scale of all parties to the treaty, the treaty in question is bound to be stable. Objections to *modus vivendi* arrangements depend upon the claim that certain and knowable power imbalances may arise, but this is the very claim negated by the fact of pluralism in association with the fact of flux. It is worth repeating, however, that the argument for political stability under practical liberalism still depends upon groups recognizing the sociological conditions that underlie the basic argument for LP. Accordingly, it is also worth considering the viability or legitimacy of this sociological view.

Let me put the point in the form of an objection to the prudential argument. Why, a critic might ask, will or should groups see their social environment in the generalized sense required by the basic argument? Instead of imagining a welter of faceless and nameless groups each with its own worldview and moral theory of the human good, why not put a more informed social face on the social environment. If we look at the United States, for example, we can identify specific groups with specific power relations. We will see Catholics, Protestants, Jews, the Aryan Nation, socialists, libertarians, black nationalists, Native-Americans, liberals of various stripes, fundamentalists, the Followers of Christ and the like, and so on. And we will see various power differentiations among all these groups. Even if we concede that the list of groups seen or recognized by other groups is bound to be incomplete and group-specific (as well as time- and place-specific), it will be this vision of society that drives group thinking about the desirability of endorsing LP and committing to a politics of unity. While it will make sense for small and relatively powerless groups to commit to a politics of unity, it will make no sense for groups that sense they are in a position of dominance to do so. So in practice, we cannot expect groups to see their social setting in the fashion that practical liberalism requires; and consequently, even if practical liberalism is theoretically coherent, it lacks practical political applicability in places like the United States.

This is a substantial objection, and one that can be answered, from the standpoint of theoretical inquiry, only by supplying all elements of the polity with reasons to be insecure about their own sociological vision of the social world around them and by reminding them of the peculiar and potentially insidious workings of the politics of interests. I will suppose that enough has been said about the latter point already, but more needs to be said about the former one.

The sociology underlying practical liberalism is informed by the socio-political history of humankind as well as the social demographics of modern pluralist polities like the United States. From socio-political history, practical liberalism takes the fact of flux, the nature of normative rivalry, and the challenge posed by the struggle groups face as they seek to live as they think they should amidst others who do not like the choices they have made. Practical liberalism holds that the package of problems on display in this socio-political history takes specific form and contemporary urgency in modern states, like the United States, whose social demographics display the presence of a wide array of groups holding disparate and conflicting normative convictions and ontological beliefs. The presence of such groups in these states introduces, in ways specific to particular states, the social pathology that invites (perhaps, one might insist, even requires) theoretical inquiry. Thus the enduring challenge associated with the human effort to live together takes specific shape and focus within distinct states. As I have indicated already, the proper theoretical response to this enduring challenge, as it manifests itself in particular states, must be state-specific and driven by the particular demographics and history of the state in question. But the theoretical enterprise must still be driven by the fact of pluralism for any state that qualifies as pluralist; and to guarantee an appropriate state-based response, this fact cannot be distorted, misrepresented, or underestimated; nor can the nature or extent of intergroup rivalry that is the source of the social pathology in need of therapy be minimized, misconceived, or misunderstood. The dramatization of the social environment that sets the sociological background for practical liberalism is constructed with this in mind. It is intended to guarantee that theoretical conclusions are not misinformed by myopic or misleading visions of the social circumstances and social pathology that invite theoretical inquiry.

If this is reason for practical liberalism to embrace the dramatization of the social environment that roughly mimics political life in the United States, then it is also reason for groups living in the US to do so as well. This takes on added significance in practice as actual groups ponder the desirability of committing to a politics of unity. Group choices about making such a commitment must be informed by salient and trustworthy information about the social setting they inhabit; as we have seen, making a rational choice requires reliable and believable information about the choice situation one faces. Groups may have their own particular vision of the social environment around them, but given the stakes at issue in the choice situation, they should want to make sure this vision is accurate—or as accurate as possible. Given the stakes at issue, groups may wonder why they should trust their own, perhaps naïvely conceived, sense of their social world. What reason do group members or group elites have for thinking that their perception of their social environment is reasonably accurate? The problem here is exacerbated by the fact that the geographic domain that constitutes a group's social setting is already fixed, as a practical matter, by existent state boundaries. Practical liberalism does not theorize the origin of the state; it encounters specific pluralist states as they are and asks, in state-specific contexts, whether a politics of unity is preferable to existing political conditions—in the American context, whether a politics of unity is preferable to the present politics of interests American style.

This means that groups presently living in the United States must know a great deal about American political and social culture, about the differing groups that make up American society and the normative and ontological diversity they bring to the social setting, and about the various political strengths and weaknesses of these multitudinous groups. It is unlikely that too many groups will feel comfortable with the belief that they have a solid grasp on the social and group demographics of America or on the best way to characterize the contest of cultures that typifies American society. Group members and group leaders may decide this is a researchable issue, of course, and set about to master the voluminous literature on the nature of American society, but they will only find there a mosaic of differing and often conflicting pictures of what American society may be like. To summarize a point made earlier, they will find some scholars who suppose the United States is growing more liberal and more in touch with its 'founding ideals' (something that might unnerve illiberal groups in America).[24] But they will find others who are less certain of this, or less certain that American political culture is as liberal at the core as others would have us believe. And they will find still others who chronicle a more agonistic and far less liberal story of group life and group conflict in America, stories that describe how nativist and nationalist sentiments sit alongside liberal presumptions and grow into prominence from time to time.[25] Given this welter of disagreement, what should groups believe about the nature of social life in the United States?

Perhaps they will believe, as I think they should, that while there is an element of truth in each of these visions, intergroup struggle and conflict seems to be an ongoing feature of political life in the United States. If liberalism (understood at the moment as a political commitment to the rights of others) really is on the march in America, this may mean only that the language of liberalism provides the context of intergroup struggle within which the politics of interests works. So, perhaps too they will notice the way this struggle plays itself out in American society (as well as similar societies) in terms of a politics of interests with groups utilizing the resources at their disposal to control the conceptualizations of issues that spark intergroup conflict. And finally, they may appreciate the difficulty and uncertainty associated with group efforts to control the politics of interests to their advantage given the complexity and frequency of intergroup hostility in the country. That is, they may come to recognize the social pathology associated with the politics of interests, and in the process also recognize that intergroup conflict is too indeterminate to be described, fathomed, or characterized with much certainty.

## Conclusion: Unstable stability

To conclude the discussion of the stability of the liberal polity imagined by practical liberalism, it would be wise to emphasize again that it is not theoretically possible to guarantee that any polity will be perfectly stable. All that we can claim on behalf of practical liberalism is that if groups perceive their socio-political predicament in the manner discussed here, there is strong reason to think that civil association under a politics of principle inspired by the commitment to LP will be stable. This may seem like small solace to those who might hope for greater certainty on this score, but no manner of theoretical inquiry can offer more to the real world of political life. Even a civil arrangement that rests upon a bedrock of moral homogeneity that supports the political ideals of the state can say no more than this. This is because, with time, this moral homogeneity may decay, doctrinal divisions may arise, and dissident groups that see the moral word differently (and for better or worse) may emerge. States can try to guard against such possibilities, of course, by socializing their citizens to see things as their forbears saw them and cultivating in the citizenry the political morality that inspired their ancestors. As we shall see in the following chapter, the cultivation of the political morality that follows from the acceptance of LP is also a key ingredient of the political stability promoted by practical liberalism. But there can be no guarantee that this socialization process will do the work required of it as successfully as one might wish. Theoretical inquiry can only influence the political future; it cannot presume to control it. Civil association, by its nature, must necessarily be understood as invariably unstable. In this regard, the uncertainties that may seem to raise doubts about the stability of practical liberalism are no different than the uncertainties that threaten the stability of any other theory of civil association.

Yet there is again something of a paradox lurking in all this. If the fact of flux is the only real constant of social life, social change and transformation would seem to be inevitable. But practical liberalism promises to establish a politics of unity that removes political uncertainty and insecurity from the polity and allows groups to coexist against the background of a shared political morality. It would seem, then, that practical liberalism seeks to control the fact of flux and establish a stable political order that overcomes the uncertainty driven by unmanaged intergroup conflict. But what sense does it make to suppose that practical liberalism can control the fact of flux, and thus assure even an unstable stability, if the vicissitudes of the fact of flux are themselves indeterminate and uncontrollable? Might it not make more sense to say that political life is a process of group and individual interaction that plays itself out within a given state according to the customs and traditions that have grown up around this process in the state in question, and then to leave matters at that? That is, might it not make sense to insist that political life is itself little more than a dimension of the fact of flux that cannot be checked or controlled, at least entirely, by rational argument and theoretical inquiry?

It is unfortunately beyond the limits of the present discussion to consider these questions in the detail they deserve, and so I will offer, at present, only a fairly modest, albeit anticipatory, response. The politics of principle associated with practical liberalism is intended to protect groups against the uncertainty, and hence insecurity, of the fact of flux. It does so by providing a principled method for the resolution of intergroup disputes that is prudentially superior to the vicissitudes of a politics of interests. It thus brings political stability to the constantly changing and evolving social condition in which it operates, but it does not—it cannot—put an end to social change and transformation. It can only domesticate social change by placing it within an authoritative political context. Practical liberalism has, in short, a conservatizing influence on the social environment in which it operates. It supports the group status quo by defending a shaky peace among disparate and potentially (and often actually) hostile groups, and thus it promises a political atmosphere where groups can flourish according to their own standards of what counts as a good life, even if groups are not allowed to treat their normative rivals in the harsh manner they might happen to favor.

# 6
# Justice, Fairness, and the Making of Civility

The liberal polity, as described here, is a prudential necessity bound together by the common realization that groups are best off if their members agree 'to seek peace, and follow it,' as Hobbes famously put it.[1] Yet this view of the matter will seem like a sorry state of affairs to anyone who would prefer to move civil association closer to the center of individual lives and to have citizens more focused upon civic engagement. Thomas Spragens, for example, criticizes a form of civil association reminiscent of practical liberalism by insisting that its aspirations are too limited and its aims too modest. Social peace and political stability are, for Spragens, undoubted goods, but they are not all that we should ask of or expect from civil association. In this spirit, it might be objected that practical liberalism 'does not provide adequate normative guidance' for the modern pluralist democracies of today.[2]

The criticism is, to say the least, curious, for it is not entirely clear what kind of normative guidance is missing from the liberal polity or why we should want to look to the polity for any normative guidance given the normative foundations supplied to individuals by their affiliation with more primary groups. Perhaps, however, we can take the criticisms to point to the apparent need for some normative *grundlage* that coheres the polity and establishes a common political ground that enables citizens to gain some sense of who they are, politically speaking, and what their polity stands for. If so, the discussion of toleration has already done something to suggest a proper response to criticisms of this sort. The commitment to toleration associated with the acceptance of LP offers a good deal in the way of normative guidance for the polity. There are, however, those who think toleration itself is a cramped and modest virtue and who hope to go beyond toleration in the polity and cultivate something like respect for others and for otherness.[3] If such hopes are premised upon the moral claims associated with moral liberalism or republicanism, they push in the direction of a moral homogeneity that is simply out of place in pluralist polities. If, that is, they rest upon the moral insistence that all worldviews and ways of life have something to be said for them that others need to recognize and respect, they must be dismissed as simply naïve when measured against the background supplied by the fact of pluralism. This is the very claim that many groups feel the need to reject, and in the face of deep normative rivalries, insisting upon the importance of respect for diversity becomes a source of social conflict in its own right.

It would, of course, be foolish to rule out the possibility that at some future time Americans might converge on a common moral theory of the human good with distinctive political implications, for the possibility cannot be discounted given the power of ongoing intergroup discourse and rational reflection. At present, however, intergroup animosity and conflict between normative rivalries is a fact of social life (or at least this is the background assumption that situates this theoretical inquiry), and while it is possible that this conflict might someday be transcended, the possibility does nothing to moderate the present challenge of forging a politics of unity amidst exceptional normative and ontological diversity. But while practical liberalism does not preclude the possibility of transcending normative conflict, it does not identify this possibility as a goal to be promoted by political inquiry. Instead, it seeks only to offer a theoretical vision of how rival groups can coexist, within a common social setting, in relative peace and tranquility. Those transcendent hopes that might inspire us should not blur the practical issues that encourage inquiry into the possibilities of civil peace. Toleration, then, need not seem like such a modest or cramped political virtue. In the face of the realities of group diversity and intergroup animosity, it is all we can, and from the standpoint of practical liberalism all we should, hope for.

Nonetheless, there must be some coming together of the citizenry if the liberal polity is to qualify as a polity at all. There must be some common focus and shared understanding throughout the polity that serves as the foundation for a politics of unity. This is implied by the very notion of a politics of unity. Yet the prospect of political unity also seems to be belied by the characterization of the liberal polity as a *modus vivendi*. I argued above that thinking of a *modus vivendi* exclusively as a treaty arrangement, in the manner identified in the previous chapter, is sufficient to sustain civil unity through time given the social reality associated with the fact of flux. But it does not do much to cultivate a sense of civic identity or inspire a spirit of publicness that can (and perhaps should) supplement the prudential case for political stability and embellish the basis of legitimacy for the liberal polity. A treaty between two or more states, for example, does not forge or generate a new civic unit; instead, it is a promissory agreement between sovereign civic units. The treaty does not bring into being a new civic identity for the contracting parties; they remain independent political units acting from a sense of their own best interests as they understand these interests at any point in time. If, by parity of reason, we understand the *modus vivendi* associated with the liberal polity in these terms, the acceptance of LP does not bring about a politics of unity, or a single polity, at all. Groups would remain independent sovereign units only loosely linked together by their treaty agreements.

So, if a politics of unity is to result from the *modus vivendi* that lies at the heart of practical liberalism, the treaty system cannot be used as the model for conceptualizing the civic relationships that accepting LP brings into being. This fact has, in part, already been acknowledged with the recognition that the acceptance of LP involves admitting the authoritative character of governmental institutions charged with policing tolerance and coordination problems. But there must be something more to a politics of unity than simply recognizing the existence of authoritative political institutions; and under practical liberalism, this something more involves the acceptance of and adherence to a political morality, shared by all elements of the polity, that fixes the norms of civil association that bind the otherwise disparate groups constitutive of the polity into a single civic unit.

As we have seen, the political morality associated with practical liberalism is introduced by LP and explicable in terms of the civic obligation of groups to practice deference and tolerance toward all other groups within the social setting constitutive of the polity. Under practical liberalism, the acceptance of LP must be supposed to have talismanic powers; it transforms the wheat and chaff of prudential necessity into the gold of civic unity. Prudential argument demonstrates the necessity of committing to a politics of unity, and by so doing it provides the theoretical foundation for the practical (*de jure*) legitimacy of such a politics. But it is only through exploring the nature of this commitment, and unpacking its implications, that we can begin to recognize how this commitment unites otherwise distinct groups into a single group that is the polity. In the remainder of this chapter, I will discuss the theoretical basis for a politics of unity and consider the prospects for building civic unity amidst normative and ontological diversity within the liberal polity.

## In the shadow of Hobbes

Modern political theorizing has labored long in the considerable shadow of Thomas Hobbes. Hobbes invited us to consider civil association as the appropriate response to humankind's asocial and divisive tendencies. This manner of association was not something natural or fundamental to human life for Hobbes, as it was for Aristotle; human beings, in Hobbes's view, are hardly sociable and certainly not political by nature. Civil association and the sociality Hobbes supposed to accompany it must be manufactured, and he considered working up the blueprint for this project to be the distinctive challenge of theorizing about political life. This was the first and necessary step in building the stability and security human beings require for viable social life. Once this security is in place, once human beings *become* political animals, so to speak, all else is possible, but without this security, nothing else is sustainable. While Hobbes hardly supposed that civil association would auger in the good life, he did imagine it to be the necessary precondition of anyone's ability to pursue a good life.

Practical liberalism is not as austere as this. In particular, it does not suppose that human sociality is itself an artifact of civil association, and Hobbes has been roundly criticized, first by Cumberland and Pufendorf, for supposing that it is.[4] Pufendorf corrects Hobbes by arguing that social unrest is not a consequence of humankind's asocial tendency and that civil association is required to generate social peace and good order amidst the competing tribes and social groups that come into conflict for scarce resources in an increasingly crowded social environment. Although it emphasizes normative rivalries rather than allocational rivalries as the most intractable aspect of intergroup conflict, practical liberalism is here more indebted to Pufendorf than to Hobbes.

There are still places on the planet where people would do well to read Hobbes and Pufendorf and take seriously their insistence that human beings listen to reason (or the voice of prudence as they understood it), and learn to get along. There are still places on the planet, this is to say, where a blueprint for civil association is needed, where people need to learn to look past religious, ethnic, and ideological difference and appreciate the value of getting along with one another.[5] It may seem, however, that this lesson has been learned in some of the so-called more advanced states—one almost wants to say in the more civilized states—like the United States. In the United States, it might be supposed, we have learned Hobbes's lesson; we have learned the value of civil association and of getting along with one another. Here theorizing about politics must now turn to other, more noble, pursuits. In particular, it must take up the subject of justice and thereby encourage the cultivation of respect for fellow citizens and the establishment of meaningful equality. It must confront the specter of greed; address the dilemma of poverty in a land of plenty; and inspire a more generous attitude toward diversity and difference.

For reasons introduced at the outset, I do not share the view that Americans have learned Hobbes's lesson and come together under a common political accord. Intergroup conflict is reasonably domesticated, to be sure. It now reaches the streets only rarely, but it still reaches the streets. It breaks into violence only rarely, but it still has violent moments. But the civil condition in America is only somewhat the better for all this. The standard institutions of political life, the courts, legislatures, and executive offices of America, and the ballot box remain battlegrounds where the politics of interests is played out.[6] Such a politics, however, has little to do with justice. Until a viable politics of principle is in place, 'justice' is just another term to be exploited or expropriated in the rhetorical struggle characteristic of this new state of war. Justice is possible only when shared political ideals animate the polity and only where there is a common agreement on what these ideals mean and a shared commitment to bring them to life. To cultivate a politics of principle, in other words, is not merely to pursue a politics of unity, for it also brings justice to life and makes discourse on justice possible by introducing the normative baseline that makes talk about justice something more than empty rhetoric. A politics of principle realizes its unifying agenda by bringing citizens together around the foundation of a shared political morality.

It is little wonder, then, that the project of practical liberalism, the project of building unity amidst deep ontological and normative diversity and disagreement, has a Hobbesian ring to it. The similarities go well beyond the superficial commitment to prudential reasoning that practical liberalism shares with Hobbes. Hobbes sought to build a polity, to bring together beings with little concern for or interest in one another, and to forge a *commonwealth* out of this mass of warring units. Practical liberalism also seeks to build a polity (albeit in theory), but it endeavors to do so by bringing together groups whose members have difficulty understanding one another after a fashion and who have reasons to find one another damned, disgusting, repugnant, or misguided by virtue of who they are or what they believe. It strives to fashion unity, to craft a common polity based upon shared standards of civility, while allowing and enabling diversity to endure. It leaves groups as they are and still brings them together to form a new group that also matters and that demands that the members of this new group see one another as fellow citizens (i.e., as fellow members of the group that is the polity) in spite of those things that separate and divide them.

There are, however, aspects of practical liberalism that separate it from Hobbes and move it more evidently toward the liberal camp. Practical liberalism does not endorse a theory of absolute sovereignty, for example; LP places clear and principled limits upon political authority by charting reasonably certain parameters of group autonomy. Under practical liberalism, government must recognize and respect its jurisdictional boundaries. Pufendorf was quick to correct Hobbes in this regard and to insist that while sovereign power should not be considered absolute because of the danger this poses to freedom, it should nonetheless be regarded as supreme in those spheres where it is entitled to exercise jurisdictional control.[7] Here too practical liberalism follows Pufendorf rather than Hobbes.

Practical liberalism also brings the rule of law to the center of political attention, for LP inspires the construction of legal rules and institutions to articulate and police the requirements of toleration and deference. Legal rules are required to specify the responsibilities and corresponding group rights that follow from LP and insulate group members from interference by outsiders acting on their own initiative or by enlisting the government to do their work for them. And courts of law are necessary in order to consider tolerance and coordination problems (among other things) and to place the burdens of tolerance and deference when specific disputes arise. If, on the one hand, judicial decisions end specific disputes, on the other hand, their authority need not be considered irreversible under practical liberalism. This is because specific disputes and controversies may spark ongoing public discussion about the meaning and requirements of LP—the demands of toleration, and the standards of deference, that filter into the public that is the polity.

Groups are invariably political units (i.e., they invariably possess animating norms and authoritative voices), and the polity is obviously no exception. They require institutional mechanisms for setting policy, reviewing past decisions, implementing policy decisions, resolving conflicts, setting political agendas, and addressing member grievances. Beyond the institution of law, what types of political constructions should we adopt in order to meet these needs? One rather Hobbesian response is to say that it does not matter. All that matters is that the jobs get done and get done authoritatively. Spragens supposes this is a weakness of theories of civil association like practical liberalism; they are, he thinks, consistent with benevolent dictatorships. And his preference for democratic institutions inclines him to consider this unfortunate. He supposes that a liberal polity should be democratic in nature.[8] These concerns invite consideration of the possibility of democracy under practical liberalism. In addition to requiring principled limitations upon political authority and a commitment to the rule of law, liberal states are generally committed to democratic procedures, including open and fair elections, universal suffrage, and free and unfettered political discourse.

Practical liberalism permits two possible responses to this concern. The first repeats the Hobbesian insistence that little hangs on matters of governmental architecture. Provided the ends established by LP are honored by political decision-makers, and the legal machinery is in place to limit governmental authority and police forbearance, there is little reason to worry further about matters of institutional structure. To this we might add the additional proviso that political theory has the most pertinence when it keeps an eye on the political circumstances it is intended to address. Practical liberalism is a response to ongoing intergroup conflict within the American political context. It is not a theoretical attempt to build a polity from the ground up; it takes—and should take—the political circumstances present in the United States as the given and finds there a social pathology in need of theoretical treatment. Its purpose is therapeutic and not revisionary. Consequently, we can suppose practical liberalism would leave in place the fundamentals of the American constitutional structure, including the democratic traditions that are already well entrenched in the United States. If practical liberalism is compatible with benevolent despotism, it is also compatible with representative democracy. So, Americans can have their democracy and practical liberalism too.

But there is reason to say something more than this and to insist more affirmatively that democracy is the preferred governmental system under practical liberalism. The defense of freedom required by LP works in two fundamental ways. First, it allows groups a maximum amount of group autonomy as we have seen. But it also prevents groups from discriminating against outgroups and denying their members the opportunity to involve themselves in the functions and activities of the group that is the polity. As members of the polity, all citizens are guaranteed equal opportunity and equal access to the offices and entitlements belonging to the civil public. This follows from the egalitarian condition from which LP is partly derived. Therefore, if there is to be a benevolent despot, the office must be open to all, which suggests that the polity will need to have an elected despot if it is going to have a despot at all. The suggestion is not quite compelling, however, because open offices and institutions need not be filled by elections. They may just as easily be distributed by lot, say, provided that all citizens that have reached the age of majority (whatever this is determined to be) are included in the lottery.

Filling political offices by chance, however, seems inconsistent with LP if everyone in the polity is included in the drawing—for LP allows groups to opt out of the political process if they elect to do so. Groups that refuse to accept LP will remain foreign presences in the liberal polity, and should they practice intolerance within the polity, the community around them will be fully justified in treating them harshly by going to war with them, so to speak. But groups that accept LP and thus involve themselves in the polity are still entitled under LP to opt out of political involvement should they think such activity inconsistent with their moral theory of the human good. Reclusive groups, or groups like the Amish that shun modern ways, may prefer to go their own way as a part of their group practices but honor the demands of LP, however, without engaging positively in the governmental process. This they are entitled to do under LP, and so distributing public offices by lottery would infringe upon this freedom, making this way of distributing political offices inconsistent with LP.

Of course, a lottery could still be held to fill offices if the drawing included only those individuals who wanted the job. But the polity has a stake in making certain that capable and knowledgeable people find their way into public office, and because of this, citizens also have an interest in making sure the most capable individuals actually win public office. Lotteries leave too much to chance. Elections, on the other hand, provide the citizenry with an opportunity to examine candidates for public office and make prudent decisions about those that seem the most capable and qualified. This might not seem like much in the way of solace because there is no guarantee that sufficiently capable or qualified individuals will bother to seek public office, but this is a problem endemic to all representative democracy. Democracy also leaves a great deal to chance, but practical liberalism will not support a political draft masquerading as a lottery.

Perhaps we should prefer a direct democracy to representative democracy in order to obviate these problems, but there are numerous familiar problems with directly involving the general citizenry in the policy-determination process. Simply put, government in the modern polities of the early twenty-first century necessitates a division of labor, and the various labors involved take tremendous expertise, talent, and time.[9] Indeed, the complexity modern government both encounters and endures now pushes toward the formation of bureaucratic structures that threaten to eclipse democratic involvement.[10] The democratic process in the United States, for example, might now be considered a strategic political compromise that enables political officials and appointed bureaucrats to proceed with the job of governing while still allowing the people to hold these individuals accountable by holding referenda on their successes and failures. When faced with the challenges of governing a state like the United States, this may be about all anyone could reasonably hope for; so while there is no principled objection to direct democracy imaginable under practical liberalism (provided citizen involvement in democratic processes is not mandated), there are practical reasons why practical liberals may prefer representative political institutions.

There is one final reason to think that practical liberalism should have a preference for democratic political procedures. Sometimes coordination and tolerance problems are resolved rather easily; sometimes the burdens of deference and tolerance can be placed without much complication. And sometimes the jurisdiction problems involving the proper domain of the group and the proper domain of the polity are straightforward and reasonably clear. When this is the case, the requirements of LP are easy to discern and the success of governmental officials in managing these problems can be readily assessed. But at other times these problems trouble, and their proper resolution is subject to reasonable disagreement. Under practical liberalism, the courts are charged with resolving particular problems when they arise, but courts are hardly infallible. Their decisions may often do more to spark public concern and discussion than to resolve it, and to think that courts should be the final voice in such matters undercuts the interest the citizenry should rightfully have in them. If the courts bring closure to specific controversies, they may also open larger questions of public concern. And it is appropriate to allow the citizenry the right and the opportunity to discuss such matters, explore alternative or additional arguments, and express a public will on them—should such a will manifest itself.

This too is an important element of democracy; for as we shall see, the citizenry should be interested in the ends of justice as established by LP and should be willing, if they so desire, to explore what LP demands in difficult situations and thereby help develop and refine the demands of justice. Once again, groups need not involve themselves in the deliberative process, or they may involve themselves only selectively. But groups should consider the question of their involvement by balancing the defense of their group ways against their responsibility to participate faithfully and earnestly in the group that is the polity. On this score, it is important to keep in mind that all groups have an interest in observing how coordination and tolerance problems are resolved and how jurisdiction problems are managed. Groups will opt for LP and a politics of principle over the alternatives because this is the best way to insure that they have a maximum amount of freedom, now and in the future, to pursue their way of life and live by their moral theory of the human good. But they can remain confident that LP is working as advertised in the polity only by involving themselves in ongoing public discussions about what LP requires and how it is to be honored and observed. It may sound trite, but it is also important to emphasize that LP will thrive in the courts of law and halls of government of the polity only if it is alive and well in the hearts and minds of the citizenry. As Stephen Macedo has rightly observed, 'Citizens, not courts or legislatures, are the ultimate custodians of our public morality.'[11] So, by opting for LP, groups also commit themselves to an ongoing colloquy about what all this involves, about how coordination and tolerance problems are to be resolved, and about how jurisdictional boundaries are to be honored. To achieve this end, open and unfettered political discourse is necessary, discourse informed and guided by a common commitment to LP, and such discourse requires democratic processes and procedures both to inspire it and to provide an appropriate forum for it. Put in more general terms, practical liberalism must defend a group right of free and unfettered political involvement in the group that is the polity, a right that comprehends the familiar rights of speech, peaceable assembly, and association in American constitutional law.

## Toward a theory of social justice

Hobbes, along with his fellow social-contract theorists, fashioned a polity out of thin air by imagining an initial moment when people come together and deliberately consent to form civil society. There are two points of importance in all this: First, the polity assumes the status of an artificial construct that must be consciously created and nurtured by those who become its citizens; and second, the job of theorizing the state becomes the process of imagining in words the conditions that establish its legitimacy and constitute its *raison d'être*. Both points still matter; both are still central elements of theorizing about civil association. But both seem to have been largely eclipsed, at present, by a fixation on the demands of social justice.[12] Justice, on the other hand, makes sense only if it is imagined and understood in light of these two contractarian concerns. A state *qua* artificial construct that cannot make a strong case for its legitimacy by demonstrating that all persons subject to its authority should consent to this authority will hardly qualify as just. Correspondingly, the defense of political authority established by theoretical inquiry needs to be all-inclusive; all persons sharing a common social setting should be able to appreciate the need for civil association. This means presenting a theory of civil association sufficiently freestanding to appeal to all groups regardless of their worldview or moral theory of the human good. Obviously, the theoretical project cannot *make* group members consent to political authority, but it can and should indicate why they should do so. This ties together the two components of the contractarian project and establishes the basic conditions that make the concerns of social justice intelligible.

Hobbes illustrated the state's legitimacy by emphasizing its necessity; it is the essential force for security and order in a given region and should be respected as such. Anyone who understands the value of peace must also understand the value of civil association. This is vintage Hobbes, and as we have seen, this element of Hobbes remains vital to practical liberalism. Pufendorf, on the other hand, domesticates Hobbes, not chiefly by challenging Hobbesian cynicism about human sociability (though he certainly did this), but by transforming Hobbes's prudential argument into a moral one and insisting that civil association is a matter of moral necessity and therefore entirely in keeping with the demands of God's law. Prudential necessity is thus recast as a form of moral order, and if Pufendorf's state is still an artificial construct, it is also a rational response to the human condition as Pufendorf imagined it to be.[13] To all of this Locke introduced a set of antecedent moral concerns that explain in distinctive terms the state's reason for being, along with the limitations upon its authority. The Lockean state is there to protect and police the natural rights possessed by each and every person under its authority, and the state loses its legitimacy and exceeds its authority in the event it compromises those rights itself.

In more contemporary terms, the Lockean argument introduces an antecedent set of moral considerations that introduce and make intelligible reflections on *social* justice—on the justice of the polity brought into being by the parties to the civil contract. The purpose of civil society is now to preserve and protect one's natural rights, and the polity is just if the government does its job effectively and unjust if it does not. Lockean natural rights thus provide an independent moral posture from which to understand and assess the justness—and hence the legitimacy—of civil association. If many contemporary political thinkers are now skeptical about the existence of Lockean natural rights, they are typically not skeptical about the importance of antecedent moral considerations capable of introducing standards of social justice to serve as a guide in shaping the institutions of the state and providing the sort of normative guidance Spragens thinks so necessary. Practical liberalism, however, rejects the propriety of the appeal to antecedent moral considerations on the grounds that no such appeal can meet the problem of audience. Given the fact of pluralism, we cannot suppose that any specific normative viewpoint is shared by all elements of the social setting that situates theoretical inquiry. So when it comes to the issue of social justice, practical liberalism must confront a theoretical challenge different from the one that faces thinkers who continue to labor in the shadow of

Locke: Is it possible to have the normative guidance that makes talk about social justice intelligible without first introducing antecedent (and disputatious) moral considerations?

No doubt the contemporary thinker who has done the most in recent times to vitalize a more Lockean sense of civil association is the John Rawls of *A Theory of Justice*.[14] In *Theory*, Rawls sought to provide a contractarian alternative to utilitarian argument by articulating two principles of justice he supposed a rational (in the Humean sense) being would accept under conditions that constrained her or his ability to privilege his or her own welfare over the welfare of those who would become fellow citizens. The imagined principles, which presumably held with the force of reason (unlike Locke's natural rights which hold ultimately only with the force of Christian faith), are the antecedent moral conditions that inform the construction of the state and guarantee the formation of just social institutions. For the most part, the Rawls of *Theory* is the rebirth of Locke without the apparent Achilles's heel of natural-rights argument. Rawls's argument was quickly criticized, however, on the grounds that it did little more than beg key questions about the moral neutrality of the conditions of constraint under which one chooses principles of justice.[15] Critics noticed properly that the choice conditions Rawls imagined reflected an unwitting liberal bias and guaranteed, for all practical purposes, that his liberal principles would be chosen under the choice conditions he introduced.[16] From a disguised set of liberal premises, we get liberal conclusions—nothing very surprising here.

Rawls's response to all this was both subtle and suggestive. He conceded the fact of pluralism and recognized it as an important challenge to theorizing about political life. Importantly, he claimed that a theory of justice must be freestanding; it cannot be premised upon or reflective of any comprehensive theory of the good.[17] Where comprehensive theories of the good differ significantly, none can serve effectively as the antecedent moral grounds for a theory of social justice. Instead, a theory of justice must be constructed out of thin air, so to speak, in order to provide the necessary antecedent moral conditions that make it possible to imagine a just state.[18] The result is to render the liberal bias of the argument of *Theory* rather innocent; let us just take the principles of justice articulated there as a given (because it does not matter how we arrived at them) and ask how they might manage to inform and guide concerns of social justice in a plural society. As we noticed in the previous chapter, his answer invokes the notion of an overlapping consensus. Rawls's two principles of justice can drive the concerns of social justice in the event they are acceptable to enough social groups in the polity given the comprehensive moral doctrines that help define them as groups, that is, if there is an overlapping moral consensus in their favor.[19] The result of this argument is a remarkably unremarkable conclusion: Rawls's liberal principles of justice can serve as a normative guide and inspiration to a state if it is, in the main, sufficiently liberal to support them.

If it makes sense to read Rawls in this way, his revitalization of contractarian argument has emphasized the second feature of contractarian thought at the expense of the first. Rawlsian argument does not endeavor to construct a polity, that is, to fashion political unity out of social diversity and thereby manage social conflict; instead it provides a purified theory against which the dominant ideology in the polity can measure itself to see if it lives up to its own standards as they are ideally understood.[20] And it rests upon the hope that 'unreasonable' (i.e., illiberal) worldviews and comprehensive doctrines will remain small and politically insignificant or be kept in suitable political check.[21] Ironically, Rawls's argument rests finally upon a secular faith in the power and attractiveness of moral liberalism that is curiously similar to the religious faith that serves as the basic foundation in Locke. And importantly, illiberal groups are left out of the political picture to be shunted and demonized by liberal influences that are now better positioned, thanks to Rawls, to worry about them and appreciate the danger they pose to the liberal ascendancy.[22]

Rawlsian argument is thus unhappily ambivalent about illiberal presences in the polity. Illiberals are entitled to the rights and liberties everyone is to enjoy under liberal standards of social justice, but they presumably have little allegiance to the liberal polity and are best understood as a cancer within the body politic. Accordingly, there is reason to keep an eye on them, to wonder what they are up to, and to regard them as social pariahs that threaten decency and justice. This, of course, merely returns us to the problem of intergroup conflict and reintroduces a recurrent theme of my argument: Moral liberalism is unable to manage effectively the problems posed by illiberal and non-liberal influences in society. If these influences in the United States are not great and if they can be kept under control, this would not seem to offer much cause for concern. Since these groups reject the standards of social justice championed by moral liberalism, there is no reason to regard their marginalization or alienation as unjust. Liberals cannot impose upon illiberals with impunity, but they need have no great regard for them either and may work within the parameters of their sense of justice to eliminate or assimilate them.[23] But these groups just might be a more significant presence in America—as I suspect they are—than many moral liberals are willing to admit, and if they are not a significant threat today, they may become such tomorrow. The uncertainties associated with the fact of flux that characterizes intergroup conflict still work in America, and they work both for and against liberal sentiments.

The problem these remarks are intended to expose is central to a theoretical account of the just state and to the subject of social justice more generally. If antecedent moral concerns drive thinking about social justice, groups that do not hold or share these concerns will not be agreed that their political manifestation establishes a condition of social justice. These groups will conceptualize the just state differently, if in fact their comprehensive moral doctrine allows them to formulate such a conception at all. No doubt more dominant groups will be inclined to regard their sense of social justice as valid and to fashion or refashion (when and wherever possible) the state in their image of the just state. The resultant struggle to control the meaning and manifestation of social justice in the state thus returns us to the politics of interests masquerading behind a veil of moral propriety. But there does not seem to be anything terribly just about any of this; indeed, social justice would seem to demand something else. It would seem to require that all elements of the polity be agreed on the basic standards of social justice and that these standards themselves should not be the subject of political contestation. Put somewhat differently, it would seem that a just polity is one where a politics of unity is in place, and this implies that all elements of the polity acknowledge and endorse a politics of principle where the foundation of justice talk is supplied by some principle (or set of principles) acceptable to all groups constitutive of the polity.

This is reason to think that moral liberalism cannot make good on its concern for social justice if we suppose this notion involves the acceptance of a common standard of social justice acceptable to all elements of the polity. Yet it is not clear why we should accept *this* account of social justice; that is, it is not clear why we should think that a just polity must employ standards of social justice acceptable to all elements of the polity, or that ought to be acceptable to all elements of the polity for reasons presumed to be binding on these elements. If this judgment itself is based upon some antecedent moral viewpoint, it may not be acceptable to all moral theories of the human good present in the polity. If, on the other hand, it is not based upon some antecedent moral concern, there is reason to ask what the account has to do with social *justice*—a notion that seems necessarily embedded in some moral doctrine. It is this latter concern, of course, that troubles practical liberalism.

There are a number of possible ways to avoid this conundrum. One way is simply to reject concerns for social justice on the ground that the notion is itself embedded within moral liberalism. The egalitarian concern that all elements of the polity endorse standards of social justice, for example, may be regarded as a familiar bit of liberal moralizing, and insofar as it sneaks into practical liberalism it betrays a moral concern that ought to have no place in a theoretical project that attempts to avoid controversial or contestable normative claims. But as we have seen, practical liberalism is concerned with inclusiveness, and it must be concerned with inclusiveness if it is to picture in theory a politics of unity. Inclusiveness is a requirement of practical liberalism in order to guarantee the possibility of principled remedies to the tolerance and coordination problems that tear at the fabric of the polity. It follows that practical liberalism cannot do without a theory of social justice.

This point also demonstrates both why and how social justice is a subject of concern within practical liberalism, and an explanation of this concern points to an acceptable resolution to our conundrum. A politics of principle must necessarily make social justice a subject of the first importance, for the issue of justice is introduced by the principle(s) that stipulate and inform the type of treatment that is due the various elements of the polity. A polity is just if its citizens live according to the requirements of the principle(s) they accept as authoritative; it is unjust if any of its citizens fail to live according to the demands of principle and treat others in a fashion they do not deserve according to the political morality introduced by the principle(s) accepted as authoritative. Social justice, this is to say, is a necessary condition of a politics of principle, and its normative orientation is given by the basic principle(s) that coheres the polity. Within the theoretical edifice of practical liberalism, there can be no talk of social justice independently of the establishment of some authoritative political principle(s), for the standards of justice are supplied by the principle itself. Nor is the normative focus of the principle inherited from the nature of the argument that supports its authoritativeness; it derives entirely from the principle itself or from the basic conditions that dictate its form and content. There is no reason to suppose, then, that some antecedent moral concerns must be present in order to give sense and significance to the notion of social justice. Under practical liberalism, social justice matters because practical liberalism promotes a politics of principle, albeit one premised upon prudential rather than moral argument. While the notion of social justice remains inherently normative, its moral force does not derive from antecedent moral considerations; instead, its moral force derives from the principle that inspires the political morality it introduces.

Although practical liberalism is not itself a contractarian theory, it is faithful to the dual ends of contractarian argument insofar as it is all-inclusive and committed to articulating the normative conditions of political legitimacy. This is displayed by the claim that a politics of unity must also be a politics of principle. The acceptance of LP is thus to be understood as consenting to a normative ideal that serves as the end and animating spirit of the group that is the polity. Correspondingly, a more exact articulation of the requirements of LP begins the process of developing and presenting a comprehensive theory of justice. Such a theory, I have suggested, will have at least two chief components: a theory of toleration and a theory of deference. (I have explored the outline of a theory of liberal toleration above in order to examine the costs of endorsing LP, and these comments may now be considered initial explorations of the demands of social justice under practical liberalism.) There is, however, more to a theory of social justice than the articulation of the kinds of responsibilities and obligations it brings into being. Other, more intangible, aspects of the theory are crucial to the process of polity construction but not because they articulate the specific political morality brought into being by developing theories of toleration and deference. These involve an examination of how the political morality introduced by LP works to cohere a given social setting into a group that is now the polity and functions to sustain it by providing the normative guidance it requires and the normative glue that binds it together. Two aspects of the synergizing force of LP are particularly important in this regard.

First, and as we have noted already, LP should be understood to operate chiefly as the normative ideal that gives purpose and direction to the polity. Policing forbearance and observing non-interference are not the sole functions of government in the liberal polity, to be sure. Government in the modern age must assume a rather daunting list of functions in order to make things go well in the polity. Among other things, it must provide for the defense of its citizenry both at home and abroad, identify and address collective action problems, control and monitor emigration and immigration as sub-units of the polity come and go, anticipate the possibly deleterious consequences that technological and scientific developments might have in a variety of fields, and police those aspects of social life that matter to the more dominant groups in the polity.[24] But these necessary functions do little to encourage political identification with the polity or to cultivate an appreciation of the fact that citizens are engaged in a common enterprise of living together whether they like one another or not. By recognizing LP as a normative ideal, however, it is possible to begin to craft the type of political identification with the polity that is necessary to a politics of unity. This is because acceptance of LP means that the disparate groups constitutive of the polity have reached a common agreement on what is to become the basic requirements of the political morality that unites them. Seen as an animating spirit, LP forges the political morality that coheres the polity. Even in the face of the considerable ontological and normative differences that separate groups and generate normative rivalries, the political morality introduced by LP should be conceptualized as a source of political unity.

This political morality can and certainly should be understood in terms of social justice; it establishes the normative framework through which elements of the polity can determine what each owes to all and what all owe to each. In the abstract, we know exactly what is owed to one's political fellows: toleration and deference. And it is possible to be somewhat clear on what all this involves because the resolution of some of the more obvious tolerance and coordination problems is easy enough. This is because it is sometimes evident when the actions or action plans of the As impermissibly infringe upon the liberty of the Bs. But we have also seen that it is not always possible to see with perfect clarity how these problems should be resolved. To repeat a point made previously, the courts of law may close specific conflicts, but they do not necessarily put the last word to the problem posed by the conflict. For this, additional public discourse and additional public reflection will be in order. Work must still be done in order to clarify the normative requirements of LP and to apply them to specific situations.

As a normative ideal, this is to say, social justice remains a work in progress; the exploration of the political morality that defines the polity as such is a never-ending challenge and one in which all elements of the polity are invited to participate. This in turn introduces the second basic feature of the synergizing force of the political morality introduced by LP. Social justice is certainly a virtue of social institutions as Rawls has emphasized, but it is also something more.[25] As an animating spirit, it is also a subject of public scrutiny and discourse. It is hard to imagine that too many citizens will be either able or terribly willing to explore the nuances of energy conservation policy, foreign policy, or environmental-protection policy, to cite but a few of the technical areas of public life increasingly controlled by bureaucratic experts. Bureaucratization of the political process has transformed public and political discourse by wrapping it in a technical vocabulary and inundating it with technical facts that leave citizens outside the political loop. But the concerns of social justice are another matter. Here elements of the polity can participate if they wish to do so, and here there is reason to encourage public involvement and discussion. (Here too bureaucrats have reason to listen, for the exploration of tolerance and coordination problems will have a significant impact on the more specific policy arenas that these bureaucrats increasingly control. This may even introduce a democratizing spirit into the seemingly irreversible march toward the bureaucratization of public life.)

Political discourse is an integral element of political commitment when focused upon a common theme universally endorsed throughout the polity. The inquiry into what social justice should involve, particularly in specific controversial situations, is indicative of an unending and ongoing collective group effort to work toward the full instantiation of the ideals comprehended by the notion of social justice. This requires the construction of a common political vocabulary, one that can only be forged through the process of political discourse and one that can also profit from continuing guidance and clarification by theoretical inquiry. But the process should also give rise to the spirit of civility, that is, the willingness of members of the polity to be good citizens regardless of other group identifications and the intergroup animosities that might be present for them and important to them. Civility, that is, involves respecting and following the demands of social justice as one understands them, and it involves participation in the open-ended discourse over these demands and how they should be brought to life in specific instances. It requires, to borrow a theme popularized by Rousseau, that group members reflect upon the standards of social justice *in their capacity as citizens* and not simply in their capacity as members of the groups constitutive of the polity.[26] When it comes to social justice, the requirements of the group that is the polity come first—not because they are more important than one's group ways or beliefs but because they are the precondition for one's ability to live by these ways and beliefs peacefully and securely. This is entailed by the acceptance of LP, and it reinforces what we might now think of as the democratic spirit of practical liberalism. Correspondingly, the cultivation of civility must be regarded as an important end of the citizenship training that all groups must accept and endorse as they see to the education of their young.

The cultivation of a pervasive sense of civility is crucial for a politics of unity, and it is possible only within a politics of principle, for this principle (or set of principles) is the source of the normative ideal that brings the polity together and introduces the focus of discourse on the political morality of the polity. If civility is not cultivated, if members of the polity do not develop and value a sense of themselves as integral elements of the group that is the polity regardless of the other group identifications they might have, a politics of principle will be in danger of decaying into a politics of interests, or worse. The core meaning of LP is reasonably clear and certain: Groups are to be permitted a maximum amount of autonomy to allow their members to live their lives as they wish, to practice their moral theory of the human good as they see fit, and to practice their ways in accordance with their worldview, compatible with a like degree of freedom for other groups. Spelling this spirit out in terms of toleration and deference further clarifies the nature and spirit of social justice under practical liberalism. This is where public discourse is to begin; this is the point from which open discussion and unfettered discourse should take over and bring these ideals to life. In the process, however, everyone should be able to recognize that one's fellow citizens are also committed to the ends and ideals of social justice and thus willing to participate civilly in the political process. Self-serving arguments will be exposed as such; only arguments that indicate a willingness to take social justice seriously by invoking arguments that make reasonable appeal to the requirements of LP will carry weight in the intergroup colloquy through which the political morality introduced by LP is developed and embellished. Groups whose members fail or refuse to honor LP, and who pursue self-serving ends under the guise of social justice, will run the risk of being identified as defectors from the polity. At best, this will turn these groups into political outsiders no longer subject to the protective and supportive environment provided by the polity, and at worst it will threaten the *modus vivendi* that sustains LP and send the polity spiraling toward a politics of interests. Since this is the very condition groups have prudential reason to avoid, the prudential argument recommends that everyone take seriously the cultivation of civility and work within the spirit of LP to bring the demands of social justice to life.

Yet these comments introduce a problem that necessarily lurks beneath the surface of any discussion of social justice under practical liberalism. The end of social justice imagined under practical liberalism may be, and given the fact of pluralism almost surely will be, at odds with the specific moral agendas of at least some of the groups in the polity. If the Crazy Betas would like to eliminate or assimilate the Innocent Alphas, for example, social justice in the liberal polity would mean that they must put aside this end and in the name of justice must work to promote a political environment where the Alphas are tolerated. By endorsing LP, the Betas agree to tolerate the Alphas, but practical liberalism now seems to be asking more than this of the Betas. They are now being asked to join in an ongoing public colloquy on how best to bring toleration and deference to life in the polity and to commit to the practice of civility even in their dealings with the Alphas. This might be more than the Betas bargained for, and they might wonder what happened to the promise that they could still argue for and promote their own moral theory of the human good throughout the polity.

This is a substantial problem under practical liberalism, but it also goes to the heart of the challenge groups face once they concede the need to find acceptable ways to live together. In effect, a commitment to LP requires groups to adopt a dual consciousness. On the one hand, they may continue to press in non-coercive ways for the realization of their own moral ends, but on the other hand, they must also remain faithful to the ends and ideals of the polity—the requirements of social justice as given by LP—in the process. Thus groups may find the need to engage in two sorts of dialogues with outgroups: The first explores the demands of social justice, and the second one promotes their own preferred vision of socio-political life. Actual political discourse will need to make room for both these conversations; thus practical liberalism does not exclude any substantive speech from the public realm or define any parameters to political debate.[27] Candidates for elective office, for example, may privilege the promotion of their preferred moral theory over the political status quo under LP, and if they do, they may expect a response from their opponents that repeats the value and importance of peaceful coexistence. But even here these candidates will need to recognize that political transformation must follow the establishment of moral homogeneity (and then worry about how this homogeneity might be sustained through time). Until and unless reasoned discourse brings all outgroups into one's own group, the counsel of prudence remains in place, and acceptance of LP continues to demand a commitment to the standards and spirit of social justice associated with it. In other words, the promotion of a group's preferred form of civil association must proceed in a manner faithful to the requirements of both the letter and the spirit of social justice. The acceptance of LP and the appreciation of the need to establish a politics of unity commits a group to the demands of LP and the pursuit of social justice. This too is a cost of endorsing LP, but it makes little sense to commit to a politics of unity and not also embrace the preconditions required to make this commitment successful.

The best way to secure a politics of unity is to forge the groups constitutive of the polity into a single group whose members have a sense of themselves as citizens or as members of the group that is the polity. Accordingly, practical liberalism must insist that members of the group that is the polity recognize and respect one another as fellow citizens and behave in a manner consistent with this recognition, even if they also see some of these citizens as otherwise hated outsiders. But of course the required civility falls rather short of requiring citizens to respect one another as persons. The disdain some group members will have for the members of certain outgroups by virtue of who they are or what they believe is left in place, but this disdain needs to coexist with the respect each owes to all and all owe to each as fellow citizens.

Ideally, the cultivation of this respect will have a mollifying effect on the nature of intergroup conflict within the polity. White supremacists, say, are still permitted to argue and even agitate for their preferred moral viewpoint, but their actions are to be restrained, not only by their legal obligations to tolerate those groups they happen to despise, but also by their appreciation of the fact that they are caught up in the common enterprise of civil association with these groups and thus need to recognize the members of these groups as fellow cooperators in a common enterprise in spite of their hatred for them. The cultivation of respect, this is to say, adds a significant psychological dimension to the legal obligation to tolerate. It thus encourages toleration by nurturing the development of a tolerant attitude in the citizenry inspired by the mutual appreciation of the value of social justice for the end of civic peace and stability.

This is testimony to the fact that the normative focus of practical liberalism can and should do a great deal toward building a sense of political unity within the polity. But there is more that can be said in this regard, for normative orientation is also likely to have an effect on the ontological understanding shared by fellow citizens. The cultivation of civility will do much to reconfigure the way group members recognize one another. Citizen self-identifications will invariably take on an added complexity as the members of the polity begin to recognize that they belong to the group that is the polity as well as other more primary groups. As group members increasingly recognize themselves as citizens, or members of the group that is the polity, they may be expected to regard others as fellow citizens—as members of the common group that is the polity, and this gives birth to a shared identity even in the face of those group-specific matters that distinguish them from one another. Even though some groups may despise and loathe certain outgroups in the polity, they must also come to recognize that there is at least one sense in which they share a common identity with these hated others; while these groups will remain outgroups from a particular group's vantage point, they cannot also be considered political outsiders.

Since a great many Americans already possess complex self-identifications, the addition of another group identification should not be all that troubling. Many, if not all, Americans, for example, already have a clear political identity—or series of political identities. They may think of themselves as Americans, or as Americans *and* Californians, or Americans *and* Chicagoans, and so forth. Moreover, many Americans already mix their political identities with additional group identifications, as Horace Kallen's famous hyphenated American aptly illustrates.[28] Ethnic identifications now familiarly embellish what it means to be an American, and in ways considerably more complicated than the simple immigrant identifications of concern to Kallen.[29] But for many Americans, the hyphen is itself an overly simplified rendering of their group identifications. Sometimes religious identifications further embellish one's identification and add another dimension to the hyphen, and sometimes other political, ideological, or social group identifications add yet further components to one's self-conception. The unifying anchor in all this remains the political identification of being an American, however, and while there is often little agreement upon why it matters or what it means, there is a generally shared concession that this commonality does matter to Americans. It is a group identification that resonates with those who share it, often in spite of the many and significant differences that all too frequently set fellow Americans to warring with one another.[30]

Unhappily, under a politics of interests, group member political identifications with America often work at cross-purposes with the end of political unity. In the absence of a unifying and coherent political principle, groups tend to equate their own normative views with the public morality presumed to animate the polity, or groups tend to flesh out common political ideals in the terms supplied by the normative convictions associated with their own primary group identifications. As John Higham noted in his important study of American nativism, some groups come to understand America through the normative prism supplied by their own belief and value systems, and this inclines their members to see those who are different as alien outsiders who threaten the American way of life.[31] Recent voting outcomes that ban gay marriage in several states in America offer an apt illustration of this. As the meaning of marriage became politicized, the ballot box was used to impose dominant moral sentiment upon groups that sought to redefine the nature of marriage. Sensing a threat to the sanctity of marriage as they understood it, dominant groups insisted that *their* understanding of marriage should set the *American* view of marriage. Lost in this typical example of the politics of interests was any public concern over the question of whether the polity should have the authority to control the meaning or conceptualization of such personal relationships as they manifest themselves within distinct groups. Practical liberalism works to avoid this problem by introducing a common normative focus to political identity that gives meaning and substance to the ideal of being an American.

Absent this normative glue, being an American amounts to little more than a matter of geography or an accident of history. While there is no lack of hortatory rhetoric about equality and justice in America, all this remains the vapid terminology that drives the politics of interests. In the presence of the political morality introduced by practical liberalism, on the other hand, being an American is still not only a matter of geography and an accident of history, but it is also an indication of what matters to the group that is the polity, of what unites and sustains the group, of what makes the group a group and not just a collection of discrete groupings of individuals who happen to find themselves in geographic proximity and subject to a common political authority. The common commitment to this shared political morality enables the members of the polity to conceptualize themselves as citizens, as individuals linked together in distinctive political ways regardless of whatever else might separate them. In spite of those group identifications that might incline some to see others as damned, disgusting, repugnant, or misguided by virtue of who they are or what they believe, the emergent ontology of practical liberalism also permits citizens to recognize one another as fellows in a political enterprise, as citizens sharing the same political morality and committed to the same political end of making social justice a viable reality throughout the polity. This emergent ontological awareness should further solidify the polity and complete the reasonably strong sense in which the polity itself qualifies as a group with a distinctive normative and ontological dimension that enables group members to recognize and understand the commonalities that unite them. This too will do much to facilitate the practice of civility throughout the polity. And while it need not, and probably will not, lessen or mollify the intergroup animus present in the polity, it should do something to promote the stability and sense of legitimacy of the polity in spite of this.

There is, to be sure, nothing distinctively or exclusively American about the political morality associated with practical liberalism, and it may also service in some capacity other polities that seek to unite under a similar politics of principle. When and if this is the case, polities that mutually, yet independently, embrace LP may share an important political affinity; they will, in any event, agree importantly on crucial standards of social justice and have mutual reasons to worry about regimes that continue to practice or pursue a politics of interests or a politics of dominance. There may, of course, be a good many other things upon which they happen to disagree, and circumstances beyond a common, though not shared, political morality will dictate whether such polities will become allies or enemies. Practical liberalism, in other words, is not a preface to cosmopolitanism, and its logic does not necessarily push in this direction—how could it since it lacks a foundational moral commitment that drives the spirit of moral homogeneity? Even polities similarly committed to LP will differ in crucial ways as the evolutionary dynamic of refining and expanding the standards of social justice brought into being by LP are worked out through differing histories. The histories and the narratives they reflect will do something to generate greater public identification with the group that is one's polity. They will encourage a political identification with a particular place and a particular tradition. This is the stuff from which a sense of patriotism is likely to emerge as citizens increasingly recognize the polity to which they belong as *their* polity.[32] This too is a barrier to the growth of greater cosmopolitanism.

Practical liberalism recommends and encourages the construction of a group consciousness that blends differing and hostile group members into a united polity, although it does so specifically for the distinctive political climate of the United States. Given the fact of pluralism, it recommends a commitment to a form of political unity that takes the traditional form of the modern state, seeking only to offer reasons to reconceptualize the state in terms of the greater political unity implied by the classic notion of a polity. Liberalism always has been a tradition of political discourse that supposes the state is the primary political unit in public life and that worries chiefly, if not exclusively, about its legitimacy and justness. In this regard, practical liberalism is again firmly entrenched in the liberal tradition.

## Fairness, civility, and associational morality

By taking political construction seriously, practical liberalism invites us to imagine the cultivation of a common polity united by a shared political morality—a political morality identifiable in terms of a common commitment to maximum group autonomy within the context of political unity. Political unity is achieved by the forging of a common polity, by creating an identification with the group that is the polity, and by nurturing a sense of civility within the citizenry. This civility can be further nourished by attending to the dynamics of group-associational identification and examining the distinctive moral responsibilities that arise from participation in a common social enterprise. Citizens engage in public discourse in order to further elaborate the requirements of social justice, and to be successful at this, they must reason and discuss faithfully and honestly in their capacity as a citizen. But how might it be possible to encourage this forthright public involvement, especially when citizens will likely have their own group-based reasons for seeing things in ways dictated or influenced by primary group norms or views and will almost certainly hold their normative rivals in considerable contempt?

In order to present a plausible answer to this question, I want to bring the notion of fairness onto center stage, and with it, I want to call attention to the idea of an associative morality. Moral liberals have difficulty making sense of what might be called, from their point of view, special or associative moral relationships largely because liberal morality tends to be universal and interactive in nature.[33] If persons deserve concern and respect because they are autonomous agents (as a good many moral liberals believe), all persons deserve concern and respect equally because all presumably qualify as autonomous at least to the threshold extent that matters to most moral liberals. Consequently, no person can have a special claim to moral attention or regard that trumps or preempts the equal regard owed to others. From the standpoint of moral liberalism, we are all just persons among others, and we owe the same moral duties and responsibilities to everyone accordingly. If a moral liberal of this sort finds herself facing a moral dilemma where, say, both her mother and a total stranger are drowning and she can save only one of the two, she would have to resort to chance to decide whom she will save. Both are persons in need of help, and this is all that matters from the standpoint of a universal and egalitarian morality. The fact that someone might have a special relationship to one of two potential victims is no reason to prefer the welfare of this person over the welfare of the other.

But this seems an uncommonly rigorous and insensitive moral position. The special relationship between a child and her mother is of distinctive moral importance, and it is just nonsense to think that someone behaves wrongly if she opts to rescue her mother from drowning without showing equal regard for the plight of a similarly situated stranger.[34] Nor does this conclusion rest upon pure sentimentality or the ancillary claim that one should privilege one's mother's case in such situations because of a special debt of gratitude for past support, nurturing, or the like. In point of fact, all things are not equal between persons morally speaking, a fact that moral liberalism, with its insistence upon an interactive morality, often obscures. Yet some caution is in order here. It may be that some version of a universal, interactive morality is true or that there are universal moral duties and responsibilities owed by each person as such to all others. But even if this is the case—and I have no interest in speculating on this matter here—it does not follow that such an interactive morality adequately captures and conveys all the possible dimensions of concern that might fall within our moral horizons.[35] Although interactive moralities are generally blind to this aspect of our moral lives, our associative attachments also seem to matter from a moral point of view. In particular, they introduce a dimension to moral understanding that supports the acknowledgment of special duties and obligations owed specifically to our fellow associates.

One way to accommodate these disparate moral concerns is to embrace the type of value pluralism endorsed by Isaiah Berlin and his followers.[36] We might, that is, insist that our moral world is populated by a variety of differing but equally legitimate views of the good that cannot be reduced to any specific and foundational moral claim. Value pluralism offers some promise, when woven into a political theory, of accommodating a wide range of normative and ontological diversity, but there are limits to this promise. Value pluralism is not relativism, and while value pluralists are willing to acknowledge considerable normative difference in group beliefs, they are typically unwilling to tolerate all manner of normative diversity. William Galston, for example, insists that the liberal state must respect human life as a 'central liberal purpose.'[37] This not only means, 'no free exercise for Aztecs' (because they presumably practice human sacrifice as part of their religious ways), it also means that the state should intervene in the affairs of the Followers of Christ in order to save their children from premature death.[38] It is not clear how value pluralists can sustain their belief in moral pluralism, on the one hand, and still find justifiable moral reason to prohibit the normative practices of groups like the Followers of Christ without slipping quietly into some form of moral monism.[39] But this problem need not trouble us here because practical liberalism does not suppose some version of value pluralism. And the notion of an associative morality that does have a place in practical liberalism is quite different from value pluralism. Rather than insist upon the presence of diverse and mutually exclusive visions of the good, an associative morality points toward the types of commitments one adopts in the course of living with others in the context of some shared social enterprise.

By way of illustration, consider an athletic contest of some sort—say, a tennis tournament. Players in such a tournament may or may not know one another, and they may or may not like one another. Typically, they enter the tournament with the desire to win and with the intention of doing everything they can to win within the bounds of fair play. From the standpoint of an interactive morality, this is personal bias with a vengeance, but it is also the way things work in a competition. Competitors who want to win will do everything in their power to do so, including working to exploit weaknesses in an opponent's game and striving within the parameters of fair play to put one's opponent at a disadvantage. There is, in other words, no concern for an opponent's interests, and no such concern is expected. We would think it quite silly if a player objected to his opponent's play on the grounds that by exploiting his weaknesses the opponent was biased against him and not displaying equal concern and respect for him as a person.

But moral relationships are not entirely suspended even in competitions of this sort. Players or participants are expected to play and participate fairly; that is, they are expected to play and participate in a fashion that is faithful to the ends or controlling ideals of the competition. Like most athletic contests, the point behind a tennis tournament is to identify the player who best exemplifies the excellences the game is designed to test, namely, facility with a racquet, speed and quickness, endurance, strength, a mastery of different shots, shrewd and clever play, and so forth. If we suppose that luck either cancels out or has only a minimal effect on the outcome of play (sometimes a large supposition), tournament winners will be those who best exemplify these ends within the context of the tournament, and thus they deserve whatever tokens of excellence are customarily awarded to the winners.

Players, of course, may not care particularly about displaying the requisite talent and ability; they may simply want to win. But they cannot do just anything to achieve this goal; if winning is to matter, they must play fairly. They must, that is, remain faithful to the aim and purpose of the game itself. This acts as a side constraint upon how players and participants in competitive endeavors can conduct themselves. They cannot cheat; they cannot threaten or intimidate opponents beyond the confines of play itself; they cannot interpret the rules always and exclusively to their own advantage when this works against a fair outcome; and they cannot attempt to buy off opponents, say, by offering them money to throw the game. In competitions, players and participants have personal reasons to put themselves first and to disregard the interests of their opponents. Sometimes, of course, this is fair enough. Once again, if my opponent has a weak backhand, I can put my interest in winning above my opponent's by trying to exploit this weakness to my advantage. But at other times, my interest in winning is checked by the constraints of an associative morality; my interest in winning, for example, does not override my obligation to play fairly.[40]

We might try to explain this imbalance by saying that at some point, an opponent's interests really do matter. Someone who cheats, it might be argued, disadvantages his opponent in an unlicensed manner, and this explains the unfairness at issue here. But it is difficult to make sense of this. For one thing, it assumes that one's opponent really is disadvantaged by cheating, but this is not necessarily so. One's opponent may care little if he wins or loses, for example, or he may be so superior (or inferior) that one's cheating will not influence the outcome of the match in the least. But cheating is still wrong, and it is wrong because it is unfair. Moreover, this explanation still cannot explain why some types of disadvantaging are fair and why some are not. Why is cheating an unlicensed disadvantaging while exploiting a weak backhand is not?[41] The explanation for this, of course, is that cheating is unfair but exploiting a weak backhand is simply fair play. We cannot explain why this is so, however, simply by making a crude appeal to disadvantaging, or even to rule following. (Why should we think the rule that allows this is fair?) We get to the problem with cheating, on the other hand, when we see that cheating ruins the game, so to speak; it frustrates the ability to be confident that the excellence the game is intended to test is being realized. It skews the results of play, or at least it threatens to do so. This is inconsistent with the point or purpose of play. It indicates a betrayal of all participants involved in the game, and this displays something of the nature of the wrong associated with unfairness. Defection from the point or purpose of play betrays one's fellow participants in the game, and the game is sullied or disrupted as a result. Correspondingly, we can understand fairness in terms of fidelity to some shared social practice or enterprise.[42] Fairness demonstrates a steadfastness and fidelity to the ends or ideals of the social practice or enterprise in which one happens to participate.

Accordingly, it is inappropriate to think that a wrong conceptualized in terms of unfairness has something to do with a setback suffered by the specific opponent who has been cheated. It is, as we have seen, an open question as to whether one's personal interests are set back as a result of cheating. But regardless of this, the tournament has been sullied by this defection from the spirit of fair play. Cheating mars the ability of all participants in the competition to be confident that the result is a true test of the excellence being examined. Competitions in this sense are rightly understood as cooperative social endeavors; for their ends to be fulfilled and their purposes realized, all participants must play in a manner faithful to these ends and purposes. This is what fairness requires, and it is why fairness is a preeminent virtue of an associative morality.[43]

To put the point more generally, associative morality involves the specific moral relationships we have with particular others by virtue of the social attachments that unite us in some common endeavor or enterprise. The common involvement in cooperative enterprises gives rise to new moral demands that follow from a joint commitment to the goals and/or ideals of the enterprise or practice itself. By entering a tennis tournament, I assume the responsibility of being faithful to the cooperative endeavor that is the tournament. The tournament can be successful and meaningful only if the participants (who are after all fellow cooperators in a shared social enterprise) dedicate themselves to its point or purpose and play accordingly.

The social attachments that unite competitors in a cooperative endeavor like an athletic competition—and unlike, say, a family where the attachments are considerably tighter—are thin or weak at best. Under such circumstances, it is tempting to privilege one's own interests and cheat or try to work the rules to one's advantage. But it is just here that fairness matters; for fairness calls attention to the fact that even competitions are cooperative events that can proceed as they should only if all participants remain faithful to their ends. It reminds us that our personal interests are really subservient to the well-being of the cooperative social enterprise to which we belong. Such reminders are of the first importance when we find ourselves united in a common social enterprise with others we do not know well or happen to hold in low esteem. When we have personal interests in making sure that the cooperative enterprise goes as it ideally should, fairness takes on added significance, and our corresponding desire to see our fellow cooperators play or compete fairly underscores our own commitment to doing so as well.

Fairness, then, is a cohesive virtue that matters within those social enterprises where cooperators have reason to defect from the cooperative endeavor and put themselves first. It is a crucial feature of an associative morality when the association in question is composed of cooperators who also have personal reasons to defect from the association perhaps because they dislike some or all of their fellow cooperators or perhaps because these reasons give them license to think they are special in some sense.

The pertinence of the concerns of fairness and the demands of an associative morality for a politics of unity should now seem reasonably straightforward. Within the liberal polity, associative morality requires citizens, as members of the group that is the polity, to participate fairly in the group enterprise, and this means they should practice civility as this notion has been described above. This means, first of all, honoring and respecting the responsibilities of toleration and deference required by LP. But it also demands faithful participation by all elements of the polity, *as citizens*, in the democratic process by which the standards of social justice are discussed, pursued, and implemented. This too is a fundamental aspect of what it means to participate forthrightly in the cooperative social enterprise that is the polity. While isolationist groups may opt out of many aspects of the political life of the polity, they too must understand and promulgate the ends of civility; they too must keep before them a sense of their responsibilities as citizens and practice them when called upon to do so.

Just as in the case of athletic competitions, members of the polity may not know one another or know one another well. And in the face of intergroup animosity, we can suppose that some members will dislike, or even hate, other citizens. Normative rivalries being what they are, some citizens may well have reason to advocate the elimination, segregation, or assimilation of hated others. This they are allowed to do under practical liberalism, although their efforts in this regard are circumscribed by the requirements of toleration and deference. But we are now also in a position to add that all members are required upon pain of unfairness to practice civility even in pursuit of their own group agendas. In spite of their personal or group agendas, all citizens as such must commit themselves to the ends of social justice as these are constructed through open and unfettered social discourse; and by virtue of their involvement in the polity, all citizens should be willing to engage in public discussion about the ends and spirit of social justice, particularly as these ideals affect their own group ways. Bringing the spirit of fairness to life in the liberal polity may be no simple chore, though it establishes another crucial goal of the educational process regardless of whether it happens to be under public or group control. But it is nonetheless a chore that the polity should attend to and insist upon, for accepting LP involves group members in the common project that is the polity and thus triggers all the responsibilities necessitated by associative morality.

To extend the analogy with athletic competition a bit further, groups may continue to pursue their desired end of bringing about some degree of moral homogeneity in society by working for the elimination, segregation, or assimilation of hated outgroups. But they must do so constrained by the spirit of fair play and also work to make sure that the demands of fair play are understood and respected by their own members. If intergroup animosity introduces a dimension of competition (about how life should go) into social life, it need not, and should not, turn social life into a war. And it will not turn social life into a form of warfare if groups understand that they are not just competitors, but more importantly fellow cooperators in the practice of living together within a common social setting. This, under practical liberalism, is the precondition for managing to live peaceably and viably in the presence of others and avoiding the worst possible scenario of intergroup predation and conflict.

To summarize what may seem like a fairly meandering argument, fairness, as an aspect of associative morality, indicates that fellow cooperators have a responsibility to remain faithful to the ends and ideals of the cooperative practice to which they belong. From the standpoint of practical liberalism, the polity must be regarded as a cooperative enterprise, and groups that elect (for prudential reasons) to accept LP and live according to a politics of principle are therefore obligated, as a matter of fairness, to remain faithful to the ends and ideals established by LP—or more simply, to remain faithful to social justice and the requirements of civility. Fairness, in short, mandates a commitment to social justice and to working to make the liberal polity a stable and peaceful civil arrangement. To endorse LP and embrace a politics of principle necessarily entails committing to do what is necessary in order to make the liberal polity a viable civil endeavor through time, or at least until and unless a given group can convince all other groups, including its normative rivals, to accept its moral theory of the human good and rearrange the polity's civil affairs accordingly. If accepting LP makes sense from a prudential point of view, then working to make a go of the liberal polity also makes sense, for this is simply the nature of the commitment one makes by opting for a politics of unity. Thus a group commitment to social justice will involve group efforts to support the legitimacy of the polity and maintain its integrity through time while also arguing for its own distinct moral theory of the human good as best it can.

The requirement to participate fairly in the social endeavor that is the polity will no doubt be considered a cost of endorsing LP. The cost, however, is already built into the requirement to practice toleration and deference. Fairness only reinforces the need to pay this cost in order to realize the social peace and security made possible by the liberal polity. It invites the citizens of the polity to see themselves as social cooperators in a common political endeavor in spite of the fact that they may consider each other repugnant, damned, disgusting, or misguided by virtue of who they are or what they believe. It leaves in place the possibility of disdain and disgust, but it emphasizes the reality of political unity in spite of this. If the polity is to work as advertised, if the ends of stability and peace are to be realized, all elements of the polity must cooperate in the political endeavor, and in this sense, they must recognize one another as fellow cooperators. This further illustrates the sense in which citizens in the liberal polity may need to embrace a dual consciousness, cultivating disdain for their normative rivals at one moment and yet continuing to engage these rivals in public discourse and work with them, as fellow cooperators, in the process. Fairness, however, makes this dual consciousness workable, for just as an athlete may have nothing but disdain for his opponent and still compete fairly against him, citizens can also have disdain for their normative rivals and still work with them to make the liberal polity work, until and unless they can persuade all elements of the polity to accept their moral vision.

## Goodness and justice in the liberal polity

It seems, then, that practical liberalism provides a reasonably robust normative guidance for the liberal polity, but there is still room to quibble over whether this is enough to make the liberal polity palatable to those who want more from civil association. Should we hope for more? Is it reasonable to hope for more? Practical liberalism must put a negative answer to both these questions. The only normative grounds that would allow a positive answer are to be found within the context of some comprehensive moral theory of the human good associated with some distinctive worldview. Insofar as practical liberals also hold comprehensive moral views that indicate, at the very least, how they would like to see their social world become, they too can work within the confines of liberal toleration for social change. But practical liberalism also insists that expecting more from civil association beyond toleration and deference threatens a return to the practical dangers associated with a quest for moral homogeneity; and this reintroduces the problems associated with the politics of interests that practical liberalism strives to overcome. But there is more to be said on this score.

Practical liberalism supports a key distinction between the just polity and the good society. Under practical liberalism, the good society can be regarded as a social unit that lives up to an ideal and comprehensive vision of associational and interdependent life within a shared social setting; it involves a specific image of how things should be for people, how individual lives should go, and how people should live together. Plato's *Republic* carefully blurs the distinction between the good and the just polity by imagining the former in the name of the latter. The good society is both a utopian vision and a moral ideal, or rather it is an ideal society as viewed from within the context of some comprehensive moral theory of the human good. It may be good and appropriate for groups boasting comprehensive worldviews and distinct moral theories of the human good to draw in words pictures of such polities. This, in any event, has entertained political thinkers from Plato onward. Such visions offer in pure form an elaborate presentation of what social life should look like given some comprehensive and inspiring moral viewpoint. But they are utopian within the context of pluralism for the very reason that they are inspired by moral views not fully or even partially shared by all groups present in the social environment. For some, then, visionary or utopian thinking about politics is a noble and enlightening pursuit—a pursuit, moreover, made popular in modern times by much Enlightenment and post-Enlightenment thinking. But for others it is a prelude to tyranny, oppression, and the imposition of a moral righteousness that threatens group freedom and group integrity.

Other political thinkers have avoided visionary theorizing in favor of a more practical political agenda. Here Machiavelli and Hobbes are presumed to be exemplary, and practical liberalism follows in this general tradition. Visionary thinkers often dismiss their more practical counterparts as mere *realists* too concerned with political order and stability and not sufficiently concerned with the more noble aims of justice and goodness.[44] While practical liberalism seeks to be realistic and to address what are presumed or perceived to be the political needs of a particular state at a specific point in time, it does so without forsaking the importance of justice for a viable and unified polity. But the just polity as envisioned by practical liberalism must deliberately and carefully avoid the claim to be a good society. Under practical liberalism, the just polity is one that carves out and promotes a viable civility in the face of deep and divisive differences between people. It accords disparate groups that cannot agree with one another on the moral fundamentals of a good life their due as stipulated by LP. It thus concedes room for ontological and normative difference, even if it also anticipates a modest ontological and normative unity that orbits around a shared political understanding of social justice. It sets the bar of political legitimacy not at the level of moral end, but at the level of civic compromise. And it seeks to blend diversity into an operative civility encouraging public discussion on what one should render unto Caesar and what one should render unto one's primary group. But this is an end to the demands of practical liberalism, and it precludes pushing matters beyond the nature of the just polity and committing to some necessarily disputable vision of the good society.

Of course, the version of practical liberalism offered here also contains structural and ideological elements. The structural component is given by the institutional requirement to honor toleration and deference by bringing these notions to life through the resolution of tolerance and coordination problems, while the ideological component involves the evolutionary requirement to foster and cultivate a social commitment to civility by promoting discussion of the demands of social justice and by insisting that group members participate fairly as citizens within the group that is the polity and to which, as citizens, they also happen to belong. It might be supposed that the evolutionary process associated with the ideological component will eventually erode the delicate balance established between the worldview and moral theory of the human good associated with one's primary group and the normative and ontological dimensions that unify the polity into a common group. That is, practical liberalism may be thought to possess a transformative force in its own right that will chisel away at the integrity of at least some primary groups, and thus endanger these groups. It just might, in other words, actually threaten at least some of the very groups it strives to protect. And it might now be insisted that practical liberals must actually support such erosion in the name of social justice.

If such erosion is a possibility, it introduces a reason for at least some groups to reject LP and opt out of the requirements of practical liberalism. On the other hand, the case for LP does as much as is theoretically possible to minimize the likelihood of this possibility. Practical liberalism defends, as we have seen, a distinction between political unity and moral homogeneity, claiming that it is at least theoretically possible to manage the former without pushing toward the latter. Without taking a stand on the social value or moral necessity of primary groups, practical liberalism supposes that these groups are an enduring feature of the social landscape and that they will seek to protect and preserve themselves in the face of external and internal pressures and challenges. But it also seems reasonable to add that the existence of such groups is not an altogether bad thing, regardless of the worldview and moral theory of the human good that defines them.

Primary groups, as we have seen, play an integral role in the lives of their members. They make things intelligible and comprehensible for their members, and they give them some sense of what matters, of what the good life looks like. They place their members in the world, so to speak, and give them something to live for, some reason for being, some purpose in life. Any erosion of primary groups will likely threaten the normative and ontological grounding that these groups provide their members, and this is not something that can be replaced by the liberal polity. The liberal polity, after all, can make sense only of civil association; it does not make sense of anything else. It leaves the mysteries of life, of being, of the cosmos, in place. This is reason to protect primary groups, and as it happens, practical liberalism does just this.

It would be helpful, then, if some reasons could be presented to mitigate concern about whether practical liberalism might erode the integrity of (at least) some primary groups. I have insisted that the democratic character of practical liberalism involves the facilitation of open and unfettered public discussion on the nature and nuances of social justice and the demands of civic fairness and civility. But it might also be worthwhile to distinguish, at this point, between intergroup and intragroup discourse. Authoritarian and elitist groups may feel that the democratic element of practical liberalism will threaten group ways. These groups are also expected under practical liberalism to make sure that their members practice civic fairness and civility, thereby honoring the civic responsibility to forbear others, although this requirement will likely have little effect on the lives of the rank-and-file members of isolationist and/or authoritarian groups. And as we have also seen, these groups too must see to the civic education of their young and integrate them into the group that is the polity. How they elect to do this, however, is a matter properly left to their own internal ways and is something to be resolved by their internal political mechanisms. If group elites want to control group views on the nature of social justice and shield their ranks from open involvement in civic discourse, they are entitled to do so, provided they work to guarantee that their rank-and-file members conduct themselves civilly in accordance with the demands of LP. Group leaders or elites, then, are at liberty to represent their group in the intergroup discourse that drives and characterizes democratic discussion about the nature of social justice, while more egalitarian or more diffuse groups may prefer to allow the direct involvement of their members in this discourse.

Practical liberalism, in other words, is chiefly dedicated to an unfettered *intergroup* discourse. Group involvement in such discourse is integral to the cultivation of the exact meaning of LP and the promulgation of a general spirit of civility throughout the polity. It expands viewpoints on the proper requirements of LP by adding differing views to the discussion and enabling the various groups constitutive of the polity to make clear to others those things that matter to them. This should work as a counterweight to the views and arguments of those public officials (group members in their own right) that serve in authoritative public institutions and bring the ideals of social justice under LP to life in practice. Groups represent themselves and their ways in the polity best by joining in public discussion and indicating how their autonomy and integrity is best protected. They can best protect against the possibility that certain dominant groups will remake the demands of LP in a manner inspired by their own internal moral beliefs by full participation in the democratic process and by engaging other groups in open discussion. This is of singular importance, moreover, if a politics of principle under LP is to be sustained and not decay back into a politics of interests. If it is left to dominant groups to control the meaning of LP, these groups are likely to reissue the demands of LP in terms derived from their own comprehensive moral doctrine. This, in turn, may return the polity to a politics of interests and raise the possibility of a politics of dominance. The best check against this possibility is group involvement in the civic processes of democratic discourse. Thus, the spirit of democracy that accompanies practical liberalism may be the best defense against the threat of group erosion, and need not be viewed as a possible or likely source of erosion.

This argument should provide some solace to those groups that may worry about their erosion under practical liberalism. Yet in spite of this, it is hardly possible to guarantee that the political unity defended under practical liberalism will not bring about the social erosion of at least some groups. Rawls, following Berlin, has wisely noted that there is no social transformation without cost.[45] To this we should add that the dynamic nature of group life and intergroup involvement all but guarantees that social transformation will continue to be a fact of social life. That adherence to LP will have some effect upon the transformation that takes place is to be expected, though the nature of this effect is all but impossible to imagine. While practical liberalism protects group autonomy, it also permits intergroup discussion and dialogue on those things that matter to people, and as I mentioned above, this by itself just may have a homogenizing effect on the polity in spite of the group protections afforded by practical liberalism. Of course, it might also have the opposite effect and inspire greater normative rivalries or drive the emergence of new and competing groups with widely distinct worldviews and moral theories of the human good. Given the history of intergroup conflict even in relatively stable places like the United States, there is reason to suppose the latter possibility is the most likely—a cynicism (I must admit) that does something to support the importance of taking practical liberalism seriously. But such reflections remain a matter of supposition and should be acknowledged as such.

Political inquiry (*pace* Marx) proceeds without the benefit of a crystal ball; it makes the most sense only when it is possible to suppose that theoretical reflection may offer some guidance for dealing with the social pathology that troubles a particular social setting at a specific time. It must proceed with the awareness that it is caught up in a historical saga that it cannot hope to control or predict. Will the normative aspect of practical liberalism cause the erosion of some of those groups that constitute the liberal polity? Perhaps—who can say? Does this possibility introduce reasons for groups to reject LP? It would do so only if group members supposed, first, that their group will be subject to social erosion under a politics of principle and, second, that this group would not erode under the present politics of interests. I think enough has now been said to indicate that these possibilities are remote, but there is little reason for theoretical inquiry to insist upon this conclusion any further. I have argued that practical liberalism provides the most stable political environment that is also maximally protective of group ways and beliefs. If social erosion is always and invariably possible, it would also seem that group integrity is the most secure in a political environment that permits groups a maximal control over their internal affairs. Under these circumstances, erosion is likely to be a consequence more of internal group politics than of the external corruption of group ways and beliefs.

Would it be a good thing if such erosion results because of the normative force of practical liberalism? As should now be evident, practical liberals can take only a tepid stand on this question. If such erosion pushes in the direction of a general moral homogeneity that reinforced political stability and social peace, practical liberals can applaud it, for they need not be (and probably are not) devoted to diversity for its own sake. Beyond this, however, practical liberalism has nothing particular to say. Judgments about the moral desirability of social erosion can only be answered from a perspective internal to the moral theory of the human good that one happens to hold. There is no reason, then, to consider it an appropriate subject for political inquiry, at least once the question of how people might profitably live together is separated from moral concerns about the good life. But of course, we can make the judgment required by the question only once we know about the erosion or social transformations that happen to take place, and given the flux of intragroup and intergroup life, it is simply impossible to predict this.

The modern mind has inherited from its Enlightenment legacy the apparent belief that human beings can deliberately control and determine their own future, and it has left behind Machiavelli's appreciation of the power of *fortuna*. On this score, practical liberalism drifts back toward Machiavelli. While liberalism is traditionally and perhaps inescapably meliorist, it has never been messianic or chiliastic, and here again practical liberalism fits within this broadly liberal tradition.

## Conclusion

The argument of this chapter has attempted to demonstrate that it is possible, in theory, to manufacture civic unity amidst deep and divisive moral and ontological diversity and thus to point toward the possibility of a politics of unity in spite of all that separates disparate and possibly hostile groups. No doubt the argument will seem like a form of political alchemy to anyone who supposes that given the fact of group diversity we can hope for no more from practical liberalism than a treaty arrangement between jealously sovereign and independent groups. If, however, the argument of this chapter is cogent, this is an unnecessarily cynical view.

When it comes to forging political unity amidst normative and ontological diversity, the trick is this: One must first illustrate and emphasize the desirability of civil association, and once this is accomplished, explain what needs to happen in order for civil association to work. If the prudential argument is able to persuade groups that things will go better for them under a politics of principle than under the alternatives, then a politics of unity can be manufactured. By recognizing the (prudential) desirability of a politics of principle, groups have reason to work together and to admit that their members must come to regard one another as fellow cooperators in the civic enterprise in spite of all that may happen to separate them. Because group defection threatens the careful balance that sustains the liberal polity, there is reason, in principle, for groups not to defect, and this means that there is reason for groups to cultivate in their members the spirit of fairness and civility required to make the liberal polity work.

# Epilogue

I began this inquiry by indicating a desire to put some answers to two questions that are fundamental to the job of theorizing about civil association: First, under what conditions, if any, is it possible for human beings holding disparate, conflicting, and perhaps even hostile beliefs and viewpoints to live together peaceably within a common polity? Second, and assuming a reasonably positive answer to the first question, is it possible to hope for something more in this regard than simply peaceful coexistence? It would perhaps be good, by way of conclusion, to summarize the answers that have been put to these questions.

Under the conditions introduced and identified by the theory of practical liberalism, we should now have some inkling of the circumstances under which peoples holding distinct and potentially hostile worldviews and moral theories of the human good might nonetheless manage to live together within a *modus vivendi* arrangement constituting what I have called the liberal polity. The bonds of sociality or social identity that hold within the liberal polity, as these were developed in response to the problem of boundaries, are relatively thin by communitarian and republican standards, but, nonetheless, they would seem to be sufficiently thick to establish a civic identity in which groups can recognize their respective members as fellow cooperators within a common civil enterprise dedicated to the ends and ideals associated with a politics of unity. These bonds are cemented by the norm of fairness, which operates primarily in cooperative endeavors or social practices where disagreement and even discord is common (if not altogether expected) among fellow cooperators. So it seems (to paraphrase Kant) that even antagonistic groups can learn to live together if they possess the type of understanding associated with practical liberalism.

Beyond this—to turn to the second question—we have little reason to expect much more from civil association. This will not make republicans or even strong nationalists very happy, but it is a conclusion that at least some communitarians should be able to live with. By providing a maximum amount of protection to group life, discrete groups that qualify as distinct communities are able to endure, attend to their internal affairs, and govern themselves limited only by the requirements of citizenship associated with membership in the group that is the liberal polity. These communities, these distinct publics, can presumably provide the communal identity, sense of belonging, and tight interpersonal attachments that are valued by at least some communitarians. There is no particular reason why the communities valued by communitarians must also qualify as states; and given the fact of pluralism that backgrounds the problem posed by the first question, there would seem to be no particular value in insisting that communities must also be states or polities in the sense this term has carried here.

But republicans and nationalists are not the only ones likely to be unhappy with practical liberalism. Political theorists and philosophers working within the tradition of moral liberalism will have good reason to object to the vision of civil association developed here as well. Thinkers who suppose that a more solid, objective, or normatively universal *terra firma* should serve as bedrock for a viable and stable liberal polity will be uneasy with the prudential basis of practical liberalism. Here practical liberalism sides with those thinkers who conclude that the search for a foundational, or quasi-foundational, argument capable of establishing the normative legitimacy

226

of and justification for the state is, in Michael White's terms, a will-o-the-wisp.[1] Insofar as theorists working within the tradition of moral liberalism struggle to make their notion of liberalism coherent—to state its demands and implications with precision and internal consistency—their efforts remain both valuable and cogent. And perhaps one day their promotion of a liberal moral homogeneity will pay off; who can say? From the standpoint of practical liberalism, however, these efforts are politically beside the point if the point of theorizing about political life involves finding a viable political unity within the context supplied by the fact of pluralism. Insofar as this latter point is what drives the efforts of moral liberals, they either underestimate the problems posed by the fact of pluralism or massage the notion of pluralism out of any and all reasonable shape. Taking the social environment as it is means respecting the mess we find there and not rendering it antiseptic for the sake of theoretical purity. According to practical liberalism, if we are to take the fact of pluralism seriously and still commit to a politics of unity, the first step is to sever the theoretical project from any and all controversial moral foundations and presumptions; and of course given the fact of pluralism, all moral foundations and presumptions are controversial, linked as they must be to someone's particular worldview or moral theory of the human good.

As an aside, it would be a relatively simple matter to move practical liberalism into the realm of the moral. Precedent for such a move is on display in at least some modern natural-law thinkers. All we need do here is contend that the liberal polity imagined under practical liberalism is a prudential necessity—or a necessity of prudential rationality—and then argue that such rationality offers insight into God's intentions for how human beings should live together. If we suppose further that God's intentions in this regard provide insight into natural law, which of course has the status of moral imperative, we have a solid moral defense of the liberal polity *ala* Pufendorf. If we think, in an era that has parsed theology from philosophy, that divine voluntarism is not really appropriate as a solid method of argument, we can suppose instead that prudential rationality yields insight into the proper nature of things, and so forth, and this is the *grundlage* of moral legitimacy.[2] But while such a move may make some thinkers happy, it will probably turn off others, and more to the point, it will hardly move many groups in the polity who take exception to such catholic speculations and to whom the prudential argument must be addressed in terms they can endorse.

But those thinkers who conclude from this that we ought to give up the (traditional) point of theorizing about politics and recognize or acknowledge that politics, or at least democratic politics, is about seeking and developing compromise and balance between contesting political factions will also have reason to distance themselves from practical liberalism. But the 'art of politics' thus understood merely continues the politics of interests or the politics of dominance; it does not (and does not presume to) end conflict but merely legitimizes the continuation of conflict in the hopes that things will not unravel, at least in those relatively stable political systems where they have not unraveled already. But even in relatively stable political systems, there is perhaps less in the way of compromise and more in the way of suppression or domination on display than may seem to meet the eye. If and when this is the case, the threat of increased and destabilizing political conflict may also be greater than would seem to meet the eye. Practical liberalism explores the possibility that we can do better than this. If the case for practical liberalism has merit, there is reason to conclude that we can do better than this and should do better than this if political peace and social order matter in the least.

Yet thinkers who take seriously the challenge of inquiring into the possibilities and limitations of political association are not the only ones, and perhaps not even the primary ones, who will have reason to object to practical liberalism. As I have emphasized throughout, the groups that inhabit the social environment to which a particular brand of practical liberalism is addressed will also have reason to oppose practical liberalism, for it does not (necessarily) constitute their most preferred form of socio-political organization. Groups whose members are disinclined to want to practice toleration or deference toward all possible outgroups will naturally prefer some form of socio-political organization based upon their own worldview or moral theory of the human good. It may not even be their second most preferred option if we suppose groups would prefer to take their chances under a politics of interests, perhaps because they are confident in their political capital at present, rather than tolerate those they find damned, disgusting, mistaken, or misguided by virtue of who they are or what they believe.

From the standpoint of practical liberalism, however, a politics of principle is their wisest option. If groups cannot always or invariably have things their way, and the fact of flux operating within the context of pluralism suggests that it is unlikely that they can always or invariably have things their way, there is considerable solace in opting for a socio-political condition where their ability to manage and control their own affairs as they see fit is guaranteed and policed by political authority. Nor does opting for a politics of principle mimic the rational-choice situation illustrated by the famous prisoner's dilemma. Groups are not faced with making a distinct choice at a particular moment in time, unmindful of the choices others are making, and then living with the relative payoffs. Opting for LP is not a one-time move; it is an ongoing commitment policed by government before the watchful eyes of all elements of the polity. Defection will have its consequences, which ultimately lead back to a politics of interests under the worst-case scenario. If groups have reason, as the prudential argument suggests that they do, to not wish for this, they also have reason to remain faithful and loyal to the liberal polity.

This supposes, of course, that social peace and political stability are great social goods and are considered as such by all elements of the polity. This point is crucial for an understanding of the weights I have implicitly attached to the question of whether groups should elect to endorse LP. The heart of the case for a politics of principle depends upon group recognition that social peace and security are well worth the incidental cost associated with abandoning coercive strategies designed and intended to eliminate, segregate, or assimilate hated outgroups. And of course I could be wrong about the way these various weights should be attached to the choice equation; some groups may weight the right to continue their coercive strategies above the good of social peace and good order. Practical liberalism can ask only that groups think carefully about such weightings and consider the risks they run if they weight their continued campaign against their normative rivals over social peace and if all other groups in the social environment do so as well. The case for LP is also an argument that supports the view that practical liberalism has gotten the right weights attached to the choice equation.

It follows, in any event, that nobody is going to be thrilled with practical liberalism. But ironically and also importantly, this may just be about the best thing that can be said for it. It is about all we can hope for at present, in places like the United States, where people face the need to be able to go on with their lives, secure in their ability to live, worship, and do as they wish (according to their respective worldviews and moral theories of the human good) even though they must live with others who might just find them damned, disgusting, misguided, or mistaken by virtue of who they are or what they believe.

The 'at present' in the above statement introduces an important and powerful qualification to the answer I have put to my second question, however—for it is always possible not only to hope for more but to work for more as well. Practical liberalism does not put an end to political history because political history, at least as conceived here, can have no end—this is but a final bow to the fact of flux. Groups can always work to get outsiders to see things their way, and it would be not only foolish but arrogant to think that a moral and ontological homogenization that might put an end to the type of normative and epistemic difference that currently serves as a source of so much social conflict is a flat impossibility. It would, that is, be both silly and myopic to make such a claim, and ironically because it too runs afoul of the fact of flux. If we take the fact of flux seriously, we must admit that we just do not know, and cannot know, what the future holds for us. Yet even if moral and ontological homogeneity materialized, it would still not put an end to political history, although it might render the need for practical liberalism otiose—albeit perhaps only for a time; even if such homogeneity came into being, we could not know if it would last for long. Though there is *at present* reason to be skeptical about all this, there is no reason for practical liberals to reject this possibility or even to fail or refuse to work toward the realization of what they consider the most appropriate and compelling worldview and moral theory of the human good. It is hardly an objection to practical liberalism to suppose that it might just set the stage necessary or required for its transcendence.

# Notes

## Introduction

1. John Rawls describes political arguments that stand independently of a given comprehensive moral theory as 'freestanding.' See Rawls, *A Theory of Justice* (Cambridge, MA: Harvard University Press, 1971), pp. 44–46.
2. Cf. R. Baxter, 'Multilateral Treaties as Evidence of Customary International Law,' *British Yearbook of International Law* 41 (1965–66); Anthony D'Amato, *The Concept of Custom in International Law* (Ithaca, NY: Cornell University Press, 1971); C. Tomuschat, 'Obligations Arising for States Without or Against Their Will,' *Recueil Des Cours* 241 (1993); I.M. Lobo Souza, 'The Role of Consent in the Customary Process,' *International and Comparative Law Quarterly* 44 (1995); Gary L. Scott and Craig L. Carr, 'Multilateral Treaties and the Formation of Customary International Law,' *Denver Journal of International Law and Policy* 25 (1996).
3. Literature on multiculturalism has exploded in recent years as ethnic minorities have become more politically active and as liberal theorists have attempted to accommodate minority-group concerns within the traditionally individualistic character of liberal thought. See in particular, Charles Taylor, *Multiculturalism*, ed. Amy Gutmann (Princeton, NJ: Princeton University Press, 1994); Judith Baker, ed., *Group Rights* (Toronto: Toronto University Press, 1994); Will Kymlicka, *Multicultural Citizenship* (Oxford: Oxford University Press, 1995); Ian Shapiro and Will Kymlicka, *Ethnicity and Group Rights* (New York: New York University Press, 1997); Nathan Glazer, *We Are All Multiculturalists Now* (Cambridge, MA: Harvard University Press, 1997); Brian Barry, *Culture and Equality* (Cambridge, MA: Harvard University Press, 2001); and Kymlicka, *Politics in the Vernacular* (Oxford: Oxford University Press, 2001).
4. Cf. Charles Beitz, *Political Theory and International Relations* (Princeton, NJ: Princeton University Press, 1979); Michael Walzer, *Thick and Thin* (Notre Dame: University of Notre Dame Press, 1994); David Held, *Democracy and the Global Order* (London: Polity Press, 1995); Richard Falk, *On Human Governance: Toward a New Global Politics* (London: Polity Press, 1995); John Rawls, *The Law of Peoples* (Cambridge, MA: Harvard University Press, 1999); and Charles Jones, *Global Justice* (Oxford: Oxford University Press, 1999); Kok-Chor Tan, *Toleration, Diversity, and Global Justice* (University Park: Pennsylvania State University, 2000).
5. Will Kymlicka, *Liberalism, Community, and Culture* (Oxford: The Clarendon Press, 1989), pp. 136–37, 147–49.
6. See, for example, Ronald Dworkin, 'Liberalism,' in Dworkin, ed., *A Matter of Principle* (Cambridge, MA: Harvard University Press, 1985), pp. 181–204; Jeremy Waldron, *Liberal Rights* (Cambridge: Cambridge University Press, 1993), pp. 4–17; John Gray, *Liberalism* (Minneapolis: University of Minnesota Press, 1995), pp. 51–60.
7. Stephen Macedo, *Liberal Virtues* (Oxford: The Clarendon Press, 1990), p. 203. A similar point is emphasized by C. Donald Moon, who asserts that political liberalism, the particular version of liberalism he prefers, 'is deeply committed to overcoming injustice and creating a political community whose norms are affirmed by all its members.' Moon, *Constructing Community: Moral Pluralism and Tragic Conflicts* (Princeton, NJ: Princeton University Press, 1993), p. 101.

8. This point has been artfully developed by Alasdair MacIntyre. See MacIntyre, *Whose Justice? Which Rationality?* (Notre Dame: University of Notre Dame Press, 1988), pp. 335–48.
9. An important exception to this view of liberalism is presented by William Galston, who attempts to distance himself from a concern for autonomy precisely because reliance upon this notion cannot serve as a legitimating foundation of civil association for groups that 'do not embrace autonomy.' (See, Galston, *Liberal Pluralism* (Cambridge: Cambridge University Press, 2002), esp. pp. 15–27.)
10. Cf. Dworkin, pp. 191–94; Charles Larmore, *Patterns of Moral Complexity* (Cambridge: Cambridge University Press, 1987), pp. 59–66; Kymlicka, *Liberalism, Community, and Culture*, pp. 140–54; Joseph Raz, *The Morality of Freedom* (Oxford: The Clarendon Press, 1986), pp. 312–20.
11. See, for example, Michael Sandel, *Liberalism and the Limits of Justice* (Cambridge: Cambridge University Press, 1982); Alasdair MacIntyre, *After Virtue* (Notre Dame: University of Notre Dame Press, 1984); Charles Taylor, *Sources of the Self* (Cambridge, MA: Harvard University Press, 1989), Ch. 2; Taylor, 'Cross-Purposes: The Liberal-Communitarian Debate,' in Nancy Rosemblum, ed., *Liberalism and the Moral Life* (Cambridge, MA: Harvard University Press, 1989), pp. 159–82; and Stephen Mulhall and Adam Swift, eds, *Liberals and Communitarians* (Oxford: Blackwell Publishers, 1992).
12. Cf. William A. Galston, 'Two Concepts of Liberalism,' *Ethics* 105 (1995) 516–34; Stephen Macedo, 'Liberal Civic Education and Religious Fundamentalism: The Case of God v. John Rawls?' *Ethics*, 105(1995), 468–96. See also Macedo, 'Charting Liberal Virtues,' in John W. Chapman and William A. Galston, eds, *Virtue* (New York: New York University Press, 1992), Ch. 10.
13. Richard E. Flathman, *Reflections of a Would-Be Anarchist* (Minneapolis: University of Minnesota Press, 1998), p. 105.
14. Cf. Stephen Macedo, 'Transformative Constitutionalism and the Case of Religion: Defending the Moderate Hegemony of Liberalism,' *Political Theory* 26 (1998), pp. 56–80; and Anna Galeotti, *Toleration as Recognition* (Cambridge: Cambridge University Press, 2002), pp. 53–84.
15. See John Locke, *A Letter Concerning Toleration* (Indianapolis: Bobbs-Merrill, Inc., 1950), pp. 51–52.
16. Charles Larmore, *The Morals of Modernity* (Cambridge: Cambridge University Press, 1996), p. 151.
17. Ibid.
18. An alternative liberal strategy is to minimize the problem by supposing that illiberal sorts, who fall outside the broad net of liberal morality, are too few and far between to worry about. (Cf. Kymlicka, *Politics in the Vernacular*), pp. 62–64.
19. See, for example, George Crowder, 'Pluralism and Liberalism,' *Political Studies* XLII (1994) 293–305; John Gray, 'Agonistic Liberalism,' *Social Philosophy and Policy* 12 (1995) 111–35; Michael J. White, *Partisan or Neutral? The Futility of Public Political Theory* (Lanham, MD: Rowman & Littlefield, 1997); Chandran Kukathas, *The Liberal Archipelago* (Oxford: Oxford University Press, 2003).
20. John Rawls, *Political Liberalism* (New York: Columbia University Press, 1993), pp. 99–107.
21. Cf. Rawls, ibid.; Larmore, *The Morals of Modernity*, pp. 121–51; Macedo, 'Liberal Civic Education and Religious Fundamentalism: The Case of God v. John Rawls,' pp. 473–96; Moon, pp. 97–120.
22. See Charles W. Anderson, *Pragmatic Liberalism* (Chicago: University of Chicago Press, 1990).

23. See Thomas Spragens, *Civic Liberalism* (Lanham, MD: Rowman & Littlefield Publishers, Inc., 1999), pp. 3–17.
24. Gray, pp. 111–35.
25. See Patrick Neal, 'Vulgar Liberalism,' *Political Theory* 21 (1993) 623–42; Judith Shklar, 'The Liberalism of Fear,' in Rosenblum, ed., pp. 21–38. Although Jacob Levy applies a similar title to his own liberal theory, his argument remains premised upon basic moral considerations, and so should be distinguished from an accommodationist argument. See Jacob T. Levy, *The Multiculturalism of Fear* (Oxford: Oxford University Press, 2000).
26. See, for example, Brian Barry, *Theories of Justice* (Berkeley: University of California Press, 1989), and *Justice as Impartiality* (Oxford: The Clarendon Press, 1995).
27. This point has been elegantly and elaborately developed by Chandran Kukathas. See Kukathas, p. 218.

# 1   A prolegomenon to political thought

1. John Locke, *The Second Treatise of Government*, Ch. V.
2. Cf. John Locke, *A Letter Concerning Toleration* (Indianapolis: Bobbs-Merrill, Inc., 1950), pp. 51–53. See also, Michael J. White, *Partisan or Neutral? The Futility of Public Political Theory* (Lanham, MD: Rowman & Littlefield, 1997), pp. 6–8.
3. John Rawls, *A Theory of Justice* (Cambridge, MA: Harvard University Press, 1971), pp. 118–61.
4. John Rawls, *Political Liberalism* (New York: Columbia University Press, 1993), pp. 49–54. See also Charles Larmore, *The Morals of Modernity* (Cambridge: Cambridge University Press, 1996), pp. 67–74.
5. Rawls articulates the point in terms of the possibility of an overlapping consensus, a notion that puts great faith in the presence of certain sociological conditions. For Rawls's political liberalism to support a stable political system, 'reasonable' groups must significantly outnumber any 'unreasonable' influences that might happen to be present. (Cf. *Political Liberalism*, pp. 59–66; and Rawls, *Justice as Fairness: A Restatement* (Cambridge, MA: Harvard University Press, 2001), pp. 153–57.) See also Gerald F. Gaus, *Justificatory Liberalism* (Oxford: Oxford University Press, 1996), pp. 113–51.
6. Rawls, *Political Liberalism*, pp. 65–66. See also Larmore, pp. 147–51; Richard Bellamy, *Liberalism and Pluralism: Towards a Politics of Compromise* (London: Routledge, 1999), Ch. 4. John Tomasi has introduced a slightly more nuanced account of the possible types of individuals one might expect to encounter in pluralist societies and expanded a description of non-liberal and illiberal influences with which liberal states must contend. See Tomasi, *Liberalism Beyond Justice* (Princeton, NJ: Princeton University Press, 2001), pp. 17–20.
7. Cf. William A. Galston, 'Two Concepts of Liberalism,' *Ethics* 3 (1995) 516–34; Stephen Macedo, 'Liberal Civic Education and Religious Fundamentalism: The Case of God v. John Rawls,' *Ethics* 3 (1995) 468–96; and Gerald Doppelt, 'Is There a Multicultural Liberalism?' *Inquiry* 41 (1998) 223–48.
8. The unlawful practices of the Ku Klux Klan and other racist or anti-Semitic organizations in America, along with state efforts to deal with them, have been widely documented. See in particular, *Hate Groups in America: A Record of Bigotry and Violence* (New York: The Anti-Defamation League, 1988); David M. Chalmers, *Hooded Americanism: The First Century of the Ku Klux Klan, 1865–1965* (Garden City, NY: Doubleday & Co., 1965); Arnold S. Rice, *The Ku Klux Klan in American Politics*

(Washington D.C.: Public Affairs Press, 1962); Bill Stanton, *Klanwatch: Bringing the Ku Klux Klan to Justice* (New York: Grove Weidenfeld, 1991). The Anti-Defamation League of B'nai B'rith lists 17 separate active regional groups affiliated with the Ku Klux Klan. Anti-Defamation League, *Hate Groups in America* (1988).

9.  Recourse to the notion of incommensurability has become, since Rawls, something of the standard method to account for basic group differences in worldviews and moral theories of the human good. I follow emerging tradition here and use the notion of incommensurability as a shorthand means for identifying and emphasizing the seemingly unbridgeable distance that may happen to separate the moral and epistemological viewpoints of disparate groups. Cf. Stephen Lukes, 'Making Sense of Moral Conflict,' in Nancy Rosenblum, ed., *Liberalism and the Moral Life* (Cambridge, MA: Harvard University Press, 1989), pp. 127–42; George Crowder, 'Pluralism and Liberalism,' *Political Studies* XLII (1994) 293–305.

10. Cf. John S. Dryzek, *Deliberative Democracy and Beyond: Liberals, Critics, Contestations* (Oxford: Oxford University Press, 2000); Bellamy, Ch. 5; Jürgen Habermas, *Between Facts and Norms*, trans. William Rehg (Cambridge, MA: MIT Press, 1998), pp. 304–28; Stephen Macedo, ed., *Deliberative Politics: Essays on Democracy and Disagreement* (Oxford: Oxford University Press, 1999); Jon Elster, ed., *Deliberative Democracy* (Cambridge: Cambridge University Press, 1998); James Bohman and William Rehg, eds, *Deliberative Democracy: Essays on Reason and Politics* (Cambridge, MA: MIT Press, 1997); Seyla Benhabib, ed., *Democracy and Difference* (Princeton, NJ: Princeton University Press, 1996); and James Fishkin, *Democracy and Deliberation* (New Haven: Yale University Press, 1991). More agonistic theories of democracy may also be put in this camp. Cf. William E. Connolly, *The Ethos of Pluralization* (Minneapolis: University of Minnesota Press, 1995); Chantal Mouffe, *The Democratic Paradox* (New York: Verso, 2000); and Iris M. Young, *Inclusion and Democracy* (New York: Oxford University Press, 2000).

11. See, for example, Bruce Ackerman, *Social Justice in the Liberal State* (New Haven: Yale University Press, 1980), pp. 8–19; Jürgen Habermas, *The Theory of Communicative Action*, Vol. 1, *Reason and the Rationalization of Society*, trans. T. McCarthy (Boston: Beacon Press, 1984), and *Moral Consciousness and Communicative Action*, trans. Christian Lenhardt and Shierry Weber Nicholsen (Cambridge, MA: MIT Press, 1991).

12. Michael Ignatieff's provocative accounts of genocide, ethnic cleansing, and ethnic conflict powerfully illustrate the most extreme forms of political instability generated by intergroup conflict. See Ignatieff, *Blood and Belonging: Journeys into the New Nationalism* (New York: Farrar, Straus, and Giroux, 1994), and *The Warrior's Honor: Ethnic War and the Modern Conscience* (New York: Henry Holt & Co., 1997).

13. Cf. Kenneth Karst, *Belonging to America* (New Haven: Yale University Press, 1989).

14. Cf. Lawrence Fuchs, *The American Kaleidoscope* (Hanover, NH: Wesleyan University Press, 1990).

15. This is something of the legacy of Tocqueville's powerful analysis of American democracy. Thinkers following in Tocqueville's shoes suppose the basic conditions of American liberalism set the tone and fix the unchallenged ideals of political life in America. It is left to Americans to resolve the technical difficulties that lurk in the interstices of American liberal convictions. Cf. Gunnar Myrdal, *An American Dilemma* (New York: Harper & Brothers, 1944); Louis Hartz, *The Liberal Tradition in America* (New York: Harcourt, Brace, 1955); Samuel P. Huntington, *American Politics: The Promise of Disharmony* (Cambridge, MA: The Belknap Press, 1981).

16. David Hume, *A Treatise on Human Nature*, ed. L.A. Selby-Bigge (Oxford: The Clarendon Press, 1968), p. 495.

17. John Higham, *Strangers in the Land* (New Brunswick, NJ: Rutgers University Press, 1955); *Send These To Me* (New York: Atheneum, 1975); 'Hanging Together: Divergent Unities in American History,' *Journal of American History* 61 (1974) 5–28. See also Susan Herbst, *Politics at the Margin* (Cambridge: Cambridge University Press, 1994); and Smith, *Civic Ideals*, passim.
18. The point is expressed nicely by Eldridge Cleaver, 'Both right and left claim to love their country. The Ku Klux Klan, John Birch Society, American Nazi Party, conservative republicans, Minutemen, even the Hell's Angels—all wrap themselves up in the American flag and solemnly call themselves patriots.' Cleaver, *Soul On Ice* (New York: Dell Publishing, 1968), p. 109.
19. See Rogers Smith, 'Beyond Tocqueville, Myrdahl, and Hartz: The Multiple Traditions in America,' *American Political Science Review* 87 (1993) 549–66.
20. See Stuart A. Scheingold, *The Politics of Rights* (New Haven: Yale University Press, 1974).
21. Cf. J.M. Balkin, 'Some Realism about Pluralism, Legal Realist Approaches to the First Amendment,' *Duke Law Journal* 1990 (1990) 375–430; Burt Neuborne, 'Ghosts in the Attic: Idealized Pluralism, Community and Hate Speech,' *Harvard Civil Rights-Civil Liberties Law Review* 32 (1992) 371–406; Charles Fried, 'The New First Amendment Jurisprudence: A Threat to Liberty,' *University of Chicago Law Review* 59 (1992) 225–53; Frederick Schauer, 'The Phenomenology of Speech and Harm,' *Ethics* 103 (1993) 635–53. See also Samuel Walker, *Hate Speech: The History of An American Controversy* (Lincoln, NE: University of Nebraska Press, 1994).
22. Cf. Hartz, pp. 145–77; Higham, pp. 131–57.
23. *RAV v. City of St. Paul, Minnesota*, 505 US 377 (1992). The St. Paul Bias-Motivated Crime Ordinance struck down by the Court stated,

> Whoever places on public or private property a symbol, object, or appellation, characterization or graffiti, including, but not limited to, a burning cross or Nazi swastika, which one knows or has reasonable grounds to know arouses anger, alarm, or resentment in others on the basis of race, color, creed, religion, or gender commits disorderly conduct and shall be guilty of a misdemeanor.

24. Richard Delgado, 'Words that Wound: A Tort Action for Racial Insults, Epithets, and Name Calling,' in Mari J. Matsuda, Charles R. Lawrence III, Richard Delgado, and Kimberlé Williams Crenshaw, eds, *Words That Wound* (Boulder, CO: Westview Press, 1993), pp. 92–93.
25. See Laura Gunderson and David Austin, 'Gay Marriage Debate: More Same-Sex Couples Wait in Line to Get Their Marriage Licenses,' *The Oregonian*, March 4, 2004, AO1.
26. See David Reinhard, 'Our Not So Gay Debate About Marriage,' *The Oregonian*, March 21, 2004, FO4.
27. See David Hogan, 'Initiative to Ban Gary Marriage on Its Way,' *The Oregonian*, May 21, 2004, AO1.

## 2   A politics of principle

1. John Rawls, *A Theory of Justice* (Cambridge, MA: Harvard University Press, 1971), pp. 118–50.
2. Cf. Will Kymlicka, *Politics in the Vernacular* (Oxford: Oxford University Press, 2001), pp. 18–27.

3. The notion of a group must, of necessity, remain rather slippery, and it is probably unwise to hope for more clarity here than the notion will allow. There is, for example, something of importance in Iris Young's insight that groups are relational entities that are to be understood in terms of members and outsiders. But Young's additional claim that groups can be identified by outsiders even if those so identified have no consciousness of themselves as a group seems more questionable. (Young, *Justice and the Politics of Difference* (Princeton, NJ: Princeton University Press, 1990), p. 46.) According to the account of groups to be followed here, groups are distinguishable by virtue of the specific viewpoints that define them and separate them from group outsiders. Since group members can be presumed to be conscious of this difference, they should also have a sense of themselves as a group. But this does not put to rest other difficulties introduced by the fact that groups may also exhibit a variety of sub-viewpoints that permit distinctions within groups. Catholics and Protestants are both Christians, for example, and thus belong to the same group in one sense. But both Catholics and Protestants will think of themselves, with justification, as distinct groups, and from the standpoint of practical liberalism, this is what matters.

   For a discussion of the relation between personal identities and group identities, see Samuel P. Huntington, *Who Are We?* (New York: Simon & Schuster, 2004), pp. 21–33.
4. See Huntington, ibid., pp. 24–27.
5. For a comprehensive discussion of the types of strategies some groups might adopt for dealing with others they find repugnant, damned, or disgusting by virtue of who they are or what they believe, see James W. Nickel, 'Freedom of Expression in a Pluralist Society,' *Law and Philosophy* 7 (1989) 281–93.
6. See, for example, David O. Sears *et al.*, 'Cultural Diversity and Multicultural Politics: Is Ethnic Balkanization Psychologically Inevitable?' in Deborah A. Prentice and Dale T. Miller, eds, *Cultural Divides: Understanding and Overcoming Group Conflict* (New York: Russell Sage Foundation, 1999), pp. 35–79; Donald M. Taylor and Fathali M. Moghaddam, *Theories of Intergroup Relations* (Westport, CT: Praeger Publishers, 1994); Melvin Seeman, 'Intergroup Relations,' in Morris Rosenberg and Ralph H. Turner, eds, *Social Psychology: Sociological Perspectives* (New Brunswick: Transaction Publishers, 1990), pp. 378–410; Susan Condor and Rupert Brown, 'Psychological Processes in Intergroup Conflict,' in Wolfgang Stroebe, Arie W. Kruglanski, Daniel Bar-Tal, and Miles Hewstone, eds, *The Social Psychology of Intergroup Conflict* (Berlin: Springer-Verlag, 1988); Robert A. LeVine and Donald T. Campbell, *Ethnocentrism: Theories of Conflict, Ethnic Attitudes, and Group Behavior* (New York: John Wiley & Sons, 1972).
7. For an excellent account of social conflict that reduces this conflict to distributional concerns, see Russell Hardin, *One for All* (Princeton, NJ: Princeton University Press, 1995), Chs. 3 and 4.
8. See James Tully, *An Approach to Political Philosophy: Locke in Contexts* (Cambridge: Cambridge University Press, 1993), pp. 47–79; John Gray, *Liberalism* (Minneapolis: University of Minnesota Press, 1995), pp. 8–16; Chandran Kukathas, *The Liberal Archipelago* (Oxford: Oxford University Press, 2003), p. 262.
9. Horace Kallen famously introduced the notion of the hyphenated American to indicate the way that ethnic identities remain in the United States even as these ethnic groups merge politically. (See Kallen, *Culture and Democracy in the United States* (New York: Boni and Liveright, 1924).) Michael Walzer, however, notes the way ethnic identities themselves change with Americanization. Irish-Americans, for example, also become American-Irish with their own ethnic character that

distinguishes them from their Irish cousins across the sea. See Walzer, *What It Means to Be an American* (New York: Marsilio Publishers, 1996), pp. 23–52.

10. Cf. David O. Sears, 'Symbolic Politics: A Sociopsychological Theory,' in Shante Iyengar and William J. McGuire, eds, *Explorations in Political Psychology* (Durham, NC: Duke University Press, 1993), pp. 113–49.

11. Kant, 'Perpetual Peace,' in H. Reiss, ed., *Kant's Political Writings*, trans. H.B. Nisbet (Cambridge: Cambridge University Press, 1970), p. 112.

12. E.E. Schattschneider has said that 'the trick' for establishing political legitimacy 'is to get the people and government on the same side.' (Schattschneider, *Two Hundred Million Americans in Search of a Government* (Hinsdale, IL: Dryden Press, 1969), p. 11.) While this is certainly true enough, it tells only part of the story and betrays a typically American (and liberal) inclination to see government as a force that stands opposed to the people it governs. The spirit of practical liberalism makes sense only when we appreciate that we can get people and their government on the same side only once we get the people themselves on the same side. The 'trick,' in effect, is to demonstrate how to make government something more than an instrument of power lodged in the hands of dominant groups; the 'trick' of political legitimacy is to get the people to agree that the ends of government are also, and at the same time properly, the ends they can and should endorse. Given the fact of pluralism, this is quite a trick.

13. The subject of state neutrality has generated considerable controversy among liberal and non-liberal theorists. Cf. Charles Larmore, *The Morals of Modernity* (Cambridge: Cambridge University Press, 1996), pp. 121–27; Richard C. Sinopoli, 'Liberalism and Contested Conceptions of the God: The Limits of Neutrality,' *Journal of Politics* 55 (1993) 644–63; John Rawls, *Political Liberalism* (New York: Columbia University Press, 1993), pp. 191–94; Bruce Ackerman, 'Neutralities,' in R. Bruce Douglass, Gerald M. Mara, and Henry S. Richardson, eds, *Liberalism and the Good* (New York: Routledge, 1990), pp. 29–43; Peter De Marneffe, 'Liberalism, Liberty, and Neutrality,' *Philosophy and Public Affairs* 19 (1990) 253–74; Will Kymlicka, 'Liberal Individualism and Liberal Neutrality,' *Ethics* 99 (1989) 883–905; and Michael J. Perry, 'Neutral Politics,' *The Review of Politics* 51 (1989) 479–509.

14. Kant was perhaps the first to advance a liberal principle of this sort. His universal principle of justice states that 'Every action is just (right) that in itself or in its maxim is such that the freedom of the will of each can coexist together with the freedom of everyone in accordance with a universal law.' (Kant, *Metaphysical Elements of Justice*, trans. John Ladd (Indianapolis, IN: The Library of Liberal Arts, 1965), p. 35.) In more recent times, John Rawls has defended a similar principle as his first principle of social justice: 'Each person is to have an equal right to the most extensive basic liberty compatible with a similar liberty for others' (Rawls, *A Theory of Justice*, p. 60).

15. Brian Barry, 'How Not to Defend Liberal Institutions,' in Douglass, Mara, and Richardson, eds, p. 47.

16. Ibid.

17. Hobbes famously elevated the counsel of prudence to a law of nature, insisting that reason dictates that a person should 'seek peace and follow it' (Thomas Hobbes, *Leviathan*, Ch. XIV).

18. For a fine discussion of prudence and prudential reasoning, see Thomas Nagel, *The Possibility of Altruism* (Oxford: The Clarendon Press, 1970), pp. 35–46. See also David Gauthier, *Morals by Agreement* (Oxford: Oxford University Press, 1986), pp. 35–38.

19. This use of the prudence argument moves practical liberalism close to the notion of a 'liberalism of fear' introduced by Judith Shklar. (Shklar, 'The Liberalism of Fear,' in Nancy L. Rosenblum, ed., *Liberalism and the Moral Life* (Cambridge, MA: Harvard University Press, 1989), pp. 21–38.)

20. Henry Sidgwick, *The Methods of Ethics* (New York: Dover Publications, Inc., 1966), p. 328. See also Bernard Williams, *Ethics and the Limits of Philosophy* (Cambridge, MA: Harvard University Press, 1985), pp. 19–21; Owen Flanagan, *Varieties of Moral Personality* (Cambridge, MA: Harvard University Press, 1991), pp. 49–50; and Gauthier, Ch. 2.

21. William Paley, *The Principles of Moral and Political Philosophy* (Indianapolis: Liberty Fund, Inc., 2002), pp. 25–26.

22. Jesse Jackson's Rainbow coalition is perhaps the most salient example of such a movement on a national scale.

23. Even groups like the Amish that isolate themselves from the larger society must still be considered only partial communities. As John Hostetler has observed, 'The Amish society is not independent, but in fact a part of society. Its continued existence depends upon maintaining unchanged certain forms, such as the prohibition of automobiles and electricity; yet its survival depends upon some contact with the outside world.' Hostetler, *Amish Society* (Baltimore: The Johns Hopkins University Press, 1963), p. 194.

24. For a thoughtful listing of the kinds of important services government provides modern states, see William A. Galston, *Liberal Pluralism* (Cambridge: Cambridge University Press, 2002), p. 125.

25. On the instability of *modus vivendi* arrangements, see Samuel Scheffler, 'The Appeal of Political Liberalism,' *Ethics* 105 (1994) 4–22.

26. See Rawls, *Political Liberalism*, pp. 147–50.

27. Kukathas has argued that a political unity based upon a common commitment to toleration rests upon a more solid foundation than a *modus vivendi*. He contends that toleration should be endorsed, at least by liberals, because it is based upon a degree of doubt regarding the certainty of one's convictions and a traditional liberal willingness to reason through, with others, whatever disagreements might happen to exist. (Kukathas, 'Cultural Toleration,' in Ian Shapiro and Will Kymlicka, eds, *Ethnicity and Group Rights* (New York: New York University Press, 1997), pp. 69–104.) While the defense of group autonomy defended under practical liberalism is similar to the conclusions reached by Kukathas, the argument here differs from his in important respects. While his defense of toleration may win the support of some liberals who appreciate the moral uncertainty he endorses, it will not move a great many religious, cultural, and ideological groups present in pluralist states. Toleration matters as a political virtue because it must confront normative certainty; thus Kukathas's argument seems too weak to achieve the unity he desires.

## 3   Freedom and toleration

1. William James, *Pragmatism and The Meaning of Truth* (Cambridge, MA: Harvard University Press, 1975), pp. 31–32.

2. See Susan Mendus, *Toleration and the Limits of Liberalism* (Atlantic Highlands, NJ: Humanities Press International, 1989), Ch. 1; Monique Deveaux, *Cultural Pluralism and Dilemmas of Justice* (Ithaca: Cornell University Press, 2000), pp. 40–43.

3. Mieczyslaw Maneli, *Freedom and Toleration* (New York: Octagon Books, 1984), p. 158. See also J. Budziszewski, *True Tolerance* (New Brunswick: Transaction Publishers, 1992), Ch. 1; Karl-Otto Apel, 'Plurality of the Good? The Problem of Affirmative Tolerance in a Multicultural Society from an Ethical Point of View,' *Ratio Juris* 10 (1997) 199–212; and Anna Elisabetta Galeotti, *Toleration as Recognition* (Cambridge: Cambridge University Press, 2002), pp. 85–114.

4. Maneli, p. 106.

5. Cf. Hans Oberdiek, *Tolerance Between Forbearance and Acceptance* (Lanham, MD: Rowman & Littlefield Publishers, 2001), pp. 13–20.

6. Cf. Bernard Williams, 'Toleration: An Impossible Virtue?' in David Heyd, ed., *Toleration* (Princeton, NJ: Princeton University Press, 1996), pp. 18–27.

7. Mary Warnock, for example, argues that putting up with those things that one dislikes, but does not consider immoral, should be included in the definition of toleration. This weak sense of toleration thus requires one to put up with only those things one finds unacceptable for strictly non-moral reasons. See Warnock, 'The Limits of Toleration,' in Susan Mendus and David Edwards, eds, *On Toleration* (Oxford: The Clarendon Press, 1987), pp. 123–39.

8. Thomas Nagel has succinctly described the paradoxical nature of toleration, 'Liberalism asks that citizens accept a certain restraint in calling on the power of the state to enforce some of their most deeply held convictions against others who do not accept them, and holds that the legitimate exercise of political power must be justified on more restricted grounds—grounds which belong in some sense to a common public domain.' Nagel, *Equality and Partiality* (Oxford: Oxford University Press, 1991), p. 158.

9. Noticing this tendency in much liberal argument, John Kekes has put the point as follows, 'The labels of Nazi, racist proapartheid, proslavery, Social Darwinist, egoist, and so forth spring readily to the lips of many egalitarians by way of maligning their opponents and making the justification of the liberal case unnecessary.' Kekes, *Against Liberalism* (Ithaca, NY: Cornell University Press, 1997), p. 95.

10. Harold Laswell's famous account of politics as 'who gets what, when, how,' for example, reduces all politics to a series of coordination problems. The challenges of theorizing about politics, on the other hand, would be considerable lessened if only things were so simple. See Laswell, *Politics: Who Gets What, When, How* (New York: Peter Smith, 1950).

11. This argument merely reworks a version of Kant's justification of the use of coercion by the state. See Kant, *The Metaphysical Elements of Justice*, trans. John Ladd (Indianapolis: The Library of Liberal Arts, 1965), pp. 35–36.

12. Prejudice is generally, if not invariably, understood as a prejudgment that is rigid, uninformed, and violative of certain normative standards. (See Gordon W. Allport, *The Nature of Prejudice* (Reading, MA: Addison-Wesley, 1954), p. 9 and passim.) Social philosophers and social psychologists usually look for more subtle and sophisticated accounts of hatred and prejudice, of course, and typically regard them as socially undesirable and objectionable mental states with social or psychological causes that should be identified for purposes of intervention and prevention. This literature, on the other hand, is not very helpful for anyone interested in developing a politics of unity since individuals accused of prejudiced or hateful behavior are unlikely to put much store in it.

13. For a discussion on the right of group autonomy and self-government, see Michael McDonald, 'Should Communities Have Rights? Reflections on Liberal Individualism,' *Canadian Journal of Law and Jurisprudence* 4 (1991) 217–37; and

L.S. Lustgarten, 'Liberty in a Culturally Plural Society,' in A. Phillips Griffiths, ed., *Of Liberty* (Cambridge: Cambridge University Press, 1983), pp. 91–107.

14. Deveaux, pp. 43–47; James Tully, *An Approach to Political Philosophy: Locke in Contexts* (Cambridge: Cambridge University Press, 1993), pp. 47–61.

15. Cf. Maurice Cranston, 'A Private Space,' *Social Science Information* XIV (1975) 41–57; Galeotti, pp. 20–52.

16. The phrase belongs, of course, to J.N. Figgis. See John Neville Figgis, *Churches in the Modern State*, 2nd edn (New York: Longmans, Green and Co., 1914), p. 225. Cf. David Runciman, *Pluralism and the Personality of the State* (Cambridge: Cambridge University Press, 1997), pp. 143–49. Rawls expresses a similar notion when he describes the just state as a 'social union of social unions.' John Rawls, *A Theory of Justice* (Cambridge, MA: Harvard University Press, 1971), p. 527.

17. Cf. Daniel A. Dombrowski amd Robert Deltete, *A Brief, Liberal Catholic Defense of Abortion* (Chicago: University of Illinois Press, 2000); Frances Kissling, 'Abortion: Articulating a Moral View,' *Conscience: A Newsjournal of Catholic Opinion* XXI (2000).

18. See, Frances Svensson, 'Liberal Democracy and Group Rights: The Legacy of Individualism and Its Impact on American Indian Tribes,' *Political Studies* XXVII (1977) 432.

19. Ibid., p. 433.

20. Will Kymlicka, *Liberalism, Community, and Culture* (Oxford: Oxford University Press, 1989), pp. 196–97.

21. Chandran Kukathas, 'Are There Any Cultural Rights?' *Political Theory* 20 (1992) 122–24. See also Will Kymlicka, 'The Rights of Minority Cultures: Reply to Kukathas,' *Political Theory* 20 (1992) 140–45; Kukathas, 'Cultural Toleration,' in Ian Shapiro and Will Kymlicka, eds, *Ethnicity and Group Rights* (New York: New York University Press, 1997), pp. 69–104; Brian Barry, *Culture and Equality* (Cambridge, MA: Harvard University Press, 2001), pp. 188–89.

22. The government may legitimately be involved in such disputes when, for example, it is clear that this group has split into separate groups and property claims are involved. Consider in this regard the *Kedroff* case decided by the US Supreme Court (*Kedroff* v. *Saint Nicholas Cathedral*, 344 U.S. 94 (1952)). In *Kedroff*, a majority of the members belonging to a Russian Orthodox cathedral in New York began to disagree with the direction Church leadership in Moscow was taking and decided to break from the Church. A minority group belonging to the cathedral remained faithful to the Church leadership and opposed the split with Moscow. The majority undertook the split, however, and took control of the cathedral, and the question at law became whether this group had a rightful title to the cathedral. Because the split was complete, judicial involvement in the matter was legitimate and even necessary, under practical liberalism, to resolve what had become a coordination problem between two separate religious communities both claiming the rightful possession of the same cathedral.

23. Consociational arrangements involve usually a limited number of autonomous but geographically connected groups banding together within a constitutional structure that allows the groups to retain considerable autonomy. This is hardly characteristic of the American political environment, which is better characterized in terms of the presence of one dominant, though loosely organized and largely unselfconscious, group in the United States intermixed with a welter of disparate minority groups. See Michael Walzer, *On Toleration* (New Haven, CT: Yale University Press, 1997), pp. 22–24.

240   *Notes*

24. Federal law exempts persons who 'by reason of religious training and belief' are conscientiously opposed to participation in war. It also grants relief from combatant services to persons who object to combat but who will perform noncombatant duties. 50 U.S.C.S. App. §456.

    In exempting Native-Americans from prosecution for using peyote for religious purposes, federal law notes that by 1994 over half the states of the union had passed similar legislation. 42 U.S.C.S. §1996a. Nor are Native-Americans the only cultural groups to receive religious exemptions from state governments. Both New York and New Jersey grant members of the Jewish faith an exemption from statutes requiring doctors to make a declaration of brain death when their patients have died. See Michael A. Grodin, 'Religious Exemptions: Brain Death and Jewish Law,' *Journal of Church and State* 36 (1994) 368–70.

25. Exemptions are sometimes won in the courts as a consequence of First Amendment free-exercise litigation. (See, for example, *Wisconsin* v. *Yoder*, 406 U.S. 205 (1972).) But the Supreme Court has avoided opening the floodgates and supporting all requests for an exemption from state law for religious reasons. (See *United States* v. *Lee*, 455 U.S. 252 (1982).) In fact, only a handful of such exemptions have been allowed by American courts. See, Austin Sarat and Roger Berkowitz, 'Disorderly Differences: Recognition, Accommodation, and American Law,' *Yale Journal of Law and Humanities* 6 (1994), 285–316.

26. Cf. *United States* v. *Kuch*, 288 F. Supp. 439 (DC, 1968); *Vermont* v. *Rocheleau*, 451 A.2d 1144 (Vt., 1982).

27. Cf. Chandran Kukathas, 'Are There Any Cultural Rights?' p. 112; Nancy L. Rosenblum, *Membership and Morals* (Princeton, NJ: Princeton University Press, 1998), pp. 47–70.

28. Michael Walzer, who has noted this tendency in liberal thought, has also offered reasons to abandon it. See Walzer, *Politics and Passion* (New Haven, CT: Yale University Press, 2004), pp. 2–20.

29. Cf. Richard C. Sinopoli, 'Liberalism and Contested Conceptions of the Good: The Limits of Neutrality,' *Journal of Politics* 55 (1993) 644–63.

30. See Kukathas, 'Cultural Minorities,' pp. 87–88.

31. Barry, pp. 40–54.

32. Ibid., p. 62.

33. 494 U.S. 872 (1990).

34. *Newdow* v. *United States Congress*, 292 F.3d 597 (2002).

35. *Elk Grove Unified School District* v. *Newbow et al.*, 542 U.S. 1 (2004).

36. In *Zorach* v. *Clauson*, 343 U.S. 306 (1952), Justice Douglas famously quipped, 'We are a religious people whose institutions suppose a Supreme Being.' p. 313.

37. See *Engel* v. *Vitale*, 370 U.S. 421 (1962); *Abington School District* v. *Schempp*, 374 U.S. 203 (1963).

38. *Wallace* v. *Jaffree*, 472 U.S. 38 (1985), but see *Board of Education* v. *Mergens*, 496 U.S. 226 (1990).

39. Cf. Barry, p. 190.

40. 462 Pa. 330, 341 A 2d 105 (1975).

41. Ibid., p. 106.

42. Kent Greenawalt, 'Freedom of Association and Religious Association,' in Amy Gutmann, ed., *Freedom of Association* (Princeton, NJ: Princeton University Press, 1998), pp. 109–44.

43. Barry, pp. 191–92.

44. Cf. Craig L. Carr, 'Coercion and Freedom,' *American Philosophical Quarterly* 25 (1988) 59–68.

45. Barry, p. 193.
46. Ibid., p. 191.
47. Cf. Margaret Thaler Singer and Janja Lalich, *Cults in Our Midst* (San Francisco: Jossey-Bass Publishers, 1995), pp. 52–82; Louis Jolyon West, 'Persuasive Techniques in Contemporary Cults: A Public Health Approach,' in Marc Galanter, ed., *Cults and New Religious Movements: A Report of the American Psychiatric Association* (Washington, DC: American Psychiatric Association, 1989), pp. 165–92.
48. See, for example, Stuart A. Wright, 'Reconceptualizing Cult Coercion and Withdrawal: A Comparative Analysis of Divorce and Apostasy,' *Social Forces* 70 (1991) 125–45.
49. On the morality of secession, see Allen Buchanan, *Secession* (Boulder, CO: Westview Press, 1991), pp. 29–81; David Miller, *Citizenship and National Identity* (Cambridge: Polity Press, 2000), pp. 110–24.

## 4   Toleration and group autonomy

1. See, for example, Michael Walzer, *Politics and Passion* (New Haven, CT: Yale University Press, 2004); Amy Gutmann, *Identity in Democracy* (Princeton, NJ: Princeton University Press, 2003); Will Kymlicka, *Politics in the Vernacular* (Oxford: Oxford University Press, 2001); John Tomasi, *Liberalism Beyond Justice* (Princeton, NJ: Princeton University Press, 2001); Monique Deveaux, *Cultural Pluralism and Dilemmas of Justice* (Ithaca: Cornell University Press, 2000); Ian Shapiro and Will Kymlicka, eds, *Ethnicity and Group Rights* (New York: New York University Press, 1997); James Tully, *Strange Multiplicity* (Cambridge: Cambridge University Press, 1995); Will Kymlicka, *Multicultural Citizenship* (Oxford: Oxford University Press, 1995); Jeff Spinner, *The Boundaries of Citizenship: Race, Ethnicity and Nationality in the Liberal State* (Baltimore: Johns Hopkins University Press, 1994); Yael Tamir, *Liberal Nationalism* (Princeton, NJ: Princeton University Press, 1993); Charles Taylor, 'The Politics of Recognition,' in Amy Gutmann, ed., *Multiculturalism* (Princeton, NJ: Princeton University Press, 1992).
2. The various positions carved out by liberal theorists are thoughtfully and carefully catalogued by Emily Gill. See Gill, *Becoming Free: Autonomy and Diversity in the Liberal Polity* (Lawrence, KS: University of Kansas Press, 2001).
3. Cf. Richard Bellamy, *Liberalism and Pluralism: Towards a Politics of Compromise* (London: Routledge, 1999), pp. 15–66.
4. Disagreement among liberal thinkers typically focuses upon how group membership supports or nurtures the development of individual autonomy. At times, however, disagreement arises between those liberal thinkers wanting to defend individual autonomy and those desiring a more direct defense of group autonomy. (Cf. Chandran Kukathas, 'Are There Any Cultural Rights?' *Political Theory* 20 (1992) 105–39; Will Kymlicka, 'The Rights of Minority Cultures: Reply to Kukathas,' 20 (1992) 140–46; Kukathas, 'Cultural Rights Again: A Rejoinder to Kymlicka,' 20 (1992) 674–80.) Brian Barry, on the other hand, parts company with many fellow liberals by arguing that liberalism need not and perhaps should not put such great emphasis upon the defense of multicultural difference. See Barry *Culture and Equality* (Cambridge, MA: Harvard University Press, 2001).
5. Mark Larabee and Peter D. Sleeth, 'Faith Healing Raises Questions of Law's Duty—Belief or Life?' *The Oregonian*, June 7, 1998, A1.
6. Cf. James Fishkin, *Justice, Equal Opportunity, and the Family* (New Haven, CT: Yale University Press, 1983).

7. Kymlicka, *Multicultural Citizenship*, p. 94.
8. Ibid., p. 168.
9. Cf. Jeremy Waldron, 'Cultural Identity and Civic Responsibility,' in Will Kymlicka and Wayne Norman, eds, *Citizenship in Diverse Societies* (Oxford: Oxford University Press, 2000), pp. 155–74.
10. A legal justification for a hate-crime category under practical liberalism goes as follows. Many criminal statutes define criminal activity by considering a mental component of the criminal act. Murder is distinguished from manslaughter, for example, by reference to a mental component. While both crimes involve homicide, the physical outcome of the act is married to the mental state of the actor. Under practical liberalism, acts done from intolerance can qualify as a separate crime because acting intolerantly is a serious wrong according to LP. It is a defection from the political morality that unites the polity.
11. 505 U.S. 377 (1992).
12. The St. Paul Bias-Motivated Crime Ordinance (St. Paul, Minn., Legis.Code 292,02 (1990)) reads as follows:

> Whoever places on public or private property a symbol, object, appellation, characterization or graffiti, including, but not limited to, a burning cross or Nazi swastika, which one knows or has reasonable grounds to know arouses anger, alarm or resentment in others on the basis of race, color, creed, religion or gender commits disorderly conduct and shall be guilty of a misdemeanor.

13. See *R.A.V.*, p. 379.
14. This means, among other things, that the so-called fighting words doctrine would be impermissible under practical liberalism. The fighting words doctrine, announced in *Chaplinsky* v. *New Hampshire* (315 U.S. 568 (1942)), holds that words which 'by their very utterance inflict injury or tend to incite an immediate breach of peace' are not constitutionally protected. (ibid., p. 574.) Under practical liberalism, however, this simply puts the burden of tolerance in the wrong place.
15. See Romel Hernandez, 'Racial Discord Rattles OSU Self-Image,' *The Oregonian*, February 28, 1996, AO1.
16. The Supreme Court's decision in *Virginia* v. *Black et al.* (538 U.S. 343, 2003) is consistent with the requirements of practical liberalism in this regard. This case again raised a question about the constitutionality of cross burning. As Justice O'Conner observed in her opinion for the Court, 'In sum, while burning a cross does not inevitably convey a message of intimidation, often the cross burner intends that the recipients of the message fear for their lives. And when cross burning is used to intimidate, few if any messages are more powerful.' 538 U.S. 343, at 357. It is worth emphasizing that it is the intention to intimidate that constitutes the failure to forbear under practical liberalism.
17. Speech delivered in a manner suggesting an acknowledged or obvious purpose to realize an intolerant agenda, in particular, violates the forbearance condition and is properly actionable under practical liberalism. Consider for example, the circumstances surrounding *Barclay* v. *Florida* (463 U.S. 939, (1983)). This case involved a member of the Black Liberation Army—a group committed to inciting a race war between whites and African Americans—who murdered a white person in the hope of generating a desired race war. If there is a speech component to this case, it is incidental to Barclay's intolerant agenda and is hardly protected under practical liberalism.

18. Cf. Jeff Spinner, *The Boundaries of Citizenship: Race, Ethnicity, and Nationality in the Liberal State* (Baltimore: The Johns Hopkins University Press, 1994), pp. 39–45.
19. *Boy Scouts of America* v. *Dale*, 530 U.S. 640 (2000).
20. Ibid., p. 649.
21. See, for example, Gill, pp. 163–70.
22. *Boy Scouts of America* v. *Dale*, p. 649.
23. See Will Kymlicka, *Liberalism, Community, and Culture* (Oxford: Oxford University Press, 1989), pp. 145–52.
24. Followers of the Bhagwan founded a small community in the high desert of central Oregon and quickly walled themselves off from outside influences. (Cf. Lewis F. Carter, *Charisma and Control in Rajneeshpuram: The Role of Shared Values in the Creation of a Community* (Cambridge, MA: Harvard University Press, 1990).) Ironically, the Rajneesh example also aptly illustrates the dangers that await groups whose members begin to think of themselves as complete units and develop hostile relations with the larger society around them. As the Rajneeshees became more iconoclastic and independent, they also generated tremendous animosity in the nearby town of Antelope and the surrounding community, from which they drew certain services. The resultant struggles eventually led to the demise of the group amidst charges of scandal and attempted murder of public officials. See Hugh Milne, *Bhagwan: The God that Failed* (New York: St Martin's Press, 1986); Kirk Braun, *Rajneeshpuram: The Unwelcome Society* (West Linn, OR: Scout Creek Press, 1984).
25. See Barry, pp. 179–81.
26. *Pierce* v. *Society of Sisters*, 268 U.S. 510, 534.
27. Cf. Eamonn Callan, 'Discrimination and Religious Schooling,' in Kymlicka and Norman, eds, pp. 45–66.
28. 406 U.S. 205 (1972).
29. Ibid., pp. 245–46.
30. See, for example, Amy Gutmann, 'Undemocratic Education,' in Nancy L. Rosenblum, ed., *Liberalism and the Moral Life* (Cambridge, MA: Harvard University Press, 1989), pp. 71–88.
31. John Rawls, *Political Liberalism* (New York: Columbia University Press, 1993), pp. 199–200.
32. *Wisconsin*, p. 212. The Court also noted a religious concern that motivated the Amish litigation, conceding that the Amish believe that 'higher learning tends to develop values they reject as influences that alienate man from God.' ibid.
33. 827 F.2d 1058 (6th Cir., 1987).
34. For a thorough discussion of the exhausting legal meanderings that surround this case, see Stephen Bates, *Battleground* (New York: Poseidon Press, 1993).
35. Hawkins County insisted before the Circuit Court that its reading program did not endorse any particular beliefs or lifestyles; it merely exposed students to diverse beliefs and ways of life without entering an evaluation either way (*Mozert*, pp. 1063–64). The argument is rather disingenuous, however; it is hard to believe that the texts would have been chosen for use had they shown lifestyles that county officials found distasteful. The use of the texts, without additional normative comment works as an implicit endorsement of the lifestyles presented. Even if the reader was not intended to do this, the County should have been aware of the fact that others might feel this way—a point illustrated by the Mozerts' request to add an additional normative comment about the desirability of these lifestyles.
36. Ibid., p. 1062.

37. A version of this argument is made by Stephen Macedo. See Macedo, 'Liberal Civic Education and Religious Fundamentalism: The Case of God v. John Rawls,' *Ethics* 105 (1995) 468–96. But Macedo has had more to say about *Mozert* that moves in the direction of practical liberalism. See Macedo, *Diversity and Distrust*, pp. 157–68. See also George W. Dent, 'Religious Children, Secular Schools,' *Southern California Law Review* 61 (1988) 863–941.
38. See Bates, Chs 5, 6, and 7.
39. Robert K. Fullinwider, 'Citizenship, Individualism, and Politics,' *Ethics* 105 (1995) 513.
40. Michael Walzer has indicated recently that he wants, on the one hand, to tolerate traditional groups, and on the other, to require them to demonstrate liberal respect for individuals as autonomous beings. He concedes that there may be no space between these positions, and here I suspect he is right (Walzer, pp. 60–61). Practical liberalism, however, does not have such mixed moral motives and perhaps because it has no real moral motives at all. It is concerned with group autonomy only because groups are justifiably concerned with this autonomy and will likely do what they can to protect and promote it. The dilemma under practical liberalism is whether the political concessions associated with accepting LP may erode group integrity and identity or weaken the comprehensive ambitions of certain groups. My response, as should be increasingly clear, is twofold: First the concessions associated with endorsing practical liberalism do not require any alterations in the formulation of group ends; and second, even comprehensive groups must live in the presence of others and doing so comes with risks and the concurrent need for compromise. The failure to make the required compromises may well (and probably will) do more to jeopardize the integrity of comprehensive groups than accepting LP, and if this is right, even comprehensive groups should be willing to endorse LP.

# 5   Stability, legitimacy, and the liberal polity

1. Readers who are already satisfied with the prudential argument and who do not share these doubts and concerns about the stability of the liberal polity may want to move on to the following chapter.
2. John Rawls, *Political Liberalism* (New York: Columbia University Press, 1993), pp. 140–42.
3. See Isaiah Berlin, 'Two Concepts of Liberty,' in Berlin, ed., *Four Essays on Liberty* (London: Oxford University Press, 1969), pp. 118–72; William A. Galston, *Liberal Pluralism* (Cambridge: Cambridge University Press, 2002), pp. 39–47.
4. Rawls, p. xxv.
5. Ibid., p. 49.
6. Ibid., p. 50.
7. Ibid., p. 147.
8. Hobbes, *Leviathan*, Ch. 17.
9. Rawls, p. 50; Brian Barry, 'How Not to Defend Liberal Institutions,' in R. Bruce Douglass, Gerald M. Mara, and Henry S. Richardson, eds, *Liberalism and the Good* (New York: Routledge, 1990), pp. 44–58.
10. This, of course, is Rawls's objection to *modi vivendi* arrangements, and one that has already been anticipated by Brian Barry. See Barry, pp. 44–46.
11. This lovely way of expressing the apparent irrelevance of certain ideologically marginalized groups is from William O. Douglas's famous dissent in *Dennis* v. *United States*, 341 U.S. 494 (1951), Douglas J., dissenting.

12. This view of American political culture has its roots in Tocqueville's *Democracy in America*. See Gunnar Myrdal, *An American Dilemma* (New York: Harper and Row, 1944); Louis Hartz, *The Liberal Tradition in America* (New York: Harcourt Brace, 1955); Samuel Huntington, *American Politics: The Promise of Disharmony* (Cambridge, MA: Belknap Press, 1981); Lawrence Fuchs, *The American Kaleidoscope* (Hanover, NH: Wesleyan University Press, 1990); and Alan Wolfe, *One Nation After All* (New York: Penguin Books, 1998).
13. Hobbes, Ch. 13.
14. See Craig L. Carr, ed., Michael J. Seidler, trans., *The Political Writings of Samuel Pufendorf* (New York: Oxford University Press, 1994), pp. 152–54.
15. Cf. Hans Morganthau, *Politics Among Nations* (New York: Alfred A. Knopf, 1948), Ch. 3.
16. Cf. Samuel Huntington, *Who Are We?* (New York: Simon & Schuster, 2004), Ch. 9.
17. See Huntington, ibid.; Rogers Smith, *Civic Ideals* (New Haven, CT: Yale University Press, 1997), pp. 446–48.
18. Cf. Smith, pp. 358–65; M.T. Bennet, *American Immigration Policies: A History* (Washington, DC: Public Affairs Press, 1963).
19. See S.I. Benn and R.S. Peters, *The Principles of Political Thought* (New York: Free Press, 1959), pp. 299–315; Hannah Pitkin, 'Obligation and Consent—II,' *American Political Science Review* LX (1966) 39–52.
20. Jon Elster, *Nuts and Bolts for the Social Sciences* (Cambridge: Cambridge University Press, 1989), pp. 35–37.
21. The psychology of risk aversion is probably more complicated than this, to be sure. According to prospect theory, the tendency to run risks depends upon previous gains and losses. Someone who has just suffered considerable loss (say by gambling) is likely to run greater risks to recover the loss (gamble even greater sums), while someone who has made gains or is content with the status quo will be more risk averse. (See Daniel Kahneman, Amos Tversky, and Paul Slovic, eds, *Judgment under Uncertainty: Heuristics and Biases* (New York: Cambridge University Press, 1982).) If we assume that social peace and civil order are important baseline goods, as I have argued they are, then groups (that have, after all, suffered little loss and made substantial gains by endorsing LP) should be rather averse to risking considerable possible loss by defecting from the *modus vivendi*.
22. To put the point in somewhat more technical terms, rational calculations involving risk must take account both of the estimated probabilities associated with realizing a desired outcome and with the confidence one can have in the assigned probabilities. I am suggesting here that one cannot with ease calculate the probabilities and also that one can have, through time, little or no confidence in the assigned probabilities. Since the ripple effect of defection is all but impossible to calculate into the future if a group defects from the *modus vivendi*, it can have no confidence that the long-range consequences of defection will have desired effects. In an iterated game with an unknown but large number of moves made by a large number of players, cooperation is thus preferable to defection. See Robert Axelrod, *The Evolution of Cooperation* (New York: Basic Books, 1984), and Axelrod, *The Complexity of Cooperation* (Princeton, NJ: Princeton University Press, 1997).
23. Morganthau, Ch. 3.
24. See, for example, Fuchs; Huntington, *Who Are We?*; John Diggins, *The Lost Soul of American Politics* (New York: Basic Books, 1984).
25. The seminal efforts to tell the story in this fashion are John Higham, *Strangers in the Land* (New York: Atheneum, 1971), and Smith.

## 6   Justice, fairness, and the making of civility

1. Thomas Hobbes, *Leviathan*, Ch. XIV.
2. Thomas Spragens, *Civic Liberalism* (Lanham, MD: Rowman & Littlefield Publishers, 1999), pp. 15–17.
3. See, for example, Spragens, pp. 90–92; Richard E. Flathman, *Reflections of a Would-Be Anarchist* (Minneapolis: University of Minnesota Press, 1996), p. 140.
4. See Richard Cumberland, *A Treatise of the Laws of Nature*, trans. John Maxwell (London, 1727), pp. 73–91; Craig L. Carr, ed., *The Political Writings of Samuel Pufendorf* (New York: Oxford University Press, 1994), pp. 141–48, 152–54.
5. Cf. Michael Ignatieff, *The Warrior's Honor* (New York: Owl Books, 1997).
6. Cf. Todd Gitlin, *The Twilight of Common Dreams: Why America Is Wracked by Culture Wars* (New York: Henry Holt, 1995).
7. Carr, pp. 236–44.
8. Spragens, p. 16.
9. It falls to democratic theory to accommodate democratic principles to the civic needs of technological, scientific, and social expertise. Cf. Robert Dahl, *Democracy and Its Critics* (New Haven, CT: Yale University Press, 1989), pp. 311–40. See also James Fishkin, *Democracy and Deliberation* (New Haven, CT: Yale University Press, 1991).
10. Cf. Paul Edward Gottfried, *After Liberalism: Mass Democracy in the Managerial State* (Princeton, NJ: Princeton University Press, 1999).
11. Stephen Macedo, *Diversity and Distrust: Civic Education in a Multicultural Democracy* (Cambridge, MA: Harvard University Press, 2000), pp. 164–65.
12. Cf. Will Kymlicka, *Contemporary Political Philosophy* (Oxford: Oxford University Press, 1990), Ch. 1.
13. See Craig L. Carr and Michael J. Seidler, 'Pufendorf, Sociality and the Modern State,' *History of Political Thought* XVII (1996) 354–78.
14. John Rawls, *A Theory of Justice* (Cambridge, MA: Harvard University Press, 1971).
15. Cf. Brian Barry, *The Liberal Theory of Justice* (Oxford: Oxford University Press, 1973), pp. 10–18.
16. As Thomas Nagel has put it, 'The original position seems to presuppose not just a neutral theory of the good, but a liberal, individualistic conception according to which the best that can be wished for someone is the unimpeded pursuit of his own path, provided it does not interfere with the rights of others.' Nagel, 'Rawls on Justice,' in Norman Daniels, ed., *Reading Rawls* (New York: Basic Books), p. 10.
17. John Rawls, *Political Liberalism* (New York: Columbia University Press, 1993), pp. 140–45.
18. See John Rawls, *Justice as Fairness: A Restatement*, ed. Erin Kelly (Cambridge, MA: The Belknap Press, 2001), pp. 80–94.
19. See Rawls, *Political Liberalism*, pp. 147–68; *Justice as Fairness: A Restatement*, pp. 32–38.
20. Rawls, of course, refers to this process of measuring one's intuitions about justice against the background of a theoretical vision of justice as reflective equilibrium. See Rawls, *A Theory of Justice*, p. 48.
21. Rawls, *Political Liberalism*, p. 65.
22. John Tomasi has thoughtfully attempted to widen the reach of moral liberalism by advancing an argument that makes it more accommodating to illiberal presences. (Cf. Tomasi, *Liberalism Beyond Justice* (Princeton, NJ: Princeton University Press, 2001).) Yet Tomasi too concedes that there will be some illiberal groups moral liberalism cannot appease. See Tomasi, pp. 20–26.

23. Will Kymlicka, as we have seen, explicitly calls for this; recall his insistence that 'The aim of liberals should not be to dissolve non-liberal nations, but rather to seek to liberalize them.' Kymlicka, *Multicultural Citizenship* (Oxford: The Clarendon Press, 1995), p. 94.
24. Cf. William Galston, *Liberal Pluralism* (Cambridge: Cambridge University Press, 2002), p. 125. I have explored this last issue in greater depth elsewhere. See Craig L. Carr, 'Between Virtue and Vice: The Legal Enforcement of Morals,' *Kansas Journal of Law and Public Policy* XIV (2004) 1–45.
25. Rawls, *A Theory of Justice*, p. 3.
26. See J.-J. Rousseau, *The Social Contract*, trans Maurice Cranston (New York: Penguin Books, 1968), pp. 74–78.
27. In this regard, practical liberalism follows a theory of public discourse developed by Rogers Smith. See Smith, *Stories of Peoplehood* (Cambridge: Cambridge University Press, 2003), pp. 154–64.
28. Horace Kallen, *Culture and Democracy in the United States* (New York: Boni and Liveright, 1924).
29. Cf. Michael Walzer, *What Does It Mean to Be an American?* (New York: Marsilio, Publishers 1996), pp. 23–49; Lawrence Fuchs, *The American Kaleidoscope* (Hanover, NH: Wesleyan University Press, 1990).
30. Cf. Samuel P. Huntington, *American Politics: The Promise of Disharmony* (Cambridge, MA: The Belknap Press, 1981), pp. 13–30; Kenneth Karst, *Belonging to America: Equal Citizenship and the Constitution* (New Haven, CT: Yale University Press, 1989), pp. 173–74.
31. John Higham, *Strangers in the Land* (New York: Atheneum, 1971), pp. 158–93.
32. Cf. Alasdair MacIntyre, 'Is Patriotism a Virtue?' in Ronald Beiner, ed., *Theorizing Citizenship* (Albany, NY: State University of New York Press, 1995), pp. 209–28.
33. See Thomas Nagel, *Equality and Rationality* (Oxford: Oxford University Press, 1991), pp. 10–11; Samuel Scheffler, *Boundaries and Allegiances* (Oxford: Oxford University Press, 1991), pp. 48–65.
34. Scheffler, pp. 97–110.
35. Cf. Michael Walzer, *Thick and Thin* (Notre Dame: University of Notre Dame Press, 1994).
36. Isaiah Berlin, 'Two Concepts of Liberty,' in Berlin, ed., *Four Essays on Liberty* (London: Oxford University Press, 1969), pp. 118–72. See also John Gray, *Isaiah Berlin* (Princeton, NJ: Princeton University Press, 1996); Gray, 'After the New Liberalism,' *Social Research* 61 (1994) 719–36; and George Crowder, 'Pluralism and Liberalism,' *Political Studies* XLII (1994) 293–305.
37. Galston, p. 23.
38. Cf. William Galston, 'Two Concepts of Liberalism,' *Ethics* 105 (1995) 513–34. At the very least, Galston's claim may set off another round of the politics of interests. The Followers of Christ, for example, (or even the Aztecs for that matter) may agree with Galston that human life needs to be respected and insist that they are respecting this life when they pray for the recovery of their young. Who, then, should decide what it means, in practice, to respect human life? Galston apparently takes this to be a fairly straightforward and unproblematic notion, but this merely underestimates the problem of pluralism that he attempts to address.
39. Cf. John Kekes, *Against Liberalism* (Ithaca, NY: Cornell University Press, 1997), pp. 37–45.
40. I have explored and developed this point in greater detail elsewhere. See Craig L. Carr, *On Fairness* (Aldershot: Ashgate Publishing Co., 2000), pp. 114–20.

41. One might want to say that one should not cheat because cheating violates the rules of play while exploiting a weak backhand remains faithful to the rules. But rules and their application are themselves subject to the dictates of fairness. See Carr, *On Fairness*, pp. 45–51.
42. Ibid., pp. 32–33.
43. Ibid., pp. 79–83.
44. See, for example, Spragens, pp. 3–17; Flathman, pp. 37–41.
45. Rawls, *Political Liberalism*, pp. 197–98.

## Epilogue

1. Michael J. White, *Partisan or Neutral* (London: Rowman & Littlefield Publishers, 1995), p. 2.
2. Natural-law argument seems almost infinitely expandable in this regard. Cf. David Braybrooke, *Natural Law Modernized* (Toronto: University of Toronto Press, 2001).

# Index